The Best of SURFER MAGAZINE

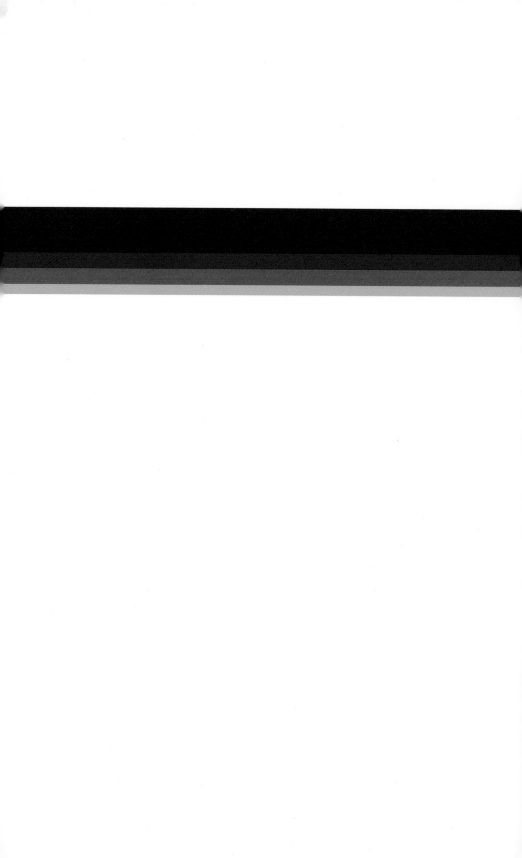

The Best of SURFER MAGAZINE

Edited by Chris Mauro and Steve Hawk

Foreword by Dave Parmenter

CHRONICLE BOOKS

SAN FRANCISCO

Library of Congress Cataloging-in-Publication Data:

The Best of Surfer magazine / edited by Chris Mauro and Steve Hawk ;
foreword by Dave Parmenter.
    p. cm.
ISBN-10: 0-8118-5816-2
ISBN-13: 978-0-8118-5816-8
1. Surfing. I. Mauro, Chris. II. Hawk, Steve, 1955– III. Surfer. IV. Title.

GV839.5.B47 2007
797.3'2–dc22

Manufactured in China

Designed by Jaimie Muehlhausen/Contusion Design

These stories appear as they were originally published in *SURFER* magazine
and have not been edited for content, spelling, punctuation, or grammar.

Distributed in Canada by Raincoast Books
9050 Shaughnessy Street
Vancouver, British Columbia V6P 6E5

10 9 8 7 6 5 4 3 2 1

Chronicle Books LLC
680 Second Street
San Francisco, California 94107

www.chroniclebooks.com

Contents

Is There Such a Thing as a Surf Writer?

By Dave Parmenter

Surfers, according to a bias long held by mainstream society, are not supposed to write. To the citizens of Tatertot, Indiana, surfers are a wacky byproduct of the Left Coast, a bunch of stoned buffoons with nasal drawls and strange bumps on their knees. Surfers can roll a joint with alacrity but never pick up a pen. Admittedly, Dudespeak, the lingua franca of the surf, seems intentionally designed to suppress expression of abstract thought. Yet we find in *SURFER* Magazine's 45 years of publication a considerable amount of good writing—not just about the kinetics of surfboard and rider but, more importantly, about the strange new hybrid of human being molded by continual play in that dynamic frontier where land meets sea. Jumping from the edge of terra firma into the ocean seems to breed individuals who come to renounce many of the absurdities and dogma that plague shore-bound life. The writers featured here may report, reflect, or even rant, but one thing they all have in common is that they have gone out of their way to cross the street to kick a sacred cow or two.

SURFER has always been written for surfers by surfers, one thing that separates it from other sports magazines. And few sports magazines have cut their writers loose quite like *SURFER*. In what essentially is a photo-based publication (originally designed by *SURFER* founder John Severson to do little more than induce surf fever in the potential audience for one of his surf films), it is astonishing to find, thriving in such scant soil, stories like Gerry Lopez's "Attitude Dancing" or Alvin Darkling's "No Observable Progress." Can you imagine an article in *Field & Stream* that wrestles with the cultural clash between Hawaiian and Australian bass fishermen, or would you find in *Golf Digest* a dark little nugget of dystopian fiction about a young golfer forced by overcrowded links into a mental institution to find a deserted fairway? And where the dilettante travel glossies have their expense-account correspondents rave about the herb-crusted antelope steaks at some $5,000-a-night safari resort in Botswana, *SURFER* flings Kevin Naughton and Craig Peterson into the fetid bowels of Angola with little more than chump change and a few rolls of Kodachrome, to await their emergence months later, dust stained and gaunt, as something like surfing's own Wilfred Thesiger.

The writing in *SURFER* has always reflected the mindset of whatever cultural/political epoch the sport was passing through. Before about '67 or '68, the fledgling sport had a chip on its shoulder about being branded an aberrant youth craze by the general public, and much of the editorial content seems equally divided between attempts to appease the Establishment by displaying crisply windbreakered and clean-cut sportsmen scrupulously obeying the bullhorns, and urgent appeals to the gremmies to take off their iron crosses.

Then, after psychedelic drugs and Vietnam irreparably widened the Generation Gap, surfing moved into its counterculture phase, where surfers were viewed as outright subversives, like Hell's Angels in Señor Lopez tops. As a viable and lively subculture, one that really threatened the Establishment, this was likely surfing's finest hour. Some of *SURFER*'s very best writing came out of the late '60s and early '70s (and, alas, some of its very worst: the use of mind-altering drugs was often mistaken for creativity, thus we find in the back issues some pretty sketchy patches of run-on LSD syntax and incomprehensible poetry). Revisiting some of these stories today brings a pang of nostalgia for that time when it was a truly subversive magazine. Stories such as the irreverent, Marx Brothers–ish Naughton/Peterson travel series and Mickey Dora's misanthropic "The Crackerjack Conspiracy" are so indelibly stamped into my mind that even 30 years later I am able to quote much of the text by memory.

But, in the end, the glory days were not to last. Though Mickey Dora had warned us often enough about the "senile organizers" pimping for their Madison Avenue overlords, by the late '70s surfing, as a refuge for the nonconformist, was under siege by the same forces that had felled Rock-and-Roll and the Hippie movement—money and the mainstream. As surfing's ascetics donned their black wetsuits and stole into Baja, the '80s were stealing across the moat with daggers clenched between the teeth. A brief period of bitter but almost token debate about the looming commercialism and professionalism sprinkled the pages of *SURFER*—and then surfing was swallowed whole by Mainstream Acceptance, and even Dora the Dark Knight couldn't save us from the beckoning tar pits of Day-Glo. And yet the reactionary impulse is hard to stamp out in most surfers. A story like "Tragic Kingdom," written smack dab in the middle of Oahu's North Shore—surfing's Hollywood— by Todd Chesser, a major beneficiary of the Dream Factory, shows that renunciation of the mainstream and materialism always seems to simmer just beneath the surface of any real surfer.

Few of the articles collected here would qualify as conventional journalism or sports writing outside of, say, *Rolling Stone*. If there is anything that the stories in this collection hold in common, it is that their writers have found a way to upstage the 500-pound gorilla of surf media— photography. All surf writers must bend to the cruel reality that all surfing magazines are, essentially, little more than picture books. In the same way adult magazines cater to the wish-fulfillment fantasies of the reader, surf magazines set out to stoke the desire of ordinary surfers who are no more likely to paddle out at Pipeline than the average *Playboy* reader is to ever tussle with a centerfold model on a bearskin.

Because of this, the surf writer is compelled to offer something fresh and unusual, and I think it is within the travel genre that he has found the greatest opportunity to do so. The photos enhance the story, and vice versa. This symbiotic relationship, when seasoned with the pungent spice of escapism, has made the travel story the source of much of the best writing in *SURFER*.

Travel and the search for fresh, unridden breaks have become the foundation for the surfing experience. Surfers have become a nomadic people, and so great is the urge to wander that I know many lifelong surfers whose urge to head off to spoor new waves far surpasses their desire to actually ride them. Such wanderlust may be seen as ironic when one considers that the only prose in the very first issue of *SURFER* was a fictional tale called "Malibu Lizards," about a bunch of surfers who never left Malibu, preferring instead to lounge on the driftwood logs there, sunning themselves into torpid malaise. Who can say exactly what drove the Malibu Lizards to hit the road to become the best-traveled sportsmen in the world? Some say it was Bruce Brown's promise of empty, perfect Cape Saint Francis in *The Endless Summer*; others say it arose from overcrowding or social Darwinism or drug smuggling or just plain itchy feet.

All of these factors no doubt contributed to the surfing diaspora, but I think the strongest stimulus commanding the surfing tribe is the horror of being displaced. All surfers, be they Polynesian or peroxide-blond Southern Californian, enjoy their sport along desirable coastal areas. They are almost always the first to detect change. They are the first to be smothered by newcomers, the first to notice the effects of dammed and diverted waterways, the first to suffer as their tribal pathways are buried in sprawl and tract homes. And so they are nearly always among the first to take flight: arrive in Western Australia or Nicaragua or Alaska, and you will find entrenched there an Orange County refugee cursing the cement malignancy that cast him from his childhood lair.

Travel offers the surfer the best chance of escape, but it also thrusts him into conflict with new cultures, customs, and peoples. Reviewing the genre in *SURFER*, we see that at best this conflict leads to a worldly, two-fisted, Jack London sort of travel yarn; at worst, it may only record a confrontation with localism and "bad vibes." To my taste, the most memorable stories presented here—even if not genuine travel adventure sagas—are those that depict the clashes arising from venturing into someone else's backyard: the *haole* in Hawaii, Hawaiians in South Africa, Australians in America, servicemen in Vietnam, infidels in Morocco.

The best of the litter, I think, is Australian John Witzig's three-part account of his extended visit to California: "The Tropic of Cancer?," "Hotel California," and "Spirit of the Place." Written in the early '80s, at the onset of yet another paroxysm of hard feelings between the United States and Australia, Witzig's narrative is remarkable for its forbearance and intellectual chivalry, considering that only 14 years earlier he had penned what is probably the most inflammatory story ever printed in *SURFER*, "We're Tops Now," which brashly reminded American readers that Aussie Nat Young had thrashed all the Californian matinee idols in the 1966 World Championship. In his California trilogy, Witzig penetrates deep into the Heart of Mellowness, infiltrating the inner sanctums of date-shake bars and the lairs of black wetsuit clans, resembling Sir Richard Burton in Arab disguise stealing into the Dome of the Rock. His trilogy infuriated its subjects, but no one has ever described as well as Witzig that peculiar muddle of self-absorption, ennui, and forced grooviness that saturates so much of life in California.

Writing about the act of surfing is an extraordinarily difficult thing to do. The surf writer must traverse a tightrope over the twin perils of rendering the act of wave-riding into something as mechanical as a golf swing or wallowing in metaphysical narcissism. Thinking of this tightrope act calls to mind John Steinbeck's comment about how writing about a deeply felt thing was like trying to collect and preserve a beautiful but delicate tide pool creature, one that fell apart when handled and turned into a soggy gray pulp when tipped into formaldehyde.

I have been a frequent contributor to *SURFER* for 25 years, and have been fortunate to work closely with both of the editors responsible for this book. Former editor Steve Hawk, who took the helm in the early '90s, utilized his extensive journalism background to raise the level of writing in *SURFER,* and established an exceptional stable of writers, many of who are still masthead mainstays. Chris Mauro, *SURFER*'s present skipper, has sustained Hawk's legacy. Amid the astounding barrage of modern photographic media, he remains a writer's editor, and has been able to draw on his far-reaching surfing experience to keep the magazine on an even keel in an era when surfing is literally frothing with diversity.

Whether you are a longtime *SURFER* reader revisiting these stories or a newcomer seeing them for the first time, I hope that the following works, gathered for the first time in one place and stripped of distracting photos, help you gain a clearer picture of what all the many millions of waves ridden before today mean to you. I also hope these stories awaken in you a deep curiosity about surfing's past and an interest in its many possible futures. But most of all, I hope that some of you are inspired to take pen and notepad and try to say something about what surfing means to you. Like the writers collected here, perhaps you may be able to tease unbroken into the specimen jar one of those brilliant and fragile sea creatures.

Makaha Beach, Hawaii
August 2006

Malibu Lizards

By Harvey Haber · SURFER Vol. 1 No. 1 · June 1960

John Severson was a high school teacher making surf films in his spare time when he founded *SURFER* magazine back in 1960. It was an easy leap from his unique brand of movie posters and flyers—always full of witty sketches—to the 36-page magazine called *The Surfer*, which he printed to promote his third film, *Surf Fever*. Among the grainy black-and-white photos, comic sketches, and a handdrawn map of California surf spots was Harvey Haber's tale, which aptly depicts the mindset of the average "bump-on-a-log" Malibu surfer of the day.

Mick lay on his stomach among the empty beer cans and driftwood and delicately peeled his sunburnt nose. Morosely he regarded a lizard, stupid with the sun, wavering on a bleached stick of wood in front of his nose. Almost without interest he reached out and grabbed it.

"Tonight, lizard . . . tonight you shall be sacrificed to Kahuna," he said listlessly. "Kahuna, god of the sun and sand and surf, will have you. Aha, lizzy . . . what say you to that?"

But the lizard only squirmed slightly and wouldn't respond, oblivious to life and death. Mickey dug out a handful of sand in front of his nose, dropped the lizard in it and stared at its twitching neck and back.

"Zap, lizard . . . zap! zap! You're sterile!" he said, flicking his fingers at the blinking reptile face and covering up his oblivious body in a handful of warm sand.

Mick glanced up the small incline leading from the highway to the beach and saw a thick, blond kid with very long hair that always reminded him of Prince Valiant. He smiled slightly, since he was getting tired of being alone on the beach on such a sunny morning and no one to surf with.

Mick yelled as the thick, blond kid came toward him.

"Wally! Wally Walrus, you missed it! Not 10 minutes ago the surf was 500 feet high, 'n some guy was handing out free kegs of beer and there were ten dapper little honeys who were so hot to trot they couldn't wait . . . not 10 minutes ago. Ohhh did you really miss it. Ha!"

Wally laughed easily through his nose—a nothing laugh—and squinted as he looked across the waveless cove and the womanless beach in front of him.

"Yeah . . . I musta missed it," he said. "God, today makes a solid week of no surf and no lovin'. Nothing but bitchin' weather and Malibu lizards. I'm going insane for something to do." His blond walrus-like head exaggerated a long sigh.

"Wally . . . how about a trip South?" Mick suggested spiritlessly, knowing that anything involving such energy would be quickly squelched.

"We could make the fights at Tijuana. Carlos Arruza's fighting tomorrow with bulls for La Laguna . . . " He paused as he saw a dubious frown form on Wally's face. "I'll go half on gas, babe."

Wally was still frowning, thinking of the long drive to the border, of the wranglings with the border officials, of the swarming pushers of Modero Street near the bullring, of the bargaining for bullfight tickets with hand-waving, screaming Mexicans, of keeping on the watch for pickpockets and petty thieves . . .

"Noooo, nay, Mick," Wally said with a kind of resigned finality. "Too much effort. Better to do nothing than fight Tijuana on a Sunday."

"Arruza cut both ears last week at Mexico City." Mick was imploring now, tired of no surf, no women, lizards and sand and sun.

Forgetting the prospective hassles, Wally thought of the bulls and of a fight he had seen two years ago in Juarez. The *torero* was a black-faced, bowlegged little Indian boy with a face like a donkey and eyes so deep-set it looked as though he had none. He remembered how restless the crowds had been with the kid's opening passes, the way he twisted and corkscrewed with the cape and his forced *naturales*; being so careful. And he remembered, too, the way the bull had caught him in the leg after he turned his back to him. He remembered the tourists and the students from S.C. with their wine sacks, fainting in the box seats as the kid was turned on the horn with the horn about fifteen inches in him and out of sight, the bull tossing his head and the boy not leaving the horn when he tossed, until the bull lowered his head and the boy slid off the horn onto his *muleta* cape and the Mexican crowds still shouting, jeering, demanding . . .

"All right," Wally said passively. "Let's make it. And if they draw poor bulls, I shall personally make you eat one thousand Malibu lizards."

"Ohhhh-le, Walrus," Mick hooted excitedly, suddenly realizing he had convinced him into going. "I'll throw my board in the gray bomb and we shall be off to T.J. Yeah . . . yeah! I'm jazzed!" Mickey hopped over some rusted beer cans and the remnants of an old beach fire and grabbed his surfboard. He ran up the hill to the highway and half threw it in his old gray Chevy convertible, still screaming excitedly. Wally Walrus halfheartedly watched a lizard run from under a six-pack carton to a tar-spotted piece of driftwood and wondered why in the hell he had let Mick talk him into going to Tijuana.

A Present from Winoski

By Patrick McNulty · SURFER Vol. 7 No. 2 · May 1966

Many surfers of the mid-'60s, themselves offspring of WWII veterans, figured that, if it came down to it, they had what it took to be good soldiers. And as the war in Vietnam devolved from a distant political skirmish to a full-blown "living room" war, some even looked forward to playing a pivotal role in the conflict. Like many movies of the day, Patrick McNulty's fictional account of how surfers might handle themselves in combat was mildly patriotic, yet still emblematic of the struggle we all face when we weigh hope against fear.

A moment after the crippled chopper slammed to the ground, Drake popped his harness, leaned forward and touched Winoski's shoulder strap. Colonel Winoski winced as he tried to move, and Drake realized he was badly injured. Carefully, he lifted Winoski from his harness and slid him over the crumpled wreckage. Winoski dropped the last few feet and screamed in pain as he landed on the rocks. Quickly Drake dropped to the ground and dragged Winoski to the shelter of a rock. The Colonel's right leg twisted in his nylon flight suit, and Drake knew the thigh was broken.

He listened for the enemy, but all he heard were the waves crashing off the point and the dull vroom, vroom of the antiaircraft guns firing at Tra Drang. He looked back at the Colonel and for several moments Drake wondered whether he was going to be sick.

"I'd sure like a cigarette." Winoski, his lips white with shock, spoke evenly and carefully.

Drake zipped down the front of his flying tunic and pulled a pack from Winoski's starched shirt pocket. Winoski always wore freshly laundered khakis on a mission because he said he wanted to look regulation if shot down. Drake put the cigarette between Winoski's lips, and he noticed his hand was shaking as he held the match. Eyes closed, Winoski took a long drag and the smoke furled out the nostrils of his blunted boxer's nose. Winoski spoke with the cigarette still in his lips:

"Another 500 yards and we would have cleared this enemy pocket. Our guys are just the other side of that river." He made a move to get up but screamed and collapsed back against the rock. After a moment he said:

"What's it look like, Lieutenant? Have we got a chance?"

Drake stood up and the warm land breeze felt good against his face. The helicopter, battered by flack, was twisted at a 45-degree angle a hundred yards from where the rocky point dropped into the sea. Up the beach he saw a small river washing into the surf. On the other side of the river was safety.

Two silver jets glinting in the sun wheeled over like protective hawks. Drake swung his eyes away from the north beach and along the rocky point to the south where the peninsula again joined the beach. Five trucks loaded with troops in camouflaged battle dress rolled along the sand toward them.

"We're going to have visitors in a moment. Plenty of Charlies. They're driving along the beach by the jungle," Drake said.

Eyes closed, Winoski took a long drag on his cigarette and the ash crumbled and fell on his nylon chest. Winoski reached down into the flap pocket along the left leg and pulled out the small canister of 35-millimeter film. He opened his eyes and looked evenly at Drake.

"Here's all the pretty pictures we took this morning, Lieutenant. You'd better throw it in the ocean before the Charlies get to us."

Drake took the film thinking, My God, what a guy this Winoski is. Even with a broken thigh, he still thinks of the film before leaving the chopper. Drake looked at the small canister in his hand and remembered the trigger on his photo camera going click, click, click just a few minutes ago as he and Winoski roared over the ammunition dump. Probably the best pictures of the war, and they were going into the drink.

Machine gun fire, sharp and squeaky, sounded above the booming waves off the point. Drake looked up and saw two jets sweeping low over the water towards the beach, their tracers stitching geysers of water. Drake watched fascinated as the bullets walked up the beach and raked the trucks jammed with troops. The green fatigues seemed to pour out of the trucks like a pot overflowing on the stove. The troops scrambled toward jungle covering along the fringe of beach, and within seconds, the trucks were abandoned.

Winoski had pulled himself around the side of the rock and was watching, too. He had a tight, tough grin on his fighter's face.

"Hooray for our side," Winoski said. "Give those two pilots a big panda doll from the top shelf."

Drake watched the jets turning tight against the sun as they came around again for another pass. Glancing south, he saw the black dot of a helicopter rising out of the jungle and moving towards them across the water. Winoski's blue eyes were riveted, too, on the chopper.

"They haven't got a chance," Winoski said with no emotion. "Those shore batteries will tear them into little pieces."

The chopper hovering above the water became larger and larger. Drake saw sun bounce from the plexiglass dome and glare from the pilot's plastic helmet. Then the ocean became alive. Geysers sprouted everywhere as the radar-directed shore batteries at Tra Drang dropped a lead curtain around the point. The chopper tried an awkward turn to seaward, hung for a moment on its rotors and went down like a wounded gull as a 90-millimeter shell ripped through the cockpit. Drake stared at the sea for a long time after the barrage stopped. There were no swimmers.

On his stomach and leaning on his elbows, Winoski shook his head, "The old man must really want this film," he said softly. "That was a suicide run."

The shore batteries opened up again as the two jets rocketed over the water toward the troops on the beach, but the jets were too fast as they flashed under the barrage. Drake felt his throat go dry as the jets' tracers pointed fiery fingers into the dense jungle fringing the beach. One of the trucks started to burn, and Drake noticed the bodies lying on the sand were still. He felt a sinking feeling as the jets climbed over the trees and lifted toward the sky.

Winoski reached down with both hands and gave a little cry as he lifted his broken thigh. A large splotch of blood stained his nylon suit leg. Winoski's fighter face was crinkled with pain.

"It's just a matter of time before they get us," Winoski said. "Our boys can only keep them in that jungle until sunset. After dark, our little pals will be out here to pick up. And I think they're going to be pretty mad about all this."

As if to clear the sinking feeling in his stomach, Drake took a long draught of the clean offshore wind. He looked at the point and the beautiful curling waves falling evenly and peacefully down the sandy beach. For a moment, his mind went back to the last time he had seen such waves. How peaceful his life had been just a few weeks ago!

Winoski had been with him that day, a summer day that the Hawaiians like to put on their tourist posters. He and Winoski had driven from Kaneohe Naval Air Station in Winoski's Volkswagen. They had two nurses from the Aiea Naval Hospital and a picnic basket and the trip around the island past the Blow Hole was the best memory Drake had brought into combat. They had picnicked at Makapuu and the waves were almost like this, clean and beautiful, blown smooth by a light offshore wind. The nurses had sat on the beach while Winoski and Drake slipped on fins and swam off for some of the greatest bodysurfing Drake had ever experienced. He and Winoski had stayed in an hour, catching ride after ride. Those waves had been perfection. It's funny, he thought, I can remember those waves, but I can't remember the nurses' names.

Winoski's eyes also were on the mesmerizing waves and Drake realized Winoski, too, probably was thinking of that day at Makapuu. Drake wondered if Winoski could remember the name of his nurse.

"Lieutenant, assemble the troops," Winoski said in his flat officer's voice. "Your Colonel is looking for a volunteer."

"I gave the troops the day off so they could write home to their mothers," Drake said. "There's only the handsome young Lieutenant left on the post."

Winoski started a laugh that turned into a cough, crisp and hacking. Blood flecked Winoski's pale lips, and Drake realized Winoski was bleeding internally.

"I'm going to give you an order, Lieutenant," Winoski said, and there was no doubt he was speaking as Squadron Commander Colonel Winoski. "I want you to take a present for me back to the old man. It's just a few snapshots, but they have a lot of sentimental value."

Drake stared at Winoski's unblinking blue eyes, realizing the Colonel was serious, but just what did he have in mind? There was absolutely no chance: they were pinned down on a rocky promontory and a break down the beach would be suicide, so how did Winoski think they could get the film away?

Winoski was silent for several moments, peering at the waves crackling off the point. What plan was forming in his mind?

"Lieutenant, how would you like to go bodysurfing?"

Drake looked at Winoski's eyes, still on the tumbling surf. The colonel was serious!

"Say again, Colonel."

Winoski looked at him and grinned. Drake saw there was more blood on Winoski's lips and a trickle now serpentined down his chin.

"It's a small chance, but at the moment, we don't have any others," Winoski said. "Now here's the way it could work: If you got out in that water and took off just right—remember, I said just right . . . If you got on a perfect angle, you could slide a quarter mile . . . This place looks as good as Makapuu."

So, thought Drake, Winoski had been thinking of that day they body-surfed in Hawaii.

Drake squinted over the waves, trying to see a bodysurfer sliding and dropping. "The Charlies would pick me up if I didn't make it, or they might chew me up on the wave."

Winoski looked at Drake and smiled.

"This plan doesn't have a money-back guarantee, but it's my best offer . . . this week only . . . " Winoski said.

Drake stood up and glanced down the beach. There were several camouflaged uniforms clustered behind a machine gun set by an overturned truck. An officer, wearing a red baseball hat, was waving an arm.

"Time's a'wasting," said Winoski, using his colonel's voice.

Drake stripped to his shorts. He dumped several shells from an ammunition belt, clamped the webbing around him and stuck the film canister into a pocket.

"It'll be tough without fins," said Winoski, and Drake realized the colonel mentally was taking the swim with him. Drake stared at Winoski, propped against the rock like a knocked-down fighter, his right thigh bent at an angle. "See you later, Colonel."

"Yeah, see you later." There was no emotion in Winoski's tone.

Drake turned and trotted over the rocks to the sea. He didn't look back at Winoski as he dove into the surging water.

Breaststroking easily, Drake looked to the beach and saw Red Baseball Hat shading his eyes, peering seaward. As Drake moved closer to the break, Red Baseball Hat waved and several camouflaged uniforms clambered into a truck that had survived the strafing. They were moving toward the point, and Drake realized he'd have a reception committee.

Treading water, Drake gauged the evenly falling waves—slow but just right for a bodysurfer! He tightened his belt with the film and gave a last look at Winoski. Winoski was on his stomach next to the rock. Drake could feel Winoski's blue eyes focused on him like a light beam.

The third wave, that's the one I want, thought Drake, as he watched the elephant-like water humps move toward him. With three powerful strokes, he was in the wave and felt it lift him and, in an instant, he became part of the exploding mass.

Extending his right arm, Drake cranked his body on an angle and shot away from the tumbling hook. Across the face of the wave he flew, eyes burning with salt foam. In his ears, a thousand lions roared. Around him, the wave split little geysers from the Charlies' bullets. Drake sideslipped and then stuck his arm out again to climb. If I'm going to be used for target practice, he thought, I might as well be a moving one. There was plenty of wave left ahead of him, but he was moving towards shore, closer and closer to Red Baseball Hat's rifles. At Makapuu on a wave like that, Drake would have wanted everyone on the beach to see, but he didn't want that now. Drake glanced at the beach through the spray and saw that he had passed the truck with Red Hat and a dozen jungle-colored uniforms. They were stopped by the river. They'd gone as far as they could go, but he was still in range.

As the shorebreak loomed ahead, Drake put down his head and kicked, trying to squeeze the last inch of wave. There was the momentary weightless feeling and the crash as he went over the falls in the shorebreak. He rolled with the whitewater, and when he felt the sand, he pushed off hard.

Knees driving, he splashed through the foamy water and sprinted up the soft sand toward where green ferns marked the edge of the jungle. Head down, Drake waited for a rifle bullet, and he wondered how it would feel. Would his blood be the same color as Winoski's? He knew he was still in range of Red Hat and his rifles; why didn't they shoot? Then he was in the ferns, stumbling and falling down a bank of dark, black soil. He was off the beach; the rifles couldn't get him now.

"You move pretty well on the ground for a flyboy."

Drake glanced up at the crouched rifleman looking through a fern and across the beach at Red Hat and his parked truck and troops on the other side of the river. The marine was wearing sergeant's stripes, there were two grenades clipped in his breast pocket, and the butt of a cigar was clamped in his teeth. What a strange place to be smoking a cigar, Drake thought as he followed the marine's gaze toward Red Hat.

"Don't worry, flyboy, you're out of range now, but they had you cold for a minute while you were running across that sand. You must have really impressed them with your bodysurfing, because when you got out of the water, they were too busy yelling and waving their arms to shoot at you."

The marine turned and gave him a grin, still holding the cigar in his teeth.

"By the way, flyboy, what makes you so important to get a chopper knocked down like that?"

"I'm bringing the old man a present," said Drake. "A present from Winoski."

The Crackerjack Conspiracy
and Psychosomatic Alternatives
By Mickey Dora · SURFER Vol. 10 No. 2 · May 1969

He was called a thief, a liar, a con man, and a hypocrite—and that by those who called him friend. But no surfer, before or since, has so gripped our minds like Mickey Dora. In catlike trim on a Malibu wave, he was nearly perfect, and in our awe we were compelled to listen to his diatribes against the too-fast-changing world. His rants were always deeply felt and sometimes even lucid—proof enough that there was a brilliant, if troubled, mind at work. But his nostalgia for a time already past seemed to drive him to the edge of reason, and tracts of almost genius wit were often checkered with swaths of confused drivel. This piece, penned in 1969 before he fled the country to escape credit card– and check-fraud charges, epitomizes the fascinating lunacy that made up nearly all of Dora's contributions to *SURFER*.

During a multitude of years on the California Coast I've watched the once dominant individuals of our art phased out by an uncomprehending bureaucracy. In an apparently useless endeavor, I devoted my energies and thoughts to warn the unenlightened of the plight of the times. Now, the "hardened" lifeguards with their extension of power fantasies, the oldies but uglies, and the thousands of other plebeian fruit flies that compose the alleged surfing sub-sub-culture are forcing me to seek greener pasture. Bad omens are in the air. With malefied systematically, the untimely rape of Tonto can only be connected with Kemo sabeism. Next, the future betrayal of Tony Tiger is inevitable; only twenty pieces of silver will save them from the unequivocal retribution. Candied popcorn magnates steer the malleable young to smack and injections, onto a level their booze-oriented guardians cannot comprehend. Even "Tony Tiger" and his gay cohorts are shooting out their falsehoods.

Religious leaders project that the current trends in world affairs are those ascribed in Biblical times to precede the end of organic earth. Astrologically, the Topanga gypsies warn of anti-Jacinth antics of the present "age of Aquarius." Tales circulate about the cross-magnetic field reversals erupting in the fifth orbit of Saturn and Venus. When Saint Patrick sped from the birch tree maze, only to ascend into the glitter of Valhalla Valley, strenuous reversals were assured a complete transversal rift of the eroticus-barbarius seems unavoidable.

Daily, Havanak International fills while the treasury drains. Nightly, the guardian of our sleep, Saint Andreas, moves closer to creating the new beach resorts at Phoenix, Arizona, where Maharishi Hynsioni builds suburban dwellings on this soon-to-be Pacific Shore. The people who are to endure this onslaught of insanity must take positive action. Acts of juvenile destruction, such as the recent surf movie rioting, produce detrimental results. Individuals must no longer complain of oppressive conditions; they are obliged by their conscience to actively seek a better life. A renaissance of the original pioneering must force discovery of new breaks and unexplored coasts of other continents. Unknown regions of tropical splendor await the adventurous person. Darwin's theory of survival of the fittest is once again the rule of the game.

After this unheralded period of prosperity and wealth, can anyone doubt that the proverbial good times must roll past? This recession is already evident in surfing now. The amount of stolen boards increases monthly as kids who can no longer afford the high prices seek a free blank to construct their own crafts. I feel this outbreak of reshaping and reglassing indicates a movement towards a more personal involvement which is destined to reconstruct the sport.

Let bygones be bygones; the bandwagon has passed and those with a common interest must unite out of necessity. Having found an island near Madagascar which offers pre-atlas thrust conditions (viz., a more consistent break than California sans the minus-mentality morons); I'm going into exile there. Since I am leaving, I have chosen to divulge the last area on the Coast in which a person may exercise his wave-riding urge unhampered. I hope this knowledge will act as payment for any misunderstandings we have had between us over the years.

Santa Monica has existed unknown and untarnished at the front door of our sprawling megalopolis because it has never received the cheap publicity which leads to the ruin of a sport by incompetents. When the migratory season occurs, annually, the flocks pass the area unknowingly on a mad dash to the nowhere of Rincon and points north. Never stopping here, they bypass a variety of conditions seldom found in such a small distance, for in its three miles of shoreline from Sunset Point (seldom good, but often surfed by aliens) to the Pacific Ocean Park Pier, there exists point, reef and rack surf of all descriptions. A partial breakdown of these spots includes: Sunset Point, Sunset Cove, 3rd Jetty, 3rd Jetty Outer Reef, State Beach, State Beach Outer Reef, Roadside, Sorrento, Old Synanon House Fish Market, Sinbads, Trolley's Reef, Upper Monicas, Bay Street, Seaview, Santa Monica Shores, and P.O.P.'s four breaks. In addition, the "T's," the Cove, Autopia, and Resnacks Reef. Meanwhile back at the ranch, the star-struck travelers with typical simian lack of logic sit it out hoping the Rincon south chop will enable them to flounder further on the rocks, not knowing that one hundred miles south at 3rd Jetty, Trolley's or Outer Resnacks, phenomenal conditions are occurring. By simply viewing the curio-nimbus cloud formations over Magao turning from south to offshore, they would realize that the offshore breaks of Santa Monica were beginning to come on. With such a well-formed play of sounds near their Megalopolis cave dwellings, their yearly unproductive pilgrimages are typical of the happy masochism which marks the current bumper crop of unloved war babies. Struck by the goddess Kali dropping down Jacob's ladder of transistorized thought patterns, they drift into the meaningless gibberish of Gebaurland.

Having established the best factors of weather (a powerful south wind, curio-nimbus cloud formations combined with low humidity and an even to minus 36 percent barometric pressure), I will now outline, briefly, a few key spots. The 3rd Jetty offers an easy Hammonds-type right cylinder at low and minus tides. At State Beach, the parking lot boasts of carnival-type atmosphere similar to Camarillo Cliffs at feeding time. The beachbreak is extremely cooperative, while the reef may produce forceful walls at times. Roadside possesses a sandbar bottom with deviously deceptive shifting peaks, best at medium to high tide. Sorrento Beach may produce some cheerful shoreward motion; however, the beach is cluttered with 12-year-old "Howdy Doody" refugees, making the walk to the break both annoying and hazardous.

The Old Synanon House is a spirited peak with makeable cylinders in both directions. The Trolley's, located just outside the harbor breakwater, derives its name and waves from the streetcars sunken to serve as fish nests by the Fish and Game Department. The sand, in covering up the trolleys, created a unique, well-proportioned left, enjoyable in late spring and early summer. Moving on south, we come to Bay Street, a true blind man's bluff. The street's décor is reminiscent of the World War II blackouts. A very shallow sand bottom gives forth some hollow and exceedingly thin waves.

The next sports are nestled in and around the demolition-bound P.O.P. pier. The north side's "T's" break provides lengthy brain-taxing lefts. In the Cove, located on the south side of the pier, breaks consistently interesting walls at the lower tides. The Autopia, positioned in the center of the amusement park under the kiddie car ride, is a hollow, but conservative, right; caution should be taken: sharks, broken boards and beads are common. Located approximately 200 yards (years if you prefer) off the front of the Autopia is what many consider to be the prime cut of the area, Resnacks Reef. The reef is actually the remnants of an undersea retaining wall originally constructed to prevent the piers being washed out by ground swells. Catching all swells, Resnacks Reef emits a uniquely formed horseshoe-shaped bowl takeoff immediately followed by a total top-to-bottom tube-type situation. Breaking in both directions (east and west) with tremendous force, the person who attempts to transverse this geometrical phenomenon must employ great speed, or face a long swim through the pilings. Seldom ridden, due to the lengthy paddle around the pier (even to view the reef requires this seaward journey), Resnacks gives its few visitors an odyssey they'll not soon forget.

As now must be evident to even the magazine-oriented, crawling, thinking substances, Santa Monica offers a splendid variety to those with the cranial capacity to truly take advantage of its abundant physical pleasures. Besides its natural resources, the area offers a well-seasoned blend of individuals. Spawned in the region's unique genetic pool resulting from years of isolation from the Mod Squad septic tank of the surfing world, they are devoid of the idiosyncrasies and juvenile personality cravings which usually are the rule. In exposing this spot to public scrutiny, it is my hope that the aliens who venture into the realm will emulate this rare strain and, thus, upgrade the habits of wave riders everywhere. God save the king, for no one else will. ◪

Contest Morning

By Mark Martinson · SURFER Vol. 10 No. 2 · May 1969

The common dawn patrol requires greater measures of balance and commitment than most surfers tend to think. Each surf mission is made up of tiny achievements that, over time, become so second nature that we lose sight of the innumerable skills required. In this piece, Mark Martinson's whimsical trip down the coast illustrates how surfers establish native bonds with people and places along the game paths they hunt for surf.

Four-thirty Saturday morning. Brrring! Wham! Uhhh Oh . . . Yeah, surfing contest. The Big Ben alarm clock does the job. Better get a little stimuli going. Some hot tea should do it.

Let's see . . . contest at Oceanside. Hmmm. Not too far. Eighty miles. Probably could make it in an hour and a half if I didn't have a VW bus. I always wonder how VW buses got so popular for surfing. Usually the average surfer travels quite a bit, checking out one place or another. I couldn't think of anything more uncomfortable to drive. They have to be the most dangerous cars on the road. Head-ons with almost anything, horse or car, are instant end. I wonder why I have one. It's probably because . . . whhhsss. Tea must be ready. Bowl of cereal would go good; let's see . . . Froot Loops, no; Crispy Critters, no; Cocoa Puffs, no. Ah yes . . . some Alpha-Bits. What a training diet.

I remember on those rainy days in the Islands when we used to play word games. Think of a product and take turns naming the brand names. The last guy that can name a brand wins. Breakfast cereals were always a popular subject—so were detergents. You could always tell who were the ones heavy on TV. Once these two guys battled it out for two hours on morning cartoon shows. The winning show was *Odie-Calodie*.

I always eat a light breakfast before contests so I won't get nauseated. Those greasy breakfasts really work my stomach. Nothing like vomiting before your heat. It leaves you dizzy for an hour. Actually, I always get nausea at contests, even if I'm judging.

Wow! It's almost five—better brush my teeth. I've forgotten to brush my teeth more times than not; it's a wonder I still have any. Hmmm . . . a picture of my dad's brother's hot rod. He is a ho-dad if there ever was one. Never even tried surfing. Guys that drive those dragsters must get some type of sensation burning down the strip about two thousand miles an hour. Maybe it's the speed or trying to be best at something.

I better get on the road. Make some more hot tea to take with me. Wax, towel, trunks, wetsuit. My board's in the car. That's one good thing about a VW bus: you don't have to load and unload your board. Just lock it up right inside. I must be one of the laziest guys around. I guess it would depend a lot on what kind of neighborhood you lived in if you were going to leave it all night.

I hope this thing starts. I should fix the starter. The last time, I had to hot-wire it because somebody ran off with my keys. Instead of just turning the key, I have to tape these stupid wires together. Green and red together, now touch black SNAP! Wow! What a spark! Better try a different combo. Va! Va! Va! Pop! Bummmmmmmm. Sounds pretty good.

I have to admit it's been a pretty good car. Baja, Mazatlàn, Texas, East Coast—no major repairs. Something that doesn't go over fifty-five shouldn't need any repairs though.

I sure have a bumpy alley. Try and make it all the way down it without spilling my tea. I didn't realize this was becoming such a sport for me in the mornings. One hand on the wheel, the other balancing the tea. I can usually make it without spilling if I don't shift into second with my foot. I won't take any chances this time. All the way in first. Here comes the worst bump! Lurch! Not a drop. Next one—Bump! Oww! Just a little sneaked over the side. I have conquered the alley. If that spilled on my lap, I doubt if I could maintain. I'd probably run into one of those buildings. I guess there's risk involved in just about any sport. I think I'll suggest that to *ABC's Wide World of Sports*. I'm sure they'd be stoked out of their minds. They should have it with VW buses because they really feel the road. Up and down, jerk, and then side to side. I've gotten more dings on my board by having it inside the car than any other way. I suppose top racks are the answer. No they aren't either. They last about two seconds and somebody has a new set of racks. Every surfer goes through the stage where they make Clyde Barrow look like a shoe clerk, minus the violence.

This must be the best surprise I've seen. That's not saying much. I'm hardly ever up this early. It seems like when I was younger, I watched a lot of sunrises from out in the water. That guy's mother that used to think nothing of getting up at five, picking up a carload of guys, and taking them surfing; I always thought she was a little off.

Looks like one of those north wind days. Clouds over Palos Verdes— clear and orange toward Saddleback. There's the old Surfside water tower. I can remember surfing there before they filled it in with sand. There were some hot guys that surfed water tower: August, Corky, Kuntz, Lenahan, Fury, Chew. One time Robert August brought Lance Carson down from South Bay. Every gremmie on the beach came out of the water to watch, including Corky and myself.

We used to surf it until noon, or until it blew out, then pile about fifteen guys into one of those 1949 Nashes or Plymouths. The kind that you just put gas and oil in and they run forever. Everyone would chip in about fifteen cents for gas. There was always somebody that didn't have fifteen cents and would donate a sandwich to the driver for his share. Besides, when you're that young, you never eat anyway. And off we'd go to the Trestle. It always seemed like Trestle never blew out.

There's Huntington Pier. It doesn't look bad. I can tell there's a storm coming. Huntington sure is changing. Exclusive-type apartments on the beach, new parking lot, fancy concessions. A lot of face lifting since the days of fire rings. Those foggy winter mornings standing around the fire with Boozer, Lonardo, Corky and Herbie, all the Long Beach Junior Surf Club members. Being so loud and obnoxious that I think back and get embarrassed about things that were said. There was this girl that hung out down there that weighed about three tons and everyone, just like it was her name, called her "Ga Hunk." I think the name was of Lonardo coinage. He was a master at making up names and phrases. It's funny how young surf "Nazis" will do anything for a laugh. You just become absolutely immune to having your feelings hurt when you've had over-exposure to situations like that. What a good time we did have.

The radio in this car works good. KBCA-FM, jazz twenty-four hours a day. What a station. Too bad it fades right out before Laguna.

Santa Ana Rivermouth looks like too much sand has washed out there. That place really breaks hard. That one time when I was out there with Greg Tucker and Jock Sutherland, Tucker caught about an eight-foot wave. The wave was a super-barrel, fifty percent sand. Greg went down to the bottom, and the thing exploded, but Greg managed to get a slight angle going backside and started powering these continuous explosions breaking left, and Tucker standing straight up: a complete strength test between Tucker and the Pacific. Right before he was going to break into the green, one last explosion nailed him, one that would have knocked anyone else unconscious. I was paddling out with Jock watching the spectacle. When we paddled by Tucker, who was swimming in, Jock asked, "Hey, why didn't you grab a rail?" Tucker answered with his slow, casual way, "Wow man, whadya think I am, a girl or something?" Jock was left speechless, and I was laughing so hard I was seeing spots. I never did grab a rail after that, though.

"Same to you buddy." It's hard trying to change lanes in these buses. They have to be the most dangerous car on the road.

Better stop and get gas before that long stretch between San Clemente and Oceanside. That's when this bus shows its failure. This time of the morning you could go three hundred miles an hour on that stretch. There are quite a few who think that also. I know of a few more who tried it and don't think at all anymore. It's probably a good idea for me to have a VW. My '50 Chevy wagon blew a rod on that stretch. I think I was getting pressured from the rear by one of those trucks that are so high they have airplane warning lights, so I had to force the red bomb beyond its limit. It didn't actually blow up; the rods just started knocking. I nursed it all the way home, stopping every two miles and putting some seventy-weight oil in it. By the time I got home, the rods were knocking so bad and loud, people were running out of their houses to see what was going on down the street. Inside the car it was worse. I had seven passengers. All of them yelling out conversation to one another. It was vibrating so bad that the dash knobs and the door handles were falling off. I couldn't stop unless I had it in neutral with the accelerator pressed to the floor so the engine wouldn't stall. Needless to say, she was running a little hot. If I did turn her off, everything would have fused together. It got us home and sat in front of my house for about a year until I had it outfitted with a new engine. It never ran right before the new engine or after. Cars are funny things for surfers. To me, they represent something as mystical as witches and witchcraft. Mike Doyle told me once that if a car acted bad, just punish it. Don't wash it, no oil, drive fast, slam the doors as hard as you can. It sounded pretty logical to me at the time.

"Rocket Gas Station." Looks good to me. "Fill it up regular." I can tell this guy has been up all night just by the way he looked at me. The kind of look that says "wham!" and you don't have any teeth left. Better be as pleasant as possible. I could see Lonardo with me now. He'd be outside aggravating the hell out of the guy. He'd get the guy to check the tires, oil, windows, even water in a VW. Lonardo would swear up and down that the engine had a radiator. I've heard of guys having service refused from restaurants and bars and things like that, but never from gas stations. Lonardo was refused service at about five on 101. If you had him in the car, they wouldn't serve you, and Lonardo didn't even have a driver's license.

"Thank you." Boy what a grouch. There's Corky's house. Car's still there. Must be getting a late start. He has that Porsche; shouldn't take him long to get down to Oceanside. Last time I saw him was in the Islands. New Year's Eve. That's right. He lit one of those packs of three thousand firecrackers under my surfboard. A couple of days later it broke in half. We've been friends for a long time. It would be ridiculous to start any friction now. Besides, he was probably remembering New Year's five years ago in the Islands when myself and Danny Lenahan lit off a pack of twelve thousand in his house, and it almost blew apart the house. He always did have a good memory.

Talk about places changing, look at the Trestle. A freeway right through the middle. It's changed so much since the first time I surfed it. Some good days there. It seemed like it was always good. I guess you forget the bad days. Like that rainy day in spring when I drove into the jungle. I had just gotten my driver's license. You shouldn't drive in there in the spring. The area where you hide your car turns into a marsh. But I thought the family car would carry me through safely. What could possibly hinder the path of a 1954 Lincoln Capri four-door? Such a beast of a car. I sank it past the axles in the marsh. The Marines were kind enough to get a town truck and pull us out. And since I had only sixty-five cents and the towing charge came to thirty-five dollars, the car was impounded. Our surfboards were impounded. And we were taken to the criminal office of Camp Pendleton. I was the oldest, sixteen, so I was responsible. You'd think that in this humorous-type situation that the Marines would use a different procedure. I'd been caught several times before, and they have you sign a written promise that you won't come back. I'd already promised twice before. That's not the American way, breaking a promise. I'm figuring by the way they're talking, they'll deport me or give me a life sentence. Meanwhile, the sergeant is making calls to the F.B.I., the General on the base and the juvenile authorities. My playmates are downstairs playing cards with the other criminals. I have some clown firing questions at me with his hick drawl. And every time I'd get a third chance, and that my pals were just under my bad influence. They were advised to associate with more upright characters. The mother of one of my pals came and picked us up. The sergeant filled her in on what had happened, and my part in it all. She had missed a dinner party and was a little upset before she got there. So that must have been why she tore into me on the way home. After almost being deported, a little nagging from a mother doesn't seem like much. But heck, all I wanted to do was surf.

Oceanside. It's starting to rain. Nobody down at the pier. Not even any judges' stands. Let's see that contest schedule. Oh yeaaah . . . the 18th and 19th, not the 11th and 12th! ▉

The Day They Walked on the Moon

By Drew Kampion · SURFER Vol. 10 No. 5 · Nov. 1969

The world had gone mad when Drew Kampion assumed the job of associate editor at *SURFER* toward the end of 1968. Through ensuing assassinations, riots, draft lotteries, and overseas carnage, the introspective writer transformed the entire shape and scope of *SURFER* from a well-behaved "how-to" manual with contest results and travel tips into a template for the new counterculture revolution. His versatility as a writer proved pivotal to the movement, and he kept readers guessing with keen-eyed poetry, profiles, contest reportage, editorials, fiction, and reviews. At a time when surfers were striving to explore who they were and where they fit in—if at all—it was Kampion who ushered them forward on their inward journey. This story offers a poignant look at what was happening back on Earth on July 20, 1969—the day man first walked on the moon.

The day they walked on the moon there was a contest at Oceanside. A 3A. Scheduled for the jetty, but ending up south of the pier and starting out of gray, choppy, early light. A cold group on the beach and a few jerseyed surfers in the water. No breakfast yet, but stomach working up for it. Another 3A. So what. Strike up a conversation here: "Mornin' Terry." Lucoff wet from his heat, dripping around inside a terry cloth robe that fails to betray he is a man at work on his second or third million, son of the Mattel vice-president, and grandson of the president of the Amsterdam stock exchange. Hair like Brillo, and a voice equally smooth. Owner of a board shop that limits itself to six a week.

Then walking up to breakfast with two of Lucoff's gun bearers. Listening to Terry ripping off "oinks" at passing local broads, dishing out an early morning "peace" to passing jarheads, and attracting a lot of attention till we step into somebody or other's café and take a booth. In the booth, Lucoff proceeds to proposition the waitress, who declines: "Sorry, I have to babysit my baby tonight." Crash. Then steak and eggs. (Scrambled easy, rare on the steak if it's good, well if it's not, a large orange juice. Melon? No. Grapefruit? No.) "You're not too diversified here, are you?" Lucoff rasps. The waitress backs away. After breakfast, Lucoff goes off to hustle a couple of Marines in the poolroom.

Then back to the beach, Lucoff bumping chest-to-chest with every chick we pass. "Want to go for a little ride?" in perfect dirty-old-manish.

Into the fantastic men's room at Oceanside: a trough against a wall in a room that smells like a stable. Deep breath and hold. No towels. Surfers are animals.

On the beach again in time to see Jeff Hakman squeezed out in a choppy heat, though he manages to raise the water temperature about eight degrees on one explosive ride, leaping over sections instead of working around them.

The 3A's were obviously progressing. So much so that a lot of the guys ripped beyond the abilities of many 4A competitors. There will come a time. Fain showed up to judge; so did Dobson. Andy Munoz. Frank Petrillo in the sand "checking up on his riders" who were doing well: Tiger Makin, Eddie Underwood. Rumor that Purpus was going to ride for him: "Maybe. We'll see." And Dru Harrison making the rounds. The Schlickenmeyers, Steve and Chris, both ripping in their heats. Marty Sugarman taking a third in his. "I really didn't like the old judges a few years ago, but now they have the younger ones, and they're worse, if anything. They're too immature to be fair." Marty considering rabbinical school, working for a CO, and reading a lot. He loans me a copy of *Trout Fishing in America*, which changes my life.

Roy Crump, back from the Islands, is talking some pleasantries, then spots a girl he might have used to know, and splits. Angie Reno has cut the glass off the top of his ski, shaved the foam down as much as an inch, and reglassed it. He looks really good on it, not floating as much as before and getting deeper into the bumpy wave.

Jock Sutherland shows up with a winged-tip, down-railed, vee-bottom-aft machine, and proceeds to demonstrate the best surfing the coast has seen in quite a while. Sugerman asks later how he gets his fin out like that. Jock: "Just stomp on the nose." Does it do it every time? "Most of the time . . . " and it does. Jock drops to the bottom of a top-heavy wall, squeezes up under the edge of the curl, twists his body so the aft end slips out, then weights forward. The result is a glue-like adhesion to the edge of the curl, a shower of spray down the face of the wave, and a very freaky free moment. Then the wave walls into an approaching section, Jock slams the fin back into contact and vaults at the lip of the approaching tunnel, over it, and down with the crashing section on top of a pile of soup. Almost always successfully. With the most incredible speed imaginable. And it's happening on crap waves that crash from their 6 feet of maturity to 3 feet of sandy foam. Jock ain't long for the 3A world. Somebody's gotta be knocked off.

Two days before at Trestles, he'd worked the same things with even more success, going backside one wave and frontside the next. Almost total versatility and awareness. The thinking man's surfer. Like Scott Preiss.

Scott Preiss is skinny. And he always wears a black and red wetsuit. He wears his wetsuit on the beach on 80-degree days. "What're you doin' here on the beach like this, Scott? It's 80 *degrees*!" "Oh, soakin' rays . . . " Scott hates cold water or something. Yet he's probably the most promising young surfer currently on the scene; sort of a cross between Greenough and Lynch, who is sort of Nat flopped over backwards. Preiss is heavy into knee riding, making boats, designing gadgets, modifying equipment and surfing. He uses a speed bead down the bottom line of his roundtail. 30 percent greater acceleration out of a turn. Nat superimposed over Greenough and flopped. Get it?

And all this time, 240,000 miles away, three men floated in a vacuum getting set for the big step. The module planted four-footed on the gray ash of the moon, the ladder dropping out and down, the hatch opening and the step-stepping down its metallic web, then KAZONK!—Jock hits the lip, fin slips out, spray and trash fly, the wall elasticizes, he pushes, fin grabs, section explodes, he carries over the top and falls armpit-deep in foam. And makes it! KABLOOEY! Preiss wiggle-waggles along a wall, faces a right coming head-on to his left. Cut-out? Fly over? Hell, no: under it, then up through the crashing lid and over the falls for 43 points at least, because you don't go around making these things. Little knee-riding experience showing. SCREECH! Steve Schlickenmeyer comes around at the bottom of a 6-footer, his rail making the only water contact there is, like a thing in a groove, so you expect him just to sit there three-sixtying six or seven times, but he breaks it, bangs off the soft underside of a ceiling and comes around again off the bottom. Why does he bother with a fin? He barely keeps it in the water long enough to twang it. Astronaut whatever-his-name was (is) takes Step One, while these little plastic slithering sticks do a basting job on Earth's spiraling head spinner. The ballet is similar. The vehicles are at opposition. Surfboards are cleaner than rocket ships.

On this particular Sunday, Jock wins, Steve Schlickenmeyer is second and Scott Preiss is third. The day is colder and windier and wetter than it was earlier, and the beach dissolves back into sand as soon as the trophies are passed out. Enthusiasm is strained or absent. The trophies seem artificial appendages to the art of surfing. Pointless, anachronistic, obtrusive. This bit of art is worth so much metal and wood. Your bit is worth this much. Etc. It all seems a bit blatant.

Home is a familiar dash. Campers crowding the highways. Family units in transit back to their homes to twist guts and raise calluses so that they can wail off more gallons of gas next weekend to get somewhere in time to get back again, etc. Fifteen miles of Camp Pendleton, and slow for the Immigration Check Point, where if you have olive skin, you have to pull over and speak to the officers. Past the Nuclear Plant that doesn't put out any watts. Past Church that doesn't have a church anymore. Past Lower Trestles that doesn't have a trestle. Past Upper

Trestle that does, and from the highway waves are visible, and it has glassed off. Then swing off the freeway, park and start the walk.

Pass three guys coming back at Uppers. "How's Lowers?" "Really good . . . really good . . . " "Anybody out?" "You're it . . . " Break into a run. Kind of a slate green evening. What Joyce called the snot-green sea, maybe, except with more brass in it. Clouds crowded down on the horizon. There would be wind in an hour or so.

Lowers was perfect. Six feet plus and back to its best for the first time in a year. Long, dark walls. Not a breath of a stir on the water. Just clouds above. Then paddling out for wave number six or eight or twenty or something, and the clouds broke apart above. They really did. There was a gigantic inner tube of cloud around Trestles, and up into the sky, except straight overhead. And overhead, planted straight in the center of the darkening blue, was a pockmarked moon. And right then, at that moment, two men were walking it. Alone at Trestles, the first trace of the wind dappling the surface, the waves perfect, after a day of exciting and great surfing, and there they were. So close. Nothing between us but 240,000 miles. ▰

Perils of the Tropics

By Bernie Baker · SURFER Vol. 11 No. 5 · Nov. 1970

The world seemed entirely new to most surfers in the early '70s, and after a decade of self-discovery they turned their attention outward, where an entire planet full of undiscovered waves seemed to beckon. Hardened by the chaos of the times, surfers were taking more risks in order to find the perfection they sought. The Caribbean became a prime jumping-off point, its countless islands offering much the same opportunities for discovery that Indonesia offers surfers today. In 1970, Bernie Baker, a self-described "very naïve 20-year-old," began a six-month exploration of the region, flitting from island to island (and, later, the unfamiliar zone of Central America), dodging revolutions and rubbing elbows with draft dodgers and drug smugglers. Ushering in the golden age of surf travel, his heart-pounding tale offered a hint of what was to come, as surfers hunted for waves still untouched, in places unfamiliar, on a planet roiled by Cold War strife and Third World poverty.

You are about to read a true-life adventure actually experienced by Bernie Baker, an everyday surfer. For the sake of surfing and mankind, he braved shark-infested waters, sidestepped revolutions and rode a bus through the middle of a war just to tell you, loyal readers, how the conditions are in the West Indies and Central America. We join Bernie in the midst of glassy, but troubled, waters.

Extreme Reflections

Sitting on the porch looking out across the Mona Passage, beyond the heated flat glass, Desecheo Island began to look like a monstrous hole in the sky. We thought we could see swells pouring out of the cave on the horizon, but they never reached shore. We were frying in the incredible sun, while health food and assorted stashes dwindled and disappeared. Heat waves were the only kind we'd seen for two weeks, and an Aussie down the road flipped out and traded his Honda 150 for three grams of hash, and wrote it off to the perils of the tropics.

Three weeks earlier, I'd been running on numb stumps at Rincon and plotting my exodus from the wetsuit, frozen-hands, aching-head winter scene. I settled on the West Indies and Central America, instead of the traditional Hawaii, and that's how come I was sitting on the porch in Puerto Rico, looking out across the Mona Passage reflecting on reflections.

I really hadn't known what to expect because few Californians know anything about the West Indies, and surf news on Central America is almost nonexistent. Easterners I've met have been pretty closemouthed about their tropics, but like everyone else, I've seen a few shots, and I was stoked.

Life Among the Eeepppeees

As soon as you get off the jet in Puerto Rico, you realize you've got another hassle on your hands—getting to the other side of the island. Either you take a $12, 20-minute flight to Mayaguez and wait for your board to get shipped at a later date, or you can sweat three hours in a *publico* through the humid city and jungle for $20. That's what the driver says, and he isn't lying (however, he conveniently forgets to tell you that $20 is the price for a full cab). With the cab full ($5 per head) and the board lashed so securely in the trunk that it becomes a part of the car, you head for Rincon.

Puerto Rico received a lot of good publicity for the World Contest and surfing, but you'd never know by the bad vibes drifting around.

Every morning "gringo" surfers and their chicks walk into town for the morning mail and "checked-out" packages (who knows what evil contraband these Americans deal in?).

A white is an "eeepppeee" and you just have to flow with it, along with being thrown into the slammer and given a close haircut and small fine for not wearing a shirt in town.

The walk to Domes includes trespassing across a short piece of property on the nuclear reactor base. The head guard screams, jumps up and down, throws rocks and chases you. If he catches you, he may beat the crap out of you, even though the reactor was disassembled last year and the United States is going to let the Puerto Rican government turn the area into an exhibition center. Barbed wire and broken glass liven up the trip if you try the trails.

You also have to flow with the Puerto Rico surf, which can be weird. The north swell that hits these beaches usually comes broken and eaten away by a hundred fetches whirling at sea, and it's a surf-out just paddling around for waves.

There aren't distinct channels between spots, and although each area of reef has a name, the left at Dogman's could very likely overlap the right at Maria's, and so on. The surf power—or lack of—calls for an all-round stick for having a good time in the beautiful-looking surf, unless Tres Palmas grinds through at 15 feet or better.

The future as a surfing area is questionable. The locals emit as many bad vibes as possible to surfers who spend in a week what a tourist goes through in a day. Maria died, and her property is being turned into a restaurant-motel complex—pay and walk in. It's all right, Ma, I'm only dying.

So you stick around your shack and watch the horizon for signs of waves to rip the monotony, or sip a beer and take a turn at the pool table at the top of the hill. Or you crash early to forget the heat (but not the mosquitoes) or you move on.

Real Exploring

Southeast of Puerto Rico lies the Virgin Islands, a couple of surf spots and some excellent skindiving. And south again lies the Windward and Lesser Antilles, where the real exploring begins.

Almost every island in the West Indies is an independent nation, and to travel through them, passports are a must, along with shots and a round-trip ticket back to the States or San Juan. These measures assure you of 21 days visiting time, and eliminate the possibility of vagrancy problems.

Far to the east of the main chain of Windward Antilles, against the prevalent tides and currents, sits the small, crowded sugar cane–hilled Barbados. The windswept island lies exposed to any swell or storm. And that's the problem.

The north swells split the island at North Point and then wrap along both east and west shores. The east is always blowing onshore, and the top of the western side blows out quickly. By the time the swell has reached halfway down the length of this 20-mile-long island to the more sheltered reefs, it's lost most of its juice. You can stand at the southern end of the western side and look out to sea and not even know that only a few minutes' drive up the coast it's 12 feet and booming.

Living accommodations are bad enough for residents and the resorts cater mostly to wealthy tourists. Although that doesn't help you or me, it keeps the crowds down for the fifteen or so surfers who reside on the island.

If you risk the hassle of getting settled there for your permitted short stay, you'll see surfboards made out of crude foam blanks from England, a few American boards, good Banks beer, a hot young goofyfoot named Buffy Edgehill (their only shaper) and will learn the delights of eating flying fish. And while the black people cut cane all day, the little children either fly their homemade kites in the everpresent wind, or go "hulling" where the surfers aren't riding.

Hulling is a form of bellyboarding that dates back to the days when their ancestors were first brought to the various islands as slaves to cut the sugar cane. For relaxation, a few hearty Bajans started rolling around in the surf, and probably picked up bodysurfing. After that, it's anybody's guess as to who thought of riding a piece of wood on their stomach, or what motivated them. But they did, and it caught on, and only recently, with the coming of surfers and their finned boards, have the local natives nailed on a bit of crude wooden fin for stability and fewer unplanned sideslips. It's really amazing to watch the older brothers stroke out to the reef, and with one hand on the nose and the other for a paddle, catch an overhead set, stand up, slideslip and free-fall to the bottom and fight their way through the curl all the way to the beach.

The diving off Barbados and the Leewards is beautiful, and unlike Puerto Rico, where the moray eels enjoy jumping out of their holes and bouncing themselves off your face mask, the only things to contend with are stone fish (instant death) and sea snakes; so once you get past these guards, be prepared to bring a 10-pound lobster or two for dinner.

Even with no jobs available to the foreign traveler, I still found it hard to leave this area with its incredibly happy people and slow living. Until a terrible flat spell hit, and one morning I could see that my dream was being shattered, so I journeyed southward to the last two islands in the chain, Trinidad and Tobago.

Trinidad turned out to be a beautiful place, with some of the poorest people I have ever seen. The beaches, with muddy, murky water, were a disappointment, and accessibility a problem. Revolution and politics were in the air, and I left the morning the riots broke out, bringing a U.S. Navy convoy to her shores to evacuate the Americans.

The neighboring island to the north, Tobago, makes up for all that Trinidad lacks. Tobago is a long, narrow isle with only a few roads, but fairly reachable beaches. She'll show on any direction of swell, and a good right point has already been discovered. What is needed here is someone with the time and patience to check out both sides during the different seasons, and get the area wired. Cheap living and happy people could bring many months of comfortable surfing and living to those who really want an island to themselves.

Avoiding La Junta

Few States surfers have stayed in Panama long enough to sample the waves, and if I hadn't been staying with a family in the Canal Zone, I might have bypassed some good surf. But it was hairy. Panama is controlled by a military junta, and that fact will be on your mind day and night. Their police system is efficient, and they make up their own rules. If they don't like your hair, bell-bottom pants or sandals, they'll let you know with a swift clop in the head and an undetermined length of time in one of their prisons.

Checkpoints are stationed throughout the country along the main highways, and we would leave for the beach (an hour from the Canal) at 3 a.m., hoping to sneak by a sleepy guard before he got too long a look at our appearance, hair and liberal ways. We didn't get ripped off, but I carried a machete at my side for security.

Panama City has an excellent break—Santo Domingo—that serves as an indicator for the primo surf spots to the north. The only problems being the sewage and 300-yard tide changes. The spots surfed north of the city are few, but clean. "Tits," named after Rio Teta, is a combination reef-peak and two beachbreaks. The waves resemble the Ranch for crispness, but the 85-degree water really gives it an edge over Rights and Lefts. The beach is called "The Oven," Panama being one of the hottest, most humid places in the world.

A couple of small towns in the vicinity carry enough foodstuffs to live on, and fruits are abundant throughout the country. They have an orange larger than a grapefruit, and plenty of papaya, mango and bananas.

Revolutionary Tools

I left Panama with Canal Zone surfer Steve Small, and headed for Costa Rica, traveling with surfboard and pack. It was much less difficult than I thought; truck drivers were glad to have company if their cargo holds were empty, and the many bus companies allow you to stick your board inside on the overhead racks.

We surfed at two beach towns, Quepos and Punta Arenas, finding clean, consistent surf. Jeep roads spurred off from these towns, but we didn't stay around to explore.

Crossing the border into Nicaragua, we got some raised eyebrows when it came time to figure out what our bag-covered surfboards were. They checked for barrels and triggers, and collectively decided they couldn't be used in a revolution, passing us and our surfboards into their country.

I was learning that the feeling among the people was that any wandering youth with long hair was one of those "student radicals" pictured in last week's international edition of *Time* or *Life*. In general a rock-throwing, cop-hating revolutionary. And these people have enough on their hands trying to keep their own youth in order without "student radicals" planting seeds of revolution in their children's minds. But don't worry, most of the kids I met were in the midst of leading their own quiet revolt against the binding Spanish traditions and beliefs of their parents.

War, Peace and Surf

As we crossed the Honduras—El Salvador border, we were given our first good look at war. The Honduras border town was completely riddled and blown apart by the Salvadoran Army, and soldiers lined the banks of the river border with small groups on rooftops and in the shrubs.

Our bus made it slowly across the border, and as we moved toward the El Salvador checkpoint, we were greeted by their army placed strategically on their banks, rooftops, and in the shrubs.

After clearing customs, we were transferred to a smaller bus and started on a detour when the Honduran forces scored a hit on the bridge. Tensions were high, and I kept my camera in my bag as we rolled slowly away from the shooting.

At the capital, San Salvador, the Instituto de Turismo people were so friendly and efficient in catering to our problems, it blew my mind. They took care of everything: maps, directions to the beaches, and even delivered a message left me by another surfer from Santa Barbara.

Monty Smith had been living there for a few months when we arrived, and was in the midst of getting his citizenship. We three were the only surfers in the country, and the coastline was entirely ours! Our house was situated next to an "*estero*" or dammed-up creek used for swimming, bathing and washing clothes. Horses grazed in the pastures beyond, and waves peeled offshore, morning, noon and night—5- and 6-foot shifting peaks that usually blew out by noon. After the morning surf-outs we usually sliced a foot-long papaya and filled it with raw cashews, honey, sliced bananas, raisins and wheat germ from our traveling stash. Then we focused on reading, dreaming in the hammock and easy afternoons.

The evenings in the local port of La Libertad provided more entertainment than one would expect in such a remote coastline as El Salvador. The three of us would wander in shortly past dusk and make our way to the local watermelon vendor for a fine dessert. After sampling his wares, and about ten others', we would make it to the local pool hall for a game or two. This proved to be a bit of cultural shock and carnival for the locals, who had rarely seen blond hair, much less of any unnatural length. But after they figured out we were as easygoing as they, it was smiles and greetings whenever we stopped in.

Late in the evening, we occasionally went down to the wharf where, under the secrecy of night, arms and ammunition were unloaded off foreign vessels anchored in deep water, and whisked away under armed convoy.

Sharks, Fruit and Surf

The surrounding coastline has plenty of points, coves and one set-up north of K-61 that resembles El Capitan, as the wave constantly reaches for the bouldered coastline as it tosses over your head.

During the rainy season—May to October—the storms off Mexico that give Southern California its south swells hit El Salvador with a bumpy north swell. If you had to pick one month, March would be the best bet.

Fernando, an oyster diver who lived behind us, told us that *tiburon* (shark) were constant companions in the surf and in the whitewater when we swam for our boards. Good old Fernando. Plenty of fish kept the *tiburon* full.

While I was there, we had a solid 10-foot swell that ripped off the point all the way to the wharf. It looked like Rincon as I snapped Monty on an incredibly long wave at La Libertad Point in front of our El Salvadoran paradise, and a long way from cold water and frozen fingers.

Routing Around Revolt

The safest and easiest way of traveling through Central America is to pick up an airmail edition of the *Miami Herald*, found in every major city down there, and find out who's revolting at the moment. Then pick your route and make a run for your destination. You can score the news at any American Embassy, along with aid and advice, and this makes for less problems.

Crossing through the southern Mexico border on the way home can be just as difficult as getting into Mexico from the States. Either entrance requires that you show $100 upon crossing. The Mexican government gets sadistic satisfaction in throwing gringo youths in jail for any petty reasons, so be cool.

If this entire journey has sounded a little too heavy for your nerves and peaceful, flowing way of life, then be content with your own beach. If you're wondering what uncrowded waves look like, and long for a little adventure, take off. 🏄

Waterbed

By Joseph A. James · SURFER Vol. 13 No. 5 · Jan. 1973

SURFER's antiwar stance was often powerful because it was usually articulated with calm, sound reason rather than vociferous tirades. Like everyone else, surfers were caught in the Vietnam crossfire, and their tales increasingly ended up in the pages of the magazine, most depicting the concealed residual effects of battle rather than glossy Hollywood heroism. This tempered short story, by Joseph Allston James (who would later change his name to Allston James and become one of *SURFER*'s contributing editors), about one soldier's long road to recovery, gives pause to anyone who thinks war might be the answer.

One

Summer. More precisely, first summer swell. As I paddled out past the shorebreak, the grime that my arms had picked up from the car roof and racks gradually faded away with each new immersion in the sea. Each individual stroke of my arms was important, not because of the resulting forward progress, but simply because I was doing it. The time-lapsed pregnancy of a small wave lifted my board. Paddling over the next wave of the set, thoughts of the war came to mind. Not whole thoughts, just fragments. That's the way memory shovels war to you after you've left the scene: just an occasional piece or fragment. Memory of anything is always going to be less than the whole, but with war, memory often seems less than nothing. A vacant lot in the head.

The Asian horror show had folded for me months ago. Not for everyone, but it had for me. It ended and started on a hospital bed in Vietnam, on a hospital bed in Japan and on a hospital bed in America. That's the main thing I think about when I think about war and hospitals . . . beds. Beds upon which every man can become the island that no man is supposedly capable of becoming. Or at least that's what they used to say in Sunday school. No man is an island. That's what they said. Before I ended up in a hospital, I always thought that when people got hurt in wars, they got hurt in the arms, legs, shoulders or stomachs. You know, sort of categorized. Like, War Injury Type A, War Injury Type B, and so on, all the way down to War Injury Type Z. But it wasn't like that. After all, how would you classify the guys who were urinating and defecating through plastic tubes and bags? Or what about the 19-year-old kid who woke up at two o'clock one afternoon and asked for the lights to be turned on? Not yelling, just asking very softly if someone would please put the lights on. From my bed, I could see blackened flesh all around the edges of his facial bandages. Where his eyes had been, there were now two big yellow gauze pads. He looked like a big fly or something. About the third or fourth time that he asked for the lights to be turned on, I rolled over in my bed and cried until I urinated right through my pale blue pajamas. There were lots of people like that in the hospitals, people who had burned-out eyes and people who cried and pissed all over themselves when they saw such things. I was lucky, although at the time I didn't quite look at it that way. A few days after I got hurt, a doctor came to my bed and told me that I might not be able to walk again for a long time. It scared me. When he left the ward, I stared at my crushed foot for a long time, several hours. It just sat there at the end of my leg, pulsating painfully. The sharp pain told me that my foot was not right, that it wasn't really even much of a foot anymore. If a foot can't act like a foot, then it can't honestly be called a foot, can it? That's when I started thinking about the island.

Two

Week after week I lay beneath the sheets, my body forming ridges and valleys under the whiteness. Between my bed and the others, I imagined an ocean. The space beyond the sides and ends of my bed constituted a great ocean, full of dragons, Vikings and submarines. And even though the other patients were not aware of it, I dragged all of them into my nautical world. They were their own islands, complete with coasts and interiors. Knowledge of their '56 Chevies, hometown football teams and girlfriends was knowledge of their islands' mountains and valleys as far as I was concerned. Idle conversations provided me with locker rooms full of charts and maps that showed me weird trails and secret caves on the islands surrounding my own. All of this was important, but not significant.

The significant thing was the surf. Starting constructing surf sports all around my island. Several well-placed reefs just off of my forearms provided some damn hot peaks on occasion, and there was a constant beachbreak all along the stretches of both of my legs. But the best surf on the island was down around what I had at one time considered to be my right foot. Down there, long glistening lines wrapped around a point that used to be a big toe. Perfect sets every time. On some days, every spot on the island would be working, and on those days, I never talked to anyone. The bed and I were an island; we had waves breaking around us.

"Son, we're sending you home in a few days."

"Where?"

"Home. We're sending you home."

"I don't have to go back to the jungles?"

"No, you're going home. Back to the States."

"Will I be able to walk around when my foot gets well?"

"Sure, but right now don't worry about that. Just think about home."

"OK, please wake me up when the plane gets there."

Three

My mother forwarded a surf magazine to me a few days before they flew me home. I looked at the pictures and wondered about them for a long time. They seemed unrealistic, these photographic images of human images stuck on the sides of billboard-like waves. The photos lacked the life of the waves that washed the shores of my bed.

Four

Outside, I turned to watch the last wave lay itself down on the shallow waters near the shore. A sun-speckled swell began to peak behind me. My foot ached in anticipation of what was to come. I wasn't ready for this. Learning to support a body that wanted to walk was one thing, but this was different. Back in the hospital beds, the crushed foot had only been called upon to serve as a point of land around which perfect waves could pour. It wasn't ready to be a part of a man on a wave. It had been ready at one time, back before Asia, but it wasn't now. It just wasn't ready. But then it had never really been ready for jungle boots and leeches either, so perhaps this was fair play after all. I'd considered a bellyboard or small spoon but couldn't manage the fins and kicking.

I looked over my shoulder to check my position, and then I paddled a few yards to the right. My pale body, suffering pangs of apprehension and doubt, protested by way of small muscle spasms in my forearms and legs, but just like small waves, they were gone in a moment. But even with the end of the muscular twitching, I could sense that my body was protesting, much like it had first begun to weaken in the first of many beds; beds that had turned my entire form into the mountainous terrain of a strange island . . . my foot, a point of land . . . my arms and legs, ridges . . . my body, an island . . . the emptiness before, a sea. All, a stiffness.

I stroked towards shore. The sand on the beach looked like a soiled sheet, and the wave, as it lifted me, seemed like a mechanical bed. I began to slide. I stiffened my arms to raise my chest from the deck, and then, leaning instinctively, I put the board on an angle along the face of the small wave. My speed doubled. The time was here. I went to stand but fell face down on the deck. The foot wouldn't work; it just went limp.

Clutching the rails for stability, I felt like crying. And the wave wasn't even over yet. It wasn't over, but I didn't want to be with it anymore. The board continued to slide across the little wave out towards the shoulder. Everything felt awkward. I just lay there waiting for the inevitable wipeout, but it wasn't coming, at least not as quickly as I expected it to. Why should this wave continue to carry me? After all, I wasn't really surfing it. I was just lying there waiting for the dump. I just happened to be there. I should have been dumped yards ago. I may as well have been on the face of a billboard. Were people supposed to be on the faces of waves if they really didn't feel like they were there?

Just as I began to wish that I was back in the ward of a military hospital where my foot could resume its character and role as a point of land, the lip of the wave, only a foot or so above my head, began to bounce a bit as the wave sucked itself up over the sandbar. I knew that I was about to swim. The board began to move faster in response to the increasing hollowness. The wave's lip, tired of teasing, leapt out ahead of the wave face, washing the side of my face. The lip was now a roof. I lay there beneath it, head twisted around to see the watery shelter. It was then that I realized that this was no more a billboard than a bed is an island. Waves don't wrap around big toes; they wrap around people who happen to be traveling through them. The absurdity and wisdom of it all crept into my mind just in time for me to giggle as the wave's roof caved in, washing me up on the beach in a sprawling confusion of happiness. ▧

No Observable Progress

By Alvin Darkling · SURFER Vol. 14 No. 1 · May 1973

Much of the writing in *SURFER* during the '60s and '70s touched on the rapid rate of suburban sprawl that was literally choking the coast. The old isolated ranchlands of Malibu had become a Riviera for Hollywood stars, "Killer" Dana Point was turned into a harbor for the rich to dock their boats, the immense orange groves in the southland were being bulldozed to make way for tract homes, and even the mysterious Hollister Ranch was being chopped up and sold off in parcels. Californians were smothered by an intense feeling of claustrophobia, and localism arose as they grew increasingly protective of their space. Perhaps this explains why many readers viewed Alvin Darkling's tale about how far one person went to find sanctuary as more of a how-to manual than fiction.

It was raining and there was nothing to do. Outside his small apartment, across the slick concrete of the coast highway, lay the beach. Beyond the sand, the ocean was moving about nervously, the waves so helplessly confused that not even a solitary rider had ventured out for a surf.

He knew that as soon as the storm passed and the waves cleaned up a touch, there would be several hundred people out scratching for every ripple. This knowledge did nothing to improve the rather negative mood he had fallen into. He was also scared. It was a fear that had been lingering somewhere within him for several years. It was a fear that had grown familiar, a fear of never being able to be alone with the waves again.

At first he had traveled. The Islands. Fifty guys out at Honolua at the first sign of a swell pouring through the Molokai Channel. France. Crowds at La Fintenia, an international scene at Hosseger. Crowds in Barbados, crowds at Jeffreys, always crowds, and his money had run out. Now California was home again, and it was raining, and he was bored.

He picked up yesterday's newspaper off the floor to see what was playing at the 75-cent movie house. Hoping for a place to invest his energy for a couple of hours.

He never got to the film section, for on page 6 of a day-old paper, he found his future. Tucked away between an airline hijacking and a dope bust was a headline that nailed his attention to the stale print: STATE TO

PURCHASE SUNRISE HILLS BEACH PROPERTY. PLANS CALL FOR CONSTRUCTION OF MENTAL INSTITUTION.

Into his mind flashed sea- and sky-colored memories of magical days at Sunrise Hills, riding the waves that broke so perfectly upon the reefs there. Sure it was a couple of hours drive, and you had to sneak in 'cause it was private property; but damn, when the spot was doing it, any hassle was worthwhile. And now the state wanted the beach. Damn!

Closing his eyes softly allowed him to see the hot, clean tubular right that he loved; the mental picture was so vivid and real that he could not imagine being denied access to these waves. But there it was in black-and-white.

He began to read the article, with sadness altering his perception at first.

"Secretary of Finance Jensen Cutino today announced that the State has purchased 10 acres of land in the Sunrise Hills area. This acreage includes the South Beach section of Sunrise Hills."

Merely the premier spot. Smokes on a low tide, playful on high.

"Cutino stated that an ultramodern facility for the treatment of the mentally disturbed would be built on the land."

Wonderful. An insane asylum overlooking one of the hottest waves on the coast. He read on through a few statistics—cost of construction, projected number of patients, etc.—and then he came to the final paragraph. A paragraph that changed his life.

"Dr. Harold Gardner, who has been appointed Chief of Staff for the new institution, has these words of assurance for homeowners in the surrounding area: 'We plan to keep the institution totally secluded. That is why we have purchased so much land. Aside from the high therapeutic effect on our patients, we can also be sure that no one will be wandering in or out of the area.'"

Totally secluded.

The next morning the weather cleared, but he did not surf. Instead, he went to the library and checked out a copy of *The Divided Personality*. And during the next year, he read every volume on personality disorder that he could find. And during the next year, the Sunrise Hills Institution for the Mentally Disturbed rose quietly upon the green hillside overlooking the rather perfect waves that snapped over the reefs of South Beach.

No one surfed there anymore. One-thousand-dollar fine and up to two years in jail for trespassing on state land. Penalties so severe that no fence was necessary, just a few highly visible signs by the highway.

The institution officially opened on April 1. On April 2, he ordered a new board from the shop. A reefbreak stick. It was ready in a few days. The board felt pure and almost magical in his hands. Quite carefully he placed it in the rack of his old Bug and drove up the coast towards Sunrise Hills.

PATIENT ADMISSION REPORT

Patient approached front gate naked, carrying a surfboard under his arm. In a coherent manner, patient announced that he was a member of the "Yeti People." Patient announced that he had traveled here from his hometown in the Himalaya Mountains by "translocation" (apparently a form of mental travel). Patient mentioned that he had come to claim the hospital and surrounding property in the name of the rightful owners, "the Yeti People."

He was placed in a "harmless" ward, and thus had beach-going privileges. He convinced the doctors that surfing was relaxing to him. And the aide/lifeguard kept an eye on him to make sure that he didn't start to paddle for Catalina.

The surf was excellent all spring.

PATIENT REVIEW. ONE-YEAR INSTITUTION

Patient spends most of his time alone in the ocean. At night, patient can be heard giggling and laughing for no apparent reason. Still claims to be from the Himalayas. Patient is making no observable progress towards reality.

He had his own small room. His neighbors were, respectively, Mr. Lazlo, who thought he was a pigeon and spent all day cooing, and Leon. Leon was God.

"I am God. Welcome to this place. Do you like old cowboy shows? I am God," said Leon when they met.

When there was no surf, he meditated, or did yoga on the cliff high above the blue-green sea. Time passed by in dreamlike fashion. Summer brought south-swell perfection.

One afternoon, Lazlo was released. He promised to stay in touch by "pigeon mail." Lately, Leon had decided he was Brett Maverick, TV cowboy star.

THIRD-YEAR PATIENT REVIEW

Patient still claims to be a "righteously idealed Yeti personage." Says the Crown Prince of Belgium and the Dalai Lama have sworn him to secrecy over the mission he is on. Patient is making no observable progress towards reality.

He was alone in his wonderful daydream, with a lifetime of sparkling multicolored wave faces to dance upon. It was, he thought with a smile, "unreal." 🐾

The Rainbow Story

By Neil Stebbins · SURFER Vol. 14 No. 6 · Feb. 1974

SURFER staff members and contributors, like any self-respecting members of the counterculture revolution, were unapologetically drug-influenced rabble-rousers, and they offered free rein to those who dared to look inward and elevate the wave-riding experience to something larger than just a simple recreation. Neil Stebbins's fantasy about magic eye drops that allowed surfers to see the hidden colors vibrating in each wave seems a recruiting poster for LSD advocates. The mantra of this story, which was a huge hit, was that surfers should not impose their will on the waves. Rather, we should calibrate our mood to that of the ocean, allowing the thread of hidden colors to guide us like a leading dance partner.

It started with my eyes. Nobody knows about that. Most people think it's got something to do with my board. In fact, there's a kid outside right now sighting the flats and curves of my new one as if there was a secret message in it somewhere. There isn't. I could turn the same moves with as much speed on almost any good stock board my size. It's not the board. And it's not me either. I ride all right, maybe a little better than most, but that only helps. Like I said, it's my eyes.

I think my friends can tell something's different, but even they aren't sure it's my eyes. If they could study them, like I did at first, they'd see how the muscles at the corners of the eyelids tighten slightly or stare narrow, while, inside, the eyes seem somehow wider. It must look wild in the water because I have to compensate for glare by glaring back (in addition to remaining dilated the pupils oscillate rapidly, almost imperceptibly).

I make people nervous, even the ones who don't know who I am—and there aren't too many of those anymore. "There he is! That's him. You know . . . The Rider." "The Rider." Some interviewer called me that and it stuck. At least no one ever says it right at me. They just keep their distance and talk about anything, or maybe smile shyly and make a request, "Could you maybe do an inversion today if you feel like it?" I don't mind. I get lots of waves now. Ever since my eyes changed.

That was ten months ago. You know the story since then. "Unknown Paddles into World Contest at Rincon—Destroys Competition!" (Hey, you have to start somewhere.) "Olympic Committee Officially Recognizes Surfing!" "The Rider Dances—North Shore." In ten months, I've taken surfing from a static, selfish, flashy sport to an acknowledged high dance form. All it took was one rider with the right eyes, and, now, nobody else is even close. It's just a fact. I was lucky. My brother deserves the credit.

My brother, "Doctor Chris," is studying to be an ophthalmologist—you know, an eye doctor. He's also a first-class chemist, and really gets into making some strange things in the lab. Some of his better potions have been very entertaining, to say the least. One day, about ten months ago, he told me he had synthesized an improved formula for the liquid they use to dilate your eyes. I wasn't particularly excited about it until he said he'd gotten the idea for it from an article he'd read about a similar substance found in the eyes of sea mammals and birds of prey. I was just about to get moral over sacrificing porpoises and falcons for lab tests when he said, "I want you to try it. There's no danger. It's really pure, and I can run some tests, and, besides, it should improve your eyeball lubrication." I was always the one to get the benefits. "Well, somebody has to conduct the tests." (Tests my ass, you should have heard him laughing outside the bathroom door when his laxative and blue-dye-tracer experiment turned me inside-out.) Anyway, I'd been sanding all afternoon and my eyes were sore, so I said, "OK."

He put one drop in each eye, ran his tests, and seemed pleased. Then he noticed that my pupils were expanding slightly and contracting rapidly—pulsing. This surprised him and kept him racing around me saying, "Interesting," until, an hour later, he had enough test data to work on alone. I was still oscillating. "Take it easy," he said, "and don't wander off." I went surfing.

There was a good glassy early evening swell at Hammonds, about shoulder-high and building. I didn't notice anything different until I stopped to change and took off my sunglasses. Everything looked normal except for the water. You know what polarized lenses do to water? Well, it was like that, only much stronger. There were lines of color on the face of the waves, like abstract illustrations or some kind of oil slick or colored kelp. I didn't know what it was, but the waves were good, so I went out anyway. Paddling out I could see the color lines ranging softer in the offshore swells. Further out in the channel the colors ran together even more. But inside, where the swells compressed into waves, the bands of color sharpened into clear-cut flowing tracks (mostly blues and greens) across the face of every wave. And the colors moved with the waves—writhing, curving, sometimes abruptly angular, always changing in intensity. The colors beneath the curl and deeper inside the tube were dazzling. I just figured Doctor Chris had laid one on me.

I took a few waves and tried to concentrate on riding, but the color lines controlled my eyes. Their streaks ran mostly parallel to the wave face and gave each wave a sensation of depth and power by their undulations beneath its surface. A few lines, usually kelp-colored or almost red, traced amazing vertical zig-zag patterns (red lines are seldom ever parallel to the stress or speed lines of the wave). There were glowing yellow areas that played across the screen or canvas of the wave, appearing unpredictably, then vanishing. And each wave was different. (I'm only beginning to appreciate how radically different these combinations can be.)

I wasn't riding well at all. I thought, "I can't surf without watching the colors, and the waves are too good to pass by, so . . . " I decided to try riding *along* one of the lines. I caught a fair wave with some shape and tracked on a blue line. The acceleration was unbelievable. I fell off the tail of my board.

Next wave, I tried it again. Again the speed burst left me behind. I swam again and decided to "think-speed" and only track into a blue line after I'd gotten set up. I waited for a set wave—nice one—dropped in easy, came back up, found the line . . . and set. Eeeeeeeeehaaa!! I came blazing out past the section, past the shoulder, and ran over a guy paddling out. I could have kissed him.

By evening, people began to watch and stay out of my way. It was a blue-line speed-day. I couldn't believe it when everybody else went in after sunset. I could still see clearly and surfed two more hours after dark, alone, screaming and laughing and streaking, till my body said, "Go home."

By morning it had worn off. I waited, crazy for Chris to get home from the airport. (He flies gliders every weekend—says it's his way of surfing.) When he came in, I told him exactly what had happened. He listened, smiling, ran some tests, said I was fine, and asked if I wanted to try it again. In the interest of science, I said, "Pour a gallon in each eye!"

All I got was another four drops. I was at the beach in a flash, Doctor Chris and camera close behind. Same place, same swell. It was fantastic. In the rush of days that followed, I found out that green lines are like natural flow lines. Step into a dark blue line and you'll rocket. Edge over to a green one and you're on a path of beauty designed and redesigned, always changing, curve-crafted by the wave itself. Shades of blue and green are shades of speed and grace. I was in love. The waves were alive. Each face had its expressions, mood, temper, emotions. Imagine, after all the years of riding and stupidly imposing myself on "my wave" like a painter whose signature is bigger than his painting; imagine instantly communicating with these travelers and learning to speak their language. Can you see what it was like? Twice, sometimes triple the speed! And flow! God, what flowing curves to let you edge and drift, fall high, lay back down and dance a wave's own music. Later came the red lines— short-cut maneuver-guides to the most full-on slalom course imaginable. Take the red road and you'll stress a board to splinters. Fly Redline and go places inside-under-over-out-and-back-again that you never dreamed of tracking into before. And it's all right there, changing at different rates (dark blue lines are the most constant) on every break from here to

Saturn. Shorebreaks—tight little light-shows of futility—jubilee-waves that leave you hungry. Or pointbreaks—Malibu, Rincon, Cojo, Government—swept-back long waves you can get loose on. Or Island waves with dark blue power bands deep below the color lines. I've seen waves with patterns so complex I wouldn't even try to ride them yet. And I've seen waves with just one green line, and they talk to you: "Look deep and feel me. I've come from a storm a thousand miles away and this is how I want to end, just this line. Ride it, friend, it's all I am."

Today, Chris asked me if I want him to make the formula available for public use. He knows I've been thinking about it and has seen me go through a lot of changes in the last ten months. He also knows that I'm just beginning to understand the lines. I guess he knows me pretty well—he couldn't have picked a worse time for me to decide.

You see, last month I began concentrating on tracking only the most brilliant colors and on changing lines (mode) only where they cross. I've been learning to control freely at full intensity of each color, riding line to line, never cruising spaces. The films of me riding during this stage are showing all that I had hoped for—choreography, counterpoint—full speed, breakaway-pinball-spot-turns, back to speed, cross over to ballet, angle, arc, accelerate. And now, just out of reach, there are the yellow areas—indistinct sunshine zones that appear and disappear moving through the lines. Cross a yellow zone and you can feel it inside. You know the feeling. It's the exultation you learn to live for. It can be a looping tube or a turn or the soft serenity of floating edgeless. It's what you either can't describe or don't have to.

Now take *that* feeling and know that you can find it, not once or twice, but all the time. Know that you can go right to it on any wave that has it, go to it on paths of different colors and then stay with it! That's where I'm heading.

I've gone past riding tight to the limits of my mind. The lines are variations on themes nobody can claim, on expressions as deep as color, as pure as wave energy. I have no right to keep the formula for myself, but for all it means to me—my life, the dance, the discovering—I cannot (will not) make it available for abuse. I've seen too many good waves conquered by crowds. I know the trophy surfers and the loud ones. I've been through all that and out the other side. I used to ride for me and for all the other eyes. I've gone too far, have too far to go to decide. I leave the fate of the formula to my brother. He found it. It's his—for him, or us, or others. I'll tell Chris that the final decision is his alone. I'll tell him as soon as he gets back from the airport.

Another thing about the eyedrops. They let you see the wind. 🐾

11 Chapters of Africa
By Kevin Naughton · SURFER Vol. 16 No. 1 · May 1975

Even a decade after *The Endless Summer* piqued our wanderlust, many of the planet's greatest waves still remained undiscovered, for one simple reason: Hard-core surf exploration required courage, patience, luck, and a healthy dose of persistence. These attributes provided the foundation for each bold venture Kevin Naughton and Craig Peterson embarked upon during the period from 1973 to the late 1980s, when the two peripatetic surf explorers became cult figures in *SURFER*. Their example, along with the rollicking humor with which they faced adversity, inspired a generation of surfers to pack bedroll and board and hit the road. One of their most audacious journeys was this 1975 trip to Africa.

Chapter 1: The End

The end. "You can go no further, masta. The trail, it has finished," said our guide, who we'd been with since daybreak.

"The end, eh?" Craig said. "Well, there's gotta be *some* way to get there from here!" We were standing on a knoll; in the distance, swell lines could be seen sweeping towards the coast. It seemed to have potential, but before us lay at least four kilometers of jungle, an impenetrable wall of tangled green that even the most gutsy bulldozer driver would balk at. The trail behind us dissipated on this knoll, and the 10 o'clock sun beamed mercilessly down on us. About 90 degrees and gettin' hotter. We had all day to get there. Just like yesterday and just like tomorrow, if we didn't get dehydrated by the sun or pooped out like all the times before.

Below us, a brown river snaked its way through the bush. Three kilometers of trudging through "bushman" jungle paths, only to end here.

How dismal! We have to turn back. No, never in hell! A month of no surf had made us fanatically determined to reach *this* spot. We were desperate. Something's gotta break soon: the surf, jungle, or our nerves.

"What about paddling down the river?" suggested Kevin.

"No masta, is very dangerous. Bill Harzy here. Yes, is dangerous," our guide answered.

"I don't care who he is," said Craig, "we're gonna try the river. Any canoes around?"

"Yes, yes, I say canoes are near," and our guide pointed up the river to where some thatched huts bruised the green.

"Well, all right, if we don't find surf, at least we'll have a helluva time!" exclaimed Kevin.

Finagled a bit for a canoe. Strangely enough, as soon as a white man enters an African village, inflation hits. One young girl selling peanuts sheepishly turned upside down a cardboard sign with 4¢ scratched on it when she saw us coming with peanuts in our eyes and change in our pockets. After hassling for the sake of hasslin', we scored a 15-foot dugout canoe, a wilted old man for a paddler, three paddles (hmm, who else is supposed to paddle this?), two burlap bags packed with dead monkeys ("might as well do a little business with the other village while we're in the area," said the Chief) and six bananas thrown in for good measure. We were off. Our guide benevolently handed us those three extra paddles, as our canoe glided away from the village.

The river wove its way through the threatening jungle. The sights and sounds of tropical Africa assaulted us like the heat, which seemed to be sizzlin' the river. The very sounds you hear on a Disneyland jungle boat cruise, only this is the real thing. We were really stoked, gazing everywhere. "Lookit, didja see that? Over there! It's movin'!!!"

The fishing village was a small one. Everybody knew each other and their business, so when we arrived amid curious stares, we really felt like strangers in an even stranger land. Every time we smiled, they smiled, and vice versa. All went quiet as the Chief appeared, an ageless black man dressed in a pair of shorts. We shook hands. A moderate "dash" put him in good spirits; good enough for us to stay in his hut for three days, meals of rice, fish and eggs brought to us twice a day, people boil water for us to drink, cut open coconuts whenever we pleased, carry our boards down to the beach when we went, and a guided tour of the village by the great Chief himself. And yes, he also showed us plenty good waves.

He took us to the beach and proudly showed us a nice flat stretch of clean, white sand. We stood on the fringe of the horseshoe-shaped beach and inspected a point that jutted out in a ragged pattern as if it had been chipped into shape. There was no sand on the point. A narrow pinstripe of rocks separated the water from the jungle, which loomed over the ocean all along the point. Like anyone who watches surf from a distance, we stared intently, almost microscopically, at each wave. The waves broke over rocks a half mile out on the point, which was a mile. The break looked fickle. One set consisted of seemingly good-sized juicy waves, then another set would slop out. But the larger waves, when they came in, were at once promising and daring. Long sections chucked out over the shallow spots in a raw, unpredictable manner. There was nothing smooth or easy-looking about the place, although the breeze was off-shore, and the sets marched in evenly. Rather, the waves could roll, pitch, bowl, and crunch, then flatten out for a moment before boiling over more rocks. It was a challenge, and on that pretense we paddled out.

Once we entered the water, we felt like participants, not spectators, in the forces around us. We stroked further around the original break we had checked from shore, and now the beach was out of our sight. The waves were two meters, and we lined up in a smooth spot next to some surging rocks. It was fast, and the spots where it didn't boil over were smooth and easy, giving you just enough time to set up for the impending explosion. Wipeouts were similar to vicious rock thrashings at places like "El Cap" and "Natural Bridges": if you got caught at the bottom of a section, you'd eat it; if you tucked under or went high, you might make it. There was a small island nearby about the size of a football stadium, with waves breaking on both sides, and coconut trees crowning the center. In between sets, we relaxed and checked out the different hues of green that swirled over the land like a Van Gogh landscape. Just digging the silence around us. Some fishermen paddled by in their canoes, waving to us on our "canoes." We named the spot after them and the tribe we stayed with on the beach: Fanti's. A pure African setting and break.

Chapter 2: Pied Pipers of Africa

"Oh my gosh!" cried Dave. "Look what's happening on the beach!"

We squinted towards shore where a mob of charcoal-colored people were rumblin', bumblin', like at a rock concert gathering.

"What's going on?" Craig asked nervously.

"It's some kind of huge gathering," said Kevin. "Is today a festival holiday?"

"I don't know, but more are coming. The whole city is pouring down to the beach."

People were congregating in large clusters. It was a restless crowd, like a gathering storm.

"You don't suppose they're here to watch us?" asked Craig.

"Naw," said Kevin. "That was just a small crowd of kids that followed us to the beach. It was neat the way they waxed our boards for us. I must have an inch-thick layer of wax on my deck, and they were waxing the bottom when I stopped them! You see how stoked they were? I thought they were gonna carry us to the water."

While Kevin fantasized about being carried around the city on his board, Dave dropped into a clean one-meter wave that sparked a roar of approval from the beach. Each tight section caused a huge suction inhale, and his kickout was followed by thunderous cheering and clapping.

"Wow, all those people are here for us!" yelled Dave, as he paddled back out.

They were. And it looked like the cheering grandstands of a high school football game, with each wave being a touchdown. If the people kept coming, it would be a Super Bowl. Kevin took off, and then Craig rode a wave as the crowd grew in size and volume. They cheered on every one of our rides. The crowd grew while we surfed. Within an hour, people were buzzing around on shore like ants, waving and dancing, cartwheels, clicking heels, while hundreds more brought up the rear. The whole city seemed to be taking off work to watch those men in the water on their "canoes." We waved, laughed and went along with the general carnival-type atmosphere. The whole thing made us flash back to some of those beach scenes in *The Endless Summer*, except on a larger scale. After a couple of hours, things were getting out of control on the beach, and we decided to head in. The tumult picked up momentum as we paddled to shore. A paddywagon drove up, and five policemen popped out the back with a stern "riot tryit" look on their faces. They appeared for a moment and then were overwhelmed.

"Things might get ugly pretty soon," said Kevin. "Let's get outta here."

We scrambled up on the beach and were engulfed by a mob of people.

"Help! Help!" someone yelled, but his pleas were muffled. The crowd was moving full bore now, tossing cans, throwing sand, flaying arms. We thought we were going to be dismembered at any moment. We shuffled towards our towels, tenaciously clutching our boards and smiling feebly while those huge black faces grinned down on us and said, "Thank you! Thank you! You have plenty magic!"

The police finally found us shaking hundreds of hands. They formed a protective ring around us and battled their way to the paddywagon. They kept asking us, "Why you do this thing? What is this?" We'd caused a riot.

We sped away in our paddywagon, waving to the crowd through bars. Another prisoner cowered in the corner of the wagon, obviously frightened. The police dropped us off at our place, and warned us "not to do this thing." No one was hurt, and we laughed at the whole incident. It was much the same story everywhere we surfed. Sometimes there'd be only a handful of fishermen, and other times a whole village, and everyone was enthusiastic, excited. Children always followed us to and from the surf. Sometimes hundreds of them. They'd grab our fingers, carry our boards, wax them, smile and compete to hold our hands. They were always the most enthusiastic and enthralled. We were Pied Pipers of sorts, in Africa.

Chapter 3: Come Easy, Go Easy

Tribal drums. Santana. Painted faces. Full moon. Heart of darkness. Devil dances. Costumed women. Night heat. Chanting. Jungle noises. Wild laughter. Congo tom-toms. Hypnotic rhythms. Lightning flashes. Blurring vision . . .

"Pass the palm wine, please," whispered Craig, in the midst of a bizarre dance being performed around a leaping fire. Tonight was celebration night for the new moon, which was now rising above the huts. Already everything outside the fires' light had the blue tint that only a bright moon and crystal night can give. Africans greet the new moon in different ways. Some go totally wild: dancing all night, screaming, chanting and totally freaking out. You can actually sense the excitement and intenseness in the air all around you. Tonight we were allowed to join in the festival, something we really dug. All present were carrying on in the true tribal fashion, totally uninhibited, while rocking out to insane tribal drummers wailing away on handmade drums that they'd grown up playing on. They seemed to be absorbed by their own music making, completely mesmerized. We were also pretty mesmerized by now, on the music, the night, and the local brew—palm wine.

Dave was fixedly staring into the ring of African dancers, clutching the flask of palm wine.

"Wow," said Kevin, "Dave's gone under sooner'n we thought," and snatched away the magic elixir. "This stuff's more potent than Drano!"

"We ought to toast," Dave said, nodding but still gazing.

"Toast who?" Craig asked.

"Bill Harzy, maybe?" Kevin said, swizzling down another gulp of wine.

"Not a bad idea at all, if we could find the guy. For now, let's toast to palm wine and Africans!"

"This reeks of an all-nighter," Kevin said, as we clunked our soup tins full of wine together. "Pray for mercy on our hangovers in the morning."

By the time the moon hit its halfway point in the sky, everyone had long passed their halfway point, and slowed stupefied in their tracks. The palm wine took its course and lived up to its reputation as "the fuel NASA refused to use." The drummers were the last to go, and went in style, blasting and pounding harder and faster till they collapsed. The memorable African celebration—in a class all its own.

African lifestyle is one based on survival. The continent is roughly in the shape of a human heart, and can be one of the most heartless places on Earth. One season there will be too much rain and flooding; the next will have hellish heat and a terrible dry spell. Food is sometimes hard to come by, so a village will band together to help those without. It is a way of life that is so hard that they have a natural brotherhood to one another. They have to. Often you'll see people holding hands or with arms wrapped around each other. It's natural to them to be close, and often necessary. Their ways of living are so radical to ours that if a white man tried to live the way they do, he would probably die of disease, malnutrition or something worse inside a month, if that long.

So they take it easy. *Very* easy, if they can. There's some expression that says there's no time in Africa. Actually, when you're in Africa, you're on "African time," which means that things will get done when they get done, if at all. Suppose a bus driver says he's leaving at 3 in the morning. Well, you arrive there at 6 that afternoon, wait an hour or two, then the driver shows up, and everything is fine. *If* the driver shows up. One night we waited till 2 a.m. for a bush taxi to come and pick us up. He was supposed to meet us at 8 that night. He never even came.

Chapter 4: Stalling Out in Africa

"Come with me, please," the officer said. "You are under arrest."

"What for?!!" cried Dave and Kevin in unison.

"Urinating in public," replied the officer indignantly.

"But we're in the jungle. It's over 50 kilometers to the nearest bathroom! Everybody does it outside!" Kevin said, as the cell door closed.

Maybe so, but not in front of a police station like we had just done. That day our senses were not in harmony for some reason. Could have been the cane juice. Luckily it wasn't a long jail sentence. After a $5 "dash" to the arresting officer and 30 minutes in a cell, we were free men again, loose on the streets.

The second time it happened, 3 a.m. when the bar closed, we were with some other friends who knew the chief of the jailhouse. Our arresting officers were quite bummed when we got off free after a smiling reprimand, a wink and a general agreement that we all would meet at the same bar the next night.

"How come everywhere we travel, we get arrested?" we wondered.

What do you do when there isn't a swell and you're sitting around in Africa trying to avoid the heat? You can take a shower if there's one, but you're hot again ten minutes later. Go for a swim in the 80-degree ocean, which is nice, but when you come out, the sun dries you so fast you're caked with salt, and all the little kids run cause they think you have leprosy. Count your malaria pills, maybe, or read another book. Write letters, sure, and freak a few people out back home by telling them you've met the native girl of your dreams and are moving in with her tribe. You can read your snakebite kit instructions over again, or go walk in the jungle and look at things. But if you do that, you may get bit by a Gabon viper, spitting cobra or some other poisonous snake that's in these jungles, and forget what your instructions told you to do. Look over the map again to figure out where it might happen at, or go explore the area you're in now. You did that the first day you got here, so now all that's needed is a swell. Go out with the fishermen on an overnight run, maybe, or just walk around town and see how things are. The heat cuts down a lot of your in-between-swells activities—when you sweat while doing a simple thing like eating, you know it's hot and there's little way around it.

Two activities got into frequently were to either come down with disease or play cards, both pastimes a gamble. If you got sick, there was nothing else to do, but nothing. You didn't surf, you didn't move, you didn't even want to be in Africa anymore; all you wanted to do was scream "Notify my next of kin!" Sometimes the same symptoms applied to the card games when heavy stakes were involved. No way did you want to be in that game of chance when there was a huge pile of seashells or bottle caps in the pot! A guy could lose everything in one of those all-nighters, even his precious surf leash. It really got hard-core when you began to bet your next wave, sizzling letters from girlfriends back home, pinups, ice cream and addresses of foxy chicks you knew. When someone raised you three addresses with stars by them, it was "no more Mr. Nice Guy" at the table anymore! Everyone became vicious and unscrupulous. You could hear knives being unsheathed under the table, all of us wearing dark glasses at 3 a.m., ticking brains and straining eyes that are familiar in Wild West movies. The one hanging lightbulb dims a bit, everyone is startled, all hands drop down on their knife handles. From out of that dingy old room a deep throaty voice asks the familiar question, signaling someone's turn to act: "Got any threes?"

Chapter 5: Your Life Vest Is Under Your Seat

Listening to noises that sounded like the plane was disintegrating right there in midair, we began to wonder how old this aircraft really was. At the airfield, the lady behind the counter smiled and told us we would be flying in the company's favorite plane. "Fly us for safety and comfort," said the poster above her desk. Now in the air, we had more doubts about this clunky aircraft than we did when we saw it resting on the grassy runway as though it had been wheeled out of a museum.

Before we boarded, Kevin prophesized, "This flight's gonna be a grueler, so we better fuel up before we go."

Craig agreed. And we scanned the area for a bar.

"Are you *sure* this is the best way to check out the coast?" asked Kevin, over a beer. But before Craig could answer, our plane sputtered, gasped, wheezed, conked out, then finally started.

And now we were staring at the other eight passengers as we bounced around inside. It seemed as thought the plane was having an epileptic fit. We were soaring at 600 feet, and still climbing—remarkable! Our two-prop vintage 1949 mail plane whined its way through the sky, high above the ocean below. We were over a vast blue sea, with the land down to our left. The coast from the air was fascinating. Our noses pressed up against the greasy windows, our eyes squinting at the surf line. All three of us had seats next to windows and could check everything out. Almost everyone else on the plane was too busy hanging on and fighting off airsickness to sightsee through a window. At times, we could have sworn that the plane's wings were flapping! The coast was mostly long stretches of beaches. Beautiful beaches, bone-white sand without a trace of anyone on them. We spotted a number of points, but the ones with overland access to them were few and far between.

"Oooh, ahhh, lookit those lines sweeping in. I feel like parachuting out right here," said Kevin.

"You will if this ride gets any worse," said Craig. "I knew I should have brought a kidney belt."

"Man, I can't get over that jungle; there's no way we'd ever get through it," said Dave.

Indeed, there was no way. Small planes have landed on top of the jungle below us. If a plane crashes in the denser jungles, the survivors must climb to the top of the jungle in order to be spotted and rescued. The bush is like a blanket, and will cover any wreckage almost overnight. Occasional dirt roads that looked more like donkey trails curved their way aimlessly towards the coast to small fishing villages. These were the places we were interested in, where there was at least some way to get to the beach, and possibly a point. A river looked sinister from the air: rich brown, Bill Harzy–ridden, sinewing through the bush like it was sneaking to the ocean. Between the plane's lurchings, we got a good idea of the surf potential for over 900 kilometers of African coast. The swell was pushing two meters, enough to show us what places would be worth trying for on the way back. Larger points stand out on maps, and we marked the accessible ones on our chart. Unfortunately, our chart looked like a two-year-old child's drawing with all the squiggly lines caused by the rattling plane.

While we were laughing about flying on "Doomsday Airlines," as we called it, the plane started down to an airstrip in the jungle. Now we were really curious to see how this thing lands.

"The pilot missed the runway!" Craig exclaimed, as the plane banked around for another try. Everyone was hanging on tight this time.

"Come on, come on, land this thing!" More bouncing around, more terrified faces; one lady closed her eyes and began to mumble something, a prayer maybe.

"If I ever get out of this one alive, I'll never eat meat again!" promised Kevin. And we all laughed. Thrashing around now, and lots of noises from the passengers and plane.

"God, put the front wheel on the ground too!" Dave cried, as the plane skipped down the runway, nose high like in a takeoff position. We weren't sure if we were comin' or goin', for the plane remained in this position for the longest time. Two people next to us were completely freaked out, looked as though they'd been given the death sentence on an indecent-exposure charge.

"Sheez! A mile-long wheelie at 120 mph! Unreal!" Craig said, as the plane settled down slowly on all three wheels and taxied to an abrupt stop in front of a small building. The captain stepped out smiling, took off his cap, and walked casually over to a bar. The praying lady regained consciousness and rushed out the door. We laughed, but were pretty shaken up. Especially when we reached under our seats where our life vests were supposed to be. They weren't there.

Chapter 6: If a Small Man Casts a Large Shadow, It Means the Sun Is Setting

"I'm telling ya, Craig, we've only got a kilometer to go," coaxed Kevin.

"A kilometer!" gasped Craig. "You're gonna have to carry me there; I'm dying!"

Tattered clothes, torn tennies, unkempt hair, complete filth—Craig had certainly hit the dregs. The strain on his face showed that he was fighting off a double hernia from the weight of the pack and camera gear loaded on his back.

"Why do *you* always find the only carriers left in the village?" Craig wheezed.

"Look," said Kevin, "I'm paying my carriers extra to carry your kneeboard. I'm tired, too, you know. And we told Dave we'd meet him tomorrow. So we should get moving if we're ever going to make it."

Kevin pulled a soiled handkerchief from his pocket, wiped the sweat off his forehead, scratched his beard and peered into the jungle as if he half expected Tarzan to come swinging to the rescue. The two native carriers stood casually by us, two boards and a backpack balanced on their heads. Anything Africans can pick up, they'll carry on their heads: buckets brim-full of water, cups, baskets of laundry, bundles of firewood, knives, 200-pound sacks of fish, bushels of fruit and surfboards. The body sways gracefully and the head remains rigid when they walk.

We were in an area erroneously designated "Cannibals" by the U.S. Air Force in a 1933 aerial land map. Our lorry broke down five kilometers ago, and we decided to hoof it to the next town where another lorry would take us onward. It was late afternoon, we were in the bush, and our driver hadn't the slightest idea how to fix the lorry when it conked out. African roads resemble a motocross track, and lorries frequently fall apart in the middle of nowhere. Lorries are hazardous vehicles to begin with, and not one would pass a single point in a Highway Patrol road check. People are fitted into the back of these small-to-medium-sized pickups like cigarettes in a pack. But they're the main mode of transportation in Africa. Experience had taught us that we'd sit for days before another lorry might come by. So we left our driver and the other passengers camped by the lorry, and hoped to walk to the next town before nightfall.

One of the scariest things that can happen to anyone is to get caught walking in the bush when night falls. If you wander 50 feet off the path, you may never be found. And if you camp out in the bush, the ants will get you before anything else. Army ants rule the jungle. One night we accidentally camped near their path, and were brutally snipped by hundreds of them. Strange things inhabit African jungles: fleas as big as ants, ants as big as cockroaches, cockroaches as big as rats, rats as big as cats, cats big enough to! . . . Ahh, but we're on our last leg and night is settling like a cloak. There's no twilight time in the tropics; it's either light or dark. The sun was grazing the treetops, and we had a kilometer to go. If you can cast a shadow, it's still light enough to walk. Africans are scared to death of the dark, and we knew that our carriers would leave us and return to the safety of their village before it got too dark.

Craig let out a few deep groans, and Kevin was about to help him with his load when three "bushmen" appeared from the thicket. They looked at us like we were the oddest things they'd ever seen. We probably were. Although we didn't speak a common language, our plight was pretty obvious to them, and after a few gestures and a small dash, they had all of Craig's gear on their heads. They could have carried us on their heads! An hour later we were "chopping" fish and rice in town, while a lightning storm illuminated the night sky. Our carriers grinned over their palm wine. Crazy white men!

Four days later, we returned by the same road after a dry surf run. The broken-down lorry was still there, along with the driver and a few other people. They had camped inside it and around it, looking as though they were expecting help to arrive at any minute. Our lorry driver picked them up.

Chapter 7: Who Is Bill Harzy?

Indeed. *What* is Bill Harzy? Everywhere we traveled, we were confronted by Bill Harzy. In paranoia gestures, natives warned us of this character at every river, lake and stream. But since we had no idea of what they were jabbering about, and after all, we never once saw Bill Harzy, we swam and paddled our way through river after river. Canoes were nice, but not always available. And only the most jungle-crazed fool would machete his way through the bush with board under arm in search of a spot on the map that might have waves. So if you don't think too much about what might be in the water, river drifts are quick, easy and breathtaking to boot!

We thought Bill Harzy was some tyrant of the waters. Oftentimes we would be the only ones swimming in an African river on days when the sun would blast down like a heat lamp. The natives always clung to the banks. "Who is this guy?" Craig finally asked the Peace Corps volunteer we were staying overnight with.

The guy laughed out loud good and hard, and was still chuckling when he told us that Bill Harzy is not a he but an *it*, a tiny microscopic worm that is in all the rivers, lakes and streams in this part of Africa. It bores unnoticed through your skin and lives in your veins, and six months after contact, blood comes out with your urine. It takes twenty painful shots in the gut to get rid of it. Bilharzial disease is nothing to tangle with.

But you can't spend time worrying about bilharzi, because tropical Africa must have every kind of disease and bug infection known to man. And it sure looks like it when you walk through a village and see cases of elephantiasis, malaria, hepatitis, polio, yellow fever, cholera, jungle rot and typhoid, just to mention a few. One particularly gruesome experience we had was when we visited a leper colony. The problems of bug infestations are ever-present and easy to pick up; all's it takes is for one little insect to bite you, and you may be laid up for a week. Kind of makes you want to carry around a can of bug repellent at all times. Oh well, at least now we know about bilharzi. Wonder what else there is we don't know about yet?

Chapter 8: Ju-ju and Ripoffs

"Are you sure this will work?" asked Craig.

"Absolutely," said Kevin. "Don't worry about a thing." And with that, Kevin placed a monkey's paw on our piled-up gear. "If this doesn't do it, nothing will. These people will never touch our stuff if they think it's protected by ju-ju (also known as voodoo)."

The three of us then walked out to the surf. Kevin, smug in the knowledge that our stuff wouldn't be touched, Dave and Craig, looking quizzically at Kevin and tapping their heads with their fingers. "The poor bugger has got jungle rot of the brain. That night last week with the witch doctor was too much for him."

When we hit the water, Kevin was still expounding on monkey paws, vulture skulls, crocodile heads, snakes, panther teeth and other ju-ju trinkets. Craig and Dave nervously humored him, promising each other to keep an eye on the stuff from the water. "Yeah," Kevin said, "and that witch doctor also told me to watch out for the number nine. He said it was a bad number for this trip, so watch out for the number nine."

"Nine? What's the number nine?" asked Craig.

"I dunno. But the old guy said the number nine was a bad sign for us," said Kevin.

"Nine! You're crazy!" said Craig.

But Kevin was off on another tangent. "And I can't wait to try out that aphrodisiac powder he gave me."

"You mean that powdered goat dung?" asked Craig.

"Hey, look," said Dave. He pointed to our stuff on the beach. A handful of natives had gathered around our packs. More natives were crowding around. We were surfing a fun beachbreak, and didn't feel like going in yet. So we watched from the water and waited as a small group of natives gathered around our stuff.

"Well, there goes our gear," said Dave.

But no one touched it. The people milled about for a while, then walked away. We came in an hour later and everything was there, untouched. Since that day, we've protected our belongings when we leave them on the beach with ju-ju objects. Africans are into ju-ju and superstition very intensely. Have been for thousands of years. Ju-ju is rarely talked about, but it's there and affects everybody in some way or another.

Last year the Minister of Broadcast and Telecommunication in one African country we visited was booted out of office after it was disclosed that he sacrificed the unborn fetus of a pregnant woman to a witch doctor in a ju-ju ceremony that was supposed to ensure his reelection.

His dealings with the witch doctor were discovered shortly after the ceremony, and he was forced to resign. Most people don't know why he was dismissed. "And just when it looked like he was going to win another term," they said.

Chapter 9: Restless Nights and Dream Waves

Peering out through our broken window at an insect that resembles one of those hideous Marvel comic creatures, as it scales the windowsill and drops into the room, Dave Terry lets out a snicker as he corners it into an empty sardine can. "One more for the dinner table!" he shouts, creating a gurgling in our stomachs. It was siesta time, with us flat on our backs on top of a rather thick layer of filth, staring up at the flaky ceiling, counting the chips of paint that slipped off when someone upstairs moved about. Occasionally the black form of a flat cockroach would zip across, giving us the same rush one gets when one sees a shooting star.

"Sure hope a swell comes up soon," continued Dave. "I've run out of things to do with all these bugs." It was true. Our room seemed to be a zoologist's dream! We must've had every kind of insect in Africa running through it. Big ones, scary ones, furry ones, multicolored ones, ones without noise and ones, unfortunately, with noise. They could fly, sing, buzz, chirp, hum, chorus and bug.

"I know," Kevin said, "it's been too long now. Good thing the bugs don't cost extra, otherwise we'd *never* be able to afford the room!"

We were paying $1.60 a night, greasy eggs and milkwater included as breakfast, and had use of the floor's toilet, like everyone else. But that benefit didn't amount to much because it was always occupied, more frequently than any of the rooms. Lucky for us our "dungeon" was on the lowest floor—easy access to the bush outside. We couldn't stay anywhere but the basement rooms unless we wanted to pay an enormous sum for a room upstairs. Up there they were running a house of ill repute.

"Sheez!" Craig cried out, as a large cluster of paint flakes drifted down into his face, freckling him completely. "Don't they *ever* siesta?" He began picking the flakes out of his eyes. "Let's hit it, eh?"

"Sounds like a plan," Kevin said, and started readying his pack.

"No way I'm stayin' here in this mosquito-ridden pit *alone*, even if I didn't have dysentery! Uh . . . 'scuse me boys, you'll have to wait a minute. Seen any paper?" Desperately he headed for the door in the style of a man late to his own wedding. "You know where to find me." As he opened the door, Kevin cut loose with a glass-shattering scream. He was frantically yanking his arm out of his backpack, knocking everything over in the struggle. He finally freed it, with a huge rhinoceros beetle clinging to his finger.

"All right Kevin! You found him! Don't let him go; I'll try and hurry," Dave cried out, as he closed the door behind him.

In Africa, there are certain hotels no white man is allowed to stay in, and it is frowned upon heavily if you sleep outdoors. The white man is expected to act like a white man by staying in expensive hotels and spending a lot of money. But we were on the usual economy run, so we stayed where we could stay the cheapest, and only in hotels or rooms if they were in our price range.

Tour guides would list some of the places we stayed in as "low-class slums only fit for condemnation or housing rats, pests and bums. Rooms come complete *without* shower, bathroom, bed; and death certificates are *not* included in the cost." That's if they would be listed at all. A few were "unlistable and unbearable": border guard houses, basements of brothels, crash pads for drunks, deck of a freighter, docks, inside train stations, outside train stations, sitting up on trains and buses, restaurant floors, park benches, terraces of buildings, porches and sidewalks. Often we would wake up to people staring down at us or sweeping around us. Beaches were peaceful places when the tides weren't too high, like they always seemed to be, because you could hear and feel the surf breaking, promising waves when you woke up—*if* the shorebreak didn't wash you and your things towards South America in the middle of the night! Nasty currents in this area, really strong.

To surf in great waves with your camp in sight on the beach is almost too good to be true. When you got tired, thirsty or hungry, all you had to do was go up on the beach and crack open a coconut, eat some fresh fruit, then rest a while to go out later. A hot sun makes everything warm and nice sitting in the shade of some tropical tree, watching a friend surf unreal waves by himself. Ah, like those lefts at Capemounts! Those beautifully perfect, fast and hollow lefts that we came upon with no one surfing and no one probably had surfed them. Away from it all, we camped out on this beach for a week, doing nothing except surfing, exploring, laughing, snoozing, eating fruit and freshly caught fish, and more surfing. Surfing in some of the best lefts any of us had ever surfed in our lives, possibly one of the nicest lefts so far discovered on this planet. This one area had four left points, each around the corner from the other. We rode only two of them—Bushman's and Capemounts, on a 1- to 2-meter swell that lasted four unreal days. Both of these waves were different from each other, and both were fantastic.

Bushman's wrapped into a scenic cove at an even, good face with hollow sections, a righteous working face, and a tricky takeoff. The smaller waves broke closer to the rocks, creating a heavy throw-out and gnarly tube ride, while the larger waves shifted the takeoff with increase in size. Bushman's was great for off-the-lips and cutbacks. You could easily get three of each before it closed out on the beach. Or you could just cruise, take it easy and flash out on the tropical jungle at the point where it met the smooth, creamy-looking sand on the deserted beach. Around this point and a 15-minute walk is another left point that more than likely hasn't been surfed yet, has no name, and is good.

Capemounts is undoubtedly the kind of wave surfers go traveling for. It is one of those waves that you can have no complaints about, a wave people dream about. It breaks, like Bushman's and the other points, over a sand bottom, so no worry about bad wipeouts. The ride begins where the last rock shows, and the rest is sand all the way. On the takeoff, you hear the thunder of the wave as it comes rifling down the line. If you look to your side as you stroke into it, you see this grinding tube that resembles a tornado, and you get a heavy rush from it all. The wave picks you up as you're stroking at an angle, and shoots you along like a slingshot. Ahead of you is this magnificent wave that appears to line up all the way down the beach. It's faster than Bushman's and breaks in shallower water, so it is also more hollow. The whole wave is a moving tube, just keeps training along down the beach. It looks absolutely perfect when you watch from shore, flawless, with no bad sections. It just keeps on swiftly tubing at a quick-but-not-too-quick pace. When you're riding it, it looks and *feels* perfect, so much so that you smile as you watch it lining up. An excellent wave for hotdogging with everything possible on one wave alone! You can put yourself in the tube wherever you choose, and you have a long wave to choose your spot. On the biggest sets we rode, maybe three meters, you went farther faster, and the wave still held its beautiful form. At four or five meters, it would really be one helluva wave to watch and ride. There are other lefts in the world that are faster, others that are hollower, and others that are longer; but this wave has all that you could want from a wave. No complaints. Farther inside this point is probably the best wave of the place, but would need a large swell to create head-high or bigger waves. If that happened, from the way the small waves we saw steaming along for a quarter of a mile came in, it would be a left point that would definitely be one of the most supreme waves of our time.

The end of the ride on a Capemounts wave is an inevitable tube ride, because the wave really sucks out and streaks along the beach. You simply tuck and see how far you can go till it passes you by. Before you begin the long paddle back out for another, you look to the beach, line up with a tree or piece of driftwood, and think to yourself, "next time I'll beat that mark." On your way out, as you're thinking about what just happened, your friend comes zooming towards you on another wave. You say something to him, and he hoots, which makes you both laugh. Next moment you're over the wave your friend is riding to try and beat his mark. You smile at the day with its soft-looking clouds sitting above the warm, clear blue water, at the unblemished egg-white sand beach and lush tropical jungle behind it, at the empty set that comes sliding by, your friend paddles back out to where you're waiting, begins telling you of his last ride before you tell him of yours. "Can you believe this place?!" he says, as you start paddling for another fantastic left. "Yeah!!"

Steve Wolff, a transplant surfer from San Diego who is now living in Africa, discovered this place with us. We all camped out together for that outrageous week of wave riding. Steve had a car, and we did some of our most rewarding surf checks with him. The time we first met him we asked how many surfers there were in the country. He grinned and said, "Four now," then bought us all a beer. When we split, he told us to say "Hi" to all his buddies in San Diego. So "Hi" all of Steve Wolff's friends in San Diego!

Chapter 10: Bargaining and Market Days

It was unmistakably market day in Africa: the biggest event of the week. Whole cities, towns and villages transform into huge outdoor markets on this day. Goats bleating, children crying, women squawking and jabbering, chicken feathers billowing with the dust, squishy objects underfoot, people packed like cows in a slaughterhouse, and rushing by like they're trying to catch the last express leaving hell. Sweat hangs like a mist and mixes with the odor of overripe fruit, fermented sugar-cane juice, bloody animal parts, palm wine, fresh fish, musty powders, black honey, fresh-baked bread and an insufferable noonday heat that bears down on everything like a giant steam press. And there you are in the center of it all, bargaining for all you're worth just to get that pineapple or those trade beads down another dime. And if you can't get it down, you won't take it 'cause you're caught up in the logic of that moment, the hasslin' hagglin' wranglin' finaglin' in buying *anything* you want. And it's not the price you pay, but the bargaining you do that determines if you'll buy it, whatever "it" is. Africans thrive on bargaining; they love it. And if you bargain really hard and well, maybe you'll just get burned on the price instead of completely ripped off. One morning Dave started bargaining for a snakeskin that a trader said he'd "give away" for only $20. By that evening, Dave had him down to $10. The next day, he bought it for $5.

And when you wander through the market, there are so many little things all around, and everything is so different and bizarre that you just want to find something that is *really* strange, that really stands out. Something to remember the whole market by. So you wander and look till you notice that everyone is watching you, and then it dawns on you what it is that really stands out in this reckless market. Yourself, of course.

Chapter 11: The Beginning

The last five days of this portion of the trip have been spent powering 2,000 kilometers overland by bus, train, canoe, bush taxi and lorry. Not one kilometer was over a paved or smooth road. We're leaving one portion of Africa and chasing waves to another area where the surf season is at its peak, over 4,000 kilometers away from where we've been.

Dave Terry, a friend who shared our experiences and waves with us on this trip, has gone off in another direction. This split with Dave and journey to a totally different area of Africa signifies for us the end of the first portion of this trip. Soon we'll be in a new area with unknown waves. As this story shows, our feelings have been as varied as Africa itself, but above all, interesting. Each time we left an area, we felt as though we had only just begun to know it. We felt that no matter how long we stayed in Africa, we'd only just begin to know it. Just beginning. ◼

Aftermath Winter 1976:
Attitude Dancing
By Gerry Lopez · SURFER Vol. 17 No. 2 · June 1976

Competitive performance surfing had a significant turning point on the North Shore of Oahu in the winter of 1975–1976. The Young Turks from Australia and South Africa, including Shaun Tomson, Rabbit Bartholomew, Ian Cairns, and Mark Richards (a.k.a. the *Free Ride* revolutionaries) were unseating the old guard, and their "rip, tear, and lacerate" mindset starkly contrasted that of the "flow with it, Brah" philosophy of the Hawaiian elite. Philosophical debate grew heated; punches flew as often as words. Pipeline's Zen archer Gerry Lopez smoothed the waters when he put the tumultuous season into perspective, diplomatically acknowledging the exceptional talents of the new guard while illuminating the underlying cultural differences at play.

Aftermath

In the wake of a satisfying and surprisingly above-average winter of surf on Oahu's North Shore, the most pervasive impression retained is that of the dynamite performance of the Australians and the South Africans. While the Hawaiians cruised through another season, with the usual assortment of achievements and disappointments, they were largely overshadowed by the aggressive attack and serious efforts of the group from "Down Under." Shaun Tomson, Ian Cairns, Mark Richards and Rabbit Bartholomew are obvious examples because of their energetic contest performances, but in addition, they were backed by another fifteen hotrods from their home countries, who happened to have their better days between contests (i.e. Mark Warren, Terry Fitzgerald, Bruce Raymond, Mike Tomson, Mike Esposito and Paul Naude). Just what was it that made these guys appear so incredible in the water this year? Why were the Aussies and the Africans (the "A's" for identification in this article) so HOTT?

Where were the Hawaiians (call them "B's" as in blah-la) this year? One might conclude that it was the fact that the Hawaiians had a very nondescript season that made the others stand out; however, this does not appear to be the case. In retrospect, the Hawaiian surfing elite is approaching a level in which their respective styles have become so polished and unobtrusive that they might go unnoticed. Ever wonder what happened to Billy Hamilton? He got so smooth in the water that sometimes a wave would go by and spectators wouldn't even register that it was being ridden, let alone by whom. It is difficult to imagine the possibility of a similar oversight when Mark Richards or Shaun Tomson are riding. The classic, flowing Hawaiian style has occupied the limelight for the past five years, and the surfing world is now unimpressed by the old poses and casual styles. It is small wonder that the A's look fresh, new and dynamic in comparison. Even the average age of the A's is about five years younger than the cream of the Hawaiians. The up and coming style in surfing seems to be that of the Australians and Africans. However, this shifting spotlight represents merely another revolution of the focal point of surfing in what appears to be a natural progression of cyclic change. In an article written almost 10 years ago, John Witzig made the same claim for the Australian surfers that we are hearing again today: "We're Tops Now!" Even his definition of what constitutes "hot surfing" has returned to vogue. Commented Witzig, "The trend is to push things to the limit: the tighter you push them, the longer you hold them, the more involved you are, the more situations you can overcome, the hotter you are." Sound familiar? This McTavish philosophy is alive and well in the forms of both the Aussies and the South Africans, as evidenced in their energetic display this past winter.

The fact that this aggressive approach to surfing is hardly new becomes apparent with a brief review of the history of surfing. This sort of historical overview will also reveal a general delineation of surfing styles, or attitudes, into two opposite types. On the one end of the scale is the classic laid-back Hawaiian style; at the other extreme, the full blast power attack of the A's. In the abstract, it can almost be called an East (Oriental) vs. West (Occidental) division. Let us review.

History

From its very conception here in the islands, surfing has been a natural form of expression and recreation for the Hawaiians. Here, the surfer has at his doorstep a most enviable supply of waves, both in quality and quantity. This constant accessibility of warm waves, as well as the slow, casual cultural environment (commonly referred to as "Polynesian paralysis") results in a certain sense of timelessness among Hawaiian surfers. They are somehow immune to the violent sense of urgency that characterizes so many of the visiting surfers. Hawaiian surfing has traditionally been, and remains, casual and relaxed. From Kealoha to Kaio's smooth cruise, to Michael Ho standing calmly in the center of a terrifying explosion of ocean, the man and the water join energies to become a single force in a noncommercial, almost religious, union. Simple surfing: gliding without glitter. From Duke at Waikiki, surfing moves to California in the "point-style" era of Kivlin and Phil Edwards. Here, surfing undergoes its first metamorphosis with the emergence of "da Cat" and the "little man on wheels," who proceed to dance all over their boards, projecting their maneuvers onto the wave. With aggressive power surfing thus inaugurated, the two traditional surfing styles have been set. Amongst the Hawaiians, the rider and the wave got equal time, they flowed together. Now in California, the surfer becomes a neon sign, using the wave as a backdrop on which to perform, whip-turns, cutbacks, rollercoasters, etc. Herein lay the seed for later Australian styles, to be transplanted by Greenough. With this loud Western-frontier approach to surfing, the California surfer makes a blatant statement of man conquering nature and establishes surfing as a total lifestyle, complete with Beach Boys, juaraches, woodies, cowabunga lingo and *SURFER* mag. Perhaps it was due to the absence of quality surf of any real consistency in California, but somehow the waves themselves received miniscule attention. It fell to David Nuuhiwa to return the attention back to the surfer becoming part of the wave again. Just when the chrome was getting a little over-done, in cruises David with his classic flowing style and graceful pose on the nose, reminding surfers how to join the ocean in movement rather than attack it. To watch David, Reno, Michael Ho, or any other representative of the Hawaiian-style surfing, is to be struck with the symmetry of the *total* picture they form with the wave.

David reigned supreme, epitomizing everything that was surfing, until the appearance of a powerhouse Aussie named Nat. At the 1966 World Contest in San Diego, Nat Young's animalistic wave shredding sent the surfing world reeling. Much to the delight of surfers such as Witzig (who felt that "the real aim of surfing had been lost in a morass of concaves and the idolatry of David Nuuhiwa") the focus of surfing had been turned upside-down again. As Nate pushes David off his throne (or, more precisely, out of his Porsches) we see a pattern developing. As surfing progresses, the focus of attention creates a direction that is pursued toward either an uncontinuable extreme (i.e., noseriding) or to such a subtle level of refinement that only the most perceptive can follow it. At this point, the attention seems to gravitate to the opposite extreme in surfing styles, and in this way surfing manages to sustain a continual supply of recycled juice.

Returning to the historical profile, after Nat returned to Australia, he left the surfing world with the realization (vocalized by Witzig and others) that it had become too extreme in one direction. Noseriders are passé. Nat has gone home, so the attention revolves again from the rider back to the waves. The search is on for new equipment with which to pursue the various aspects of wave riding. Waves and boards are the dominant concerns; Hawaii becomes the unavoidable center of attention, due to its superior natural resources, and the trend in boards leaves "the specialty noserider for everything" in favor of a specialty board for each surf spot. Jock and Cabell and Brewer are outstanding in this limbo period, but the real heroes are still the waves. Then the Hawaiian renaissance crescendos as surfers tune their equipment, minds and bodies in a cooperative effort with the waves. The return to posing and the relaxed casual Hawaiian surfing style is most evident in the Pipeline era of 1972–74. The only difference is that now instead of posing on the nose, it's done in the tube. Again the cyclical pattern is visible. No one wants to look like they're trying too hard—just flow wid it, Brah! The low-maintenance nature of the then-infantile pro circus was an additional reason for the general "minimum effort for maximum return" approach. It is no accident that the concept of a noncompetitive Expression Session appears during this time when the Hawaiians and their careless attitude dominate surfing. After five years of this dominance, what happens? The hemlines went up, so now they have to go down; enter Shaun, Ian and Co., and once again we've gone full circle. From the smooth, fluid dance of Reno, B.K., etc., we are now applauding the full-tilt boogie of the Australians and S. Africans. Maximum effort is back in. As Shaun puts it, "I really like to maneuver, not just stand there and look grace-ful." The emphasis is back on the rider as he concentrates all his power and energy into mastering the wave, maneuvering continually to main-tain the advantage. Being "top dog" is suddenly of supreme importance, as competition establishes a more permanent spot in the surfing world.

Attitude Dancing

Given this historical overview, the pattern that emerges delineates surf-ing into two opposite styles or attitudes, which alternate in prominence both in the media and in public acclaim. One attitude emphasizes the wave and the performer as a coordinated unit; the surfer dances with the wave, letting it lead him along its natural direction. This is the classic style of the Hawaiian surfer. The other attitude centers on the solo performance of the rider as he dances *on* the wave, attacking it from all angles and reducing it to shreds. This is the "conquer" approach champi-oned by the surfers of Australia and S. Africa. Ian Cairns sees the present resurgence of aggressive surfing in this way: "The classic old-style Hawaiian approach is entirely divorced from the way performance surfing has evolved. I thought to myself, 'Why are all these people going straight (i.e., posing)?' Here we've been practicing all these turns, and here's the ultimate medium for doing them—a giant face with more room to correct your errors. So I went out and endeavored to ride 20- to 25-foot waves in the same manner as if I was riding a 4-foot wave." It is noteworthy that the very concept of surfing as something to be practiced in order to correct your errors is intrinsic in the A's attitude, and yet it is virtually absent in the Hawaiian mind. Furthermore, this rather cocky attempt to impose human will on a wave, especially those of 20-foot-plus dimensions, has caused more than one surfer to eat his lunch in the face of the ocean's superior strength. Perhaps another reason for the unrestrained surfing approach of the A's is that they are the novices of the sport and have yet to learn humility towards Mother

Ocean. The Hawaiians, with the benefit of extended experience, are older and wiser (in terms of self-preservation) and have traditionally exhibited an innate respect for the waves. Instead of attempting to impose their order on the waves like the A's, the B's seek to join forces with it.

This additional evidence illustrates that if we take our inquiry deeper, we can trace the origin of the two separate surfing attitudes (represented by the A's and the B's) back to their two distinct philosophies of life. The parallels of the philosophies of the Eastern vs. Western mind are numerous. It could even be argued that the A's represent the raw, competitive, frontiersman element, while the B's fall along the lines of the ancient, more passive cultures of the East (Cowboys vs. Indians?). At any rate, the classic, Western, "take the bull by the horns" philosophy is certainly characteristic of the A's surfing approach. And the Eastern-type philosophy that it's easier to ride the horse in the direction that it's going, or "take what you can get," is fundamental to the B's style of thinking AND surfing. The A's surf with a purposeful, serious urgency; the B's with leisurely carelessness. It would not be unusual, for example, to find Reno doing his laundry or B.K. mowing his lawn at the same time that the Aussies and Africans are out scrambling for 8-foot waves at Sunset or Rocky Point. The waves were here yesterday; they'll be here tomorrow. It even goes beyond the fact that the A's are visitors whose sole purpose on the Islands is to surf, for the deep-rooted distinction remains consistent even when it is the Hawaiians who are the visitors. In a typical scene from Australia we find Terry Fitzgerald purposefully marching off, in his words, "to do battle" in the water, having been unsuccessful in persuading Reno and Lopez to join him. The Hawaiians, it seems, were occupied with more important considerations, such as what's for lunch? Even at the contests themselves the A's invariably display more serious, professional dispositions than the Hawaiians. Again, the difference boils down to basic attitudes. Shaun Tomson observes: "Surfing here (Hawaii) is considered to be a recreation, basically, whereas at home it has a full-on legitimate sports status . . . to me surfing is a whole lifestyle . . . it pervades my entire existence." Perhaps this explains why winning becomes so obsessively important to the A's. Certainly this is not to say that the B's don't like to win; however, their style of surfing is more subjective in both purpose and execution. The element of the wave itself commands equal weight in their performance, making a ride more difficult to judge. The A's style, on the other hand, is so purposeful and maneuver-oriented that it lends itself to objective grading. Thus, the grade you make, either in contests or in public opinion, becomes a measure of your surfing prowess. To the B's it is somehow a more personal matter.

In light of this thesis that surfing is continually undergoing cyclical changes, all the noise about the Aussies and the Africans representing some type of ultimate apex in surfing appears somewhat off base. The A's are fond of saying how they've "paid their dues" (although it's still unclear what dues they are referring to) and now they are "number one." Yet after their show this past winter, it deserves credit as a valid claim . . . for now. Surfing history has shown that the overall pattern is far more comprehensive than just this present phrase indicates. While the present "success" of the A's may constitute a climax within individual careers, it could hardly be called the ultimate in surfing. It would be ridiculous to say that Ian or Shaun are any more masterful than Nat or David or any other of their forerunners. They are merely different; all masters in their own right. What is happening is that the power, performance style of the A's is in vogue at this time. Attaching value judgments as to which surfing attitude is superior would be no more relevant than trying to place a value on hemlines or dance styles. Short or long, twist or waltz, maneuvering or posing . . . all that can be asserted is that they differ; it is up to the fickle vision of the public eye to pronounce which style is number one at any given moment. Drew Kampion makes a revealing comment about the unique nature of surfing as a competitive sport. He notes that "In most sports, it is the structure that determines the champs; but in surfing, it is the champs that determine the structure." It follows that the focus of surfing is largely defined by the hottest guys in the water who manage to steal the show and hypnotize the cameramen. A chronological list of outstanding surfers provides a simultaneous history of surfing styles: from Duke and Kaio, to Dora and Weber, to David, to Nat, and so on. The most charismatic surfing hero of the past winter was Shaun Tomson, who epitomizes the present stage of surfing.

In answer, then, to this article's original query—why were the A's so hot this year? We must conclude that it is just their turn to enjoy the limelight of popular attention and the media. It is all part of the complex, natural, cyclic evolution of surfing. At present, the A's are the outstanding riders, and the competitive aspect has cycled to the forefront again. The easy Hawaiian Expression Session consciousness is once again taking a back seat, while the ocean explodes with aggressive energy and battlefield tactics. Some may agree with Ian's evaluation, crediting the A's present status to the fact that they "seem to be able to push ourselves harder than the Hawaiians do." No doubt they do. It is their conquering approach that is, again, so essentially different from the Hawaiian approach. Ian continues: "We're taking over—they've been denying it for a long time, but this year they can't. I'll volunteer to be the Australian Egoist (*don't worry Ian . . . they're hardly in short supply!*); we're doing what everyone's talking about doing." Still, it takes more than this to get a rise out of the Blah-la Hawaiians whose response might well be: "Go for it, boys! Get it while you can." How long the spotlight will remain on the A's is difficult to predict. Certainly their energy and enthusiasm provide a welcome and refreshing burst of positive juice for surfing. Its longevity remains to be seen, for the only summation we can venture is the all-inclusive truth: When you're hot you're hot, and when you're not you're not . . . in the eye of the beholder.

Bustin' Down the Door

By Wayne "Rabbit" Bartholomew • SURFER Vol. 17 No. 5 • Jan. 1977

Three issues after Gerry Lopez's "Attitude Dancing" was published in *SURFER*, young Australian Rabbit Bartholomew got his chance to respond on behalf of what are known today as the *Free Ride* revolutionaries, the *enfants terrible* who threatened to unseat the Old Guard on Oahu's north shore. In his treatise "Bustin' Down the Door," he described the other side of the cultural clash that stood to halt the radical, progressive surfing championed by the young Australian and South African surfers—and his title announced, in no uncertain terms, how they meant to achieve revolution. Though Bartholomew felt he made his case in a respectful tone, many Hawaiians seethed over Rabbit's and his countrymen's behavior in the water, and his essay, rather than quell their anger, had the opposite effect. Weeks after "Bustin' Down the Door" was published, Rabbit got in a tussle with Hawaiian legend Barry Kanaiaupuni during a competition in Australia. The following season on the North Shore would prove to be one Bartholomew would never forget. Death threats and punch-outs meted out by local surfers soon forced Rabbit and a handful of other Down Under crew to live in a state of siege in a nearby resort. Fortunately, Hawaiian Eddie Aikau saw that things had gone too far. He and his highly-respected family stepped in and called together the aggrieved parties for some good old-fashioned *ho'oponopono*, the Hawaiian custom of putting things right in a group or family meeting. Held in a packed conference room at the Turtle Bay Hilton, this gathering of the tribes was a de facto public trial. The verdict: Rabbit had shown disrespect for the local people; he was banished from the North Shore, save only for his heats in the scheduled professional surfing contests. Many believe that Aikau's actions may have actually saved Rabbit's life. It would be three years before he could return, and many more before he could stop looking over his shoulder. Today, Rabbit is the president of the Association of Surfing Professionals (ASP) and stands in good graces with the Hawaiian surfing community. Still, in a 2005 *SURFER* interview, Rabbit felt the sting of old wounds, observing that the affair "cut me in half as a man."

With the emphasis being placed on sophisticated lines of both human and mechanical technology, the year 1976 has thrust mankind into the last quarter of the current century cycle; and, as we draw ever closer toward the controversy-shrouded twenty-first-century dateline, a now insignificant minority of individuals, whether they realize it or not, are psychologically adapting themselves for this coming evolution of time.

Certainly the ruthlessness of the industrialized material world has contributed to the attempted suffocation of individuality, but even in this year of politically celebrated bullshit, it cannot be denied that our race witnessed superhuman extensions of the accepted impossible, even though the recognition of personal achievement was somewhat smothered in the repetitious mode of daily madness.

From within the loose-living, rowdy atmosphere of contemporary society have filtered individuals who are making accurate evaluations of their own potentials; and, through combined natural ability and total dedication, they are mentally gearing themselves to physically project towards their concept of the highest attainment in a given, or alternative, direction. Evidence of this movement was witnessed and displayed at the Montreal Olympics, in which swimming stars, no doubt motivated by Spitz's notoriety, marginally reduced 95 percent of the existing world records; and also, for the first time in history, perfect scores were awarded to Rumanian and Soviet gymnasts.

As people's comprehension of perfection reaches new heights, in relation to the level they are currently at, they begin expanding their mental awareness, absorbing and utilizing all relevant experiences, and their physical coordinations simply become a reflection of their inner knowledge. Their imagination continually challenges their spontaneity, and they develop the ability to bounce off both positive and negative vibrations, like a computer absorbing, analyzing, assessing, and finally responding with a relevant statement.

A recent book called *Powers of Mind,* by Adam Smith, reports that professional athletes unknowingly sound like Zen masters, being that they're on the mind-body trip where psychology fades into Oriental physiology. He claims that while gurus are guruing, and M.A.s in psychology tell you what it's all about, the pro golfers, tennis players and footballers are assimilating Zen theories on meditation whilst in actual competition. By total concentration, or turning off the ego mind, one can slow down reality to a state where even the most intense situation can be dominated with total comfort and subtlety by simply being as one with the situation. Sounds like Pipeline to me.

But what does all this have to do with *SURFER* magazine, and you, and me, and us? Well, I think that the development of modern-day surfing is a bitchin' example of the "extended limits principle," and it is still a fairly young trip. When surfing became a popular pastime roughly twenty years ago, the objectives and directions were quite basic, as the pure novelty of riding waves was in itself a breakthrough and a stoker. Gradually people became aware of water flow principles, and so began the evolution of surfboard design and theory. Actual style and performance were of little consequence until the arrival of the first superstar, Phil Edwards. In '59, his down-the-line peers could not completely comprehend and accept his approach, and he was, therefore, often criticized for executing such radical longboard maneuvers, and for incorporating pronounced body English, and his creativity wasn't fully recognized until years later.

Surfing progressed through the various longboard eras, and it was the transition point between long and short board that planted the roots to some of our modern-day concepts, and the impact of those young dudes from Down Under, namely Nat McTavish and Company, blew the existing directions apart, and with their animal aggression and spontaneous direction changes, they presented radically carved faces to a then-unsuspecting audience. People's reaction ranged from being totally for this new revolution, to being totally anti-radicalized, or else they couldn't give a stuff anyway.

The fact of the matter is that Nat, like Edwards and Nuuhiwa, had set his own standard of hot surfing, with a high priority given to total performance, and he'd set this standard within himself while he was still a developing gremmie, long before he exposed it to the world. Nat simply opened the door to realistic extensions, and in the following years, many alternative directions were created and then taken to advanced heights of acceptance by people such as Jock Sutherland, Lopez, Hakman, Greenough, B.K., Owl, Lynch, Reno, James Jones, Fitzgerald, Hamilton, and many others, and though each exhibits individuality and comes from varying sources, they all seemingly influenced, and were thus influenced by, each other's energies, and they created immense incentive for young kids to go surfing.

By synchronization with many seasons and cycles, these guys introduced many innovations to the surf vehicle, and were either directly or indirectly responsible for untold breakthroughs, including, with the help of people such as Hemmings and Downing, the introduction of professional surfing contests, and the overall commercialization of surfing. Another angle which is rarely reflected upon is the development of surf photography and the growth, expansion and influence of the surfing media, which, apart from expressing both the art and game of surfing, supports quite a band of ocean-oriented people.

And here we are, today, '76, and yet another breed is establishing themselves, and creating new directions, and following contest circuits, and still finding remote surf spots, and generally laying their trip on the surfing world. Most names are known, including Bertleman, Ho, Buttons, Dunn, Liddell and Kealoha from Hawaii; Paarman and Mike and Shaun Tomson from South Africa; and Richards, Peterson, Cairns, Warren, Townend, Raymond, and a few others from Australia, with Rasmussen and Flecky being the more versatile mainlanders, along with the already established Crawford and Loehr.

In today's interaction of professionals, an interesting development is occurring, being that the currently emerging crop is attempting to further extend the limits that the already established stars have attained, a process which once occupied the total being of the older pros, also. This courageous attempt has centered a great deal of attention upon various outstanding members of this new breed, namely Shaun and a few

Austroids, and while many people have recently expressed their theories on why this new group have had so much competitive success and why they are considered to be HOT, very few verbal reactions have been reflected and recorded by the actual people in subject.

In most articles, we've been given little credit for originality, and many of our peers have expressed criticism toward our whatever. We've been faced with charges ranging from assault, battery and arrogant defiance against the faces of waves; and, according to some of our peers, the basic flow of our surfing has been lost in a sea of battleground tactics and aggressive abuse to our mother ocean. Apparently, we've also breached the Sixteenth Amendment, in that we've been overampingly gliding with too much glitter. Many minor charges have been submitted, and due to our conquering approach, as Gerry would say, we're experiencing a reign of supremacy within the professional area, which, of course, has been thoroughly analyzed and finally diagnosed as probably only a temporary dominance, as we've all supposedly reached our peak. Oh, I shouldn't really get bitchy like that.

None of the younger guys can truthfully claim to have greater skill than the already established surfers simply because B.K., Gerry, Hakman, and Nat, to name but a few, have been a major influence in contemporary surfing, and yet there is still room for individuals, whether known or unknown, to receive recognition by simply displaying originality and creativity. Today's younger surfers have developed their skills in varying surfing environments; for example, Bertleman and Michael Ho were spawned in the paradise situations of Ala Moana, V-land and Backdoor; whereas Shaun Tomson put his act together in the isolated waves of South Africa, and guys like Richards and Townend emerged from the competitive zones of Australia, and yet they were all drawn towards professionalism at roughly the same time.

It is true that we place quite a bit of emphasis on our competitive aspirations, but because of this fact, all the Australian and African stars have too often been categorized as having similar approaches and attitudes towards surfing and life in general, as though we've all been popped out of the same mold, and I really feel that our surfing goes much deeper than simply A, B, or C. Quotations like, "we've paid our dues," and "we're taking over now," have been miscomprehended because people don't realize the background and relevance of these statements. Some people even look upon our performances last winter as being overnight successes, but little do they realize how much time and money was spent in reaching our current status.

The fact is that when you are a young emerging rookie from Australia or Africa, you not only have to come through the backdoor to get invitations to the Pro meets, but you have to bust the door down before they hear ya knockin'. I mean, it was left up to people who weren't even into surfing to say who was hot, and who was not. Our situation was that we had read about and seen photos and movies of all the established stars, for years and years, and then we'd travel to Hawaii as total anonymities, or nobodies, and literally eat shit each session, each day, each season. The pro contests were already full of super-hot surfers, and there was already a giant queue waiting to get in, so our only alternative was to surf each big-wave session with total abandon. Like there were ten young Aussies and Africans vying for three vacant slots in the contest circuit, knowing that at any time, Nat, Wayne and Midget could come over and snap up all the Australian quota of contest invitations.

There was no real need to have young blood in the circuit because the older guys were still red-hot, and to put some unknown Aussie kid in the lineup meant that some guy who'd put in maybe eight or ten seasons had to be put out, and understandably, nobody was keen for this to happen, except us, and so to gain both media and competitive recognition, we had to paddle out on the gnarliest days at Pipeline and Sunset, and literally attempt impossible maneuvers. This situation set the stage for the introduction of the hard rock–ripping, full-tilt boogie band, which, in true, "Story of Pop" fashion, has for its first time climbed to the top of the hit parade, and now band members such as Shaun, Kanga and Mark Richards are top-billed features at many inside-out, upside-down jam sessions.

For sure, Gerry and Rory still provide the most in-tune front-side sessions at Pipeline; and B.K., Hakman and Reno are always the show-stoppers at Sunset, and their past notoriety is directly responsible for the emergence of the new boys, but this new band is developing the ability of versatility, in that they are displaying the same explosive intensity at 12-foot Pipeline and Sunset as they do at 6-foot V-Land and Off-The-Wall. The already established surfers like B.K. and Hawk were into such heavy directions on our arrival that we were forced to delve into certain subtleties which they found unnecessary in their flights to the heights. Some people are either introducing original theatrical moves, or adding more flash to already established body English clichés, although some of Owl's and Fitzgerald's are patented, and increasing degrees of stylish statements, even the odd Jagger- or Bowie-oriented moves are being witnessed on both large and small waves.

In today's arena, there is no single best surfer like there was a decade ago when there was only one Nat and one David, but now, on any given day, any one of ten people may stand out as having the most positive session, and no current day champion can claim to be the greatest, just because he gave the most outstanding display on the contest day, because the very next day he might fail to relate to the ever-changing mood of the ocean, while the guy who placed 16th yesterday, might today be off on a different tangent, striking perfect chords with the rhythm of the ocean's fickle majesty. Certainly, everyone has a different interpretation of who and what they consider to be great, and many leading surfers have claimed to be "the greatest," but the funny thing is that they are all accurate evaluations because each hot surfer is the best in his own direction.

Surfing is such a simple expressive act, and yet at the same time it reflects all the complexities of modern-day man, and can be as deep, mystical and undefined as the ocean itself. Varying levels of consciousness are displayed whilst surfing; for example, some people don't care to make any explanations in relation to what a wave represents, but rather just take it all for granted, while others see waves as the end result of all the significant elements of energy created within the earth's atmosphere, while yet another person may relate to a wave as being a direct link with his or her concept of God, and on a fifteen-foot day at Pipeline, it's quite easy to relate to waves in this way. It has been claimed that the meeting point between the ocean and the land is the highest point of untapped energy on earth, and surfers seem to be the only group utilizing this energy and successfully tapping this organically electrified current.

To a non-surfer, it is virtually impossible to visualize surfing as being anything other than a physical expression, but many of today's more advanced surfers are approaching the ocean on the spiritual plane, and they are comprehending and absorbing all of her pulsating rhythms, and their surfing reflects an extremely deep relationship. They're delving further into themselves, and whilst surfing, they become so self-centered that they often appear to be in a hypnotic trance, where the surfer, the board and the wave become as one, and they can actually dominate and alter the flow of wave by total concentration and mind projection. I swear I've seen it happen, and experienced it. I've witnessed Shaun, Ian, Gerry and others actually make a wave change to suit their flow, and I know it's possible for someone to mentally command a wave situation to instantaneously materialize by being so one-pointed or self-centered that they actually become the wave, by seeking the wave's power nucleus, and becoming as one with it.

Some professionals are developing their own mind psychology, becoming their own gurus, reaching naturally altered states and learning when and how to switch off certain parts of their mind, including their ego-centered mind, which is interested in everything except the here and now. Not many guys are into long hours of meditation, and yet by surfing upside-down, around and inside waves for hours and hours, they are experiencing the weird spaces, with the only difference being that there is no guru or *roshi* present to tell them what's happening while their performances are getting better.

When one is surfing really big waves, total concentration is demanded, and your perception and awareness is extended to the point where every movement of the ocean is seen, and not one ripple or bump escapes your attention, and one becomes totally harmonized with the present moment; you completely shut off all ego-centered thoughts to the point where your mind is dancing with the waves, and as you concentrate on the contours and subtleties on the wave's face, the wave's whole motion seems to slow down. This is simply the altered state which some people get to by meditation, and others get to by using a chemical.

A more down-to-earth example of this process is experienced when going surfing on a 12- to 15-foot day at Pipeline, and on this occasion, I'll go surfing, and you can come along for the ride. I'm sitting in an obscured spot amongst the bushes in front of the line-up house, and for the last fifteen minutes, though it seems like hours, my attention and concentration has been on nothing but waves. From this point of slight elevation, I've been able to observe the sets moving in from miles out to sea. The swell begins as a long line stretching from outside Rocky to outside Waimea, and as it moves towards shore, it appears to begin focusing on one reef along that stretch, namely Pipeline. Banzai reef is such a dominant face on this day that it has literally magnetized this giant line moving in from the horizon, and has centered the total energy of this swell on this perfectly one-pointed pinnacle peak, which is being used as the takeoff spot by the surfers already out there. After battling out through the insanely heavy shorebreak sweep, I begin paddling towards this peak, which from my viewpoint, now appears to be a series of giant open-mouthed, roaring caves, which, after a cyclical process of turning themselves inside-out, send hissing vapors out the now partially closed off entrance.

My perception and concentration is intense, and I'm totally mesmerized by these liquid energy streamers. I reach the takeoff point during a lull, and I line myself up with the exact spot that I know the wave that I'm after will soon be roaring through, and I wait. I'm at a spot a little further out than the peak, because not only can't I let my concentration be taken away by speaking with others, but I know the biggest and meanest tubes can be picked up from where I'm at, and now I'm watching a large west set approach the outer reefs. I paddle over the first two waves, which twist and wrap onto the inside reef, and the third one rears up. I turn around, make about eight positive strokes, and I'm into it, dropping down the vortex of the giant cylinder whose sole intention is to suck every bit of spare water up its face, and then fire it all back down again in one heaving, cyclical motion; and yet, I'm in total control, and I'm even in a relaxed state of mind, because my perception is at such an extended height that it appears as if the wave and everything around it is moving in super slow motion.

I know this sounds ridiculous, but I have this giant, thick, hungry, hollow tube exploding all around me, wanting to bury me into the nearly exposed coral bottom, and to me it's like watching and participating in some beautiful, mystical ballet. I've got all the time in the world, time is standing still, I'm backside, and now my instincts tell me to move NOW, and I feel that inner click, that feeling you get when you know a shot's good before you throw it, and I move up into a perfectly shaped cylinder, get totally tubed, and as I'm spat out the end, I give freedom to some of my inner emotions that I've been holding back and disciplining for the last hour.

Of course, every surfer has a different physical, emotional and intellectual breakdown, but that was just a first-person indication of how one could approach big-wave surfing. Every hot surfer, and there's about thirty super hotties, all incorporating a different psychic technique to build up to a big-wave session, and most good surfers reflect their wave consciousness in their various modes of living and their daily routine, and it is the combined energies of all the past and current personalities and characters that is developing surfing into one of this world's most progressive activities and definitely our spaciest sport. ◪

Aloha Ha

By Carlos Izan · SURFER Vol. 18 No. 1 · May 1977

Surfers have never needed to travel very far to experience cultural clashes, because the most significant chasm always existed right in the very birthplace of the sport—Hawaii. Nothing brings this point home quite like a five-hour spell on the cattle barge to Hawaii, where surfers are forced to play nice with a strange herd of pasty Middle Americans on their way to Mai-Tai-and-plastic-pineapple holidays. Lurking in the disguise of the pseudonym Carlos Izan, Santa Monica writer Craig Stecyk recounts a typical encounter on one of the alien airlifts.

Moana Mana

It was all too real as I boarded the Honolulu-bound 747 at Hilo International. I had just come over on the mail boat from Kahoolawe, and was sweating profusely, since my haphazard travel arrangements had left no room for error. A cursory inspection revealed that the entire jumbo jet was filled with one of those incredible look-alike mainland tour groups. In this case, it was the "Your Man Tour," and the participants were all into their 50s, primed for paradise and flashing those eerie Kodak smiles. The sole distinguishing mark on these individuals was the oval-shaped red, white and blue badge each wore saying, "Your Man Tours, My Name Is_____."

As I stumbled into the only available seat next to Ruth and Harry Zartler from Sparto, Illinois, it was obvious that I wasn't their man. Admittedly, the two-week lack of a shower and shave had ripened me a bit, yet still, the disgusted look on Ruth's face was downright . . . well . . . disgusting. I attempted to strike up a conversation to quell the uneasiness—"You folks new to these parts," etc. Reluctantly they warmed to my hospitality, and soon I began to discover some fascinating facets of Ruth's and Harry's lifestyle. For instance: there was Harry's dry cleaning business that offered the only one-hour Martinizing service in the county; or how Ruth's Oldsmobile 442 could hit 110 flat out, and would never start on those cold mornings until Harry mixed cod liver oil in with Prestone antifreeze; or how Harry figures he walks 50 miles a year shoveling the snow off his driveway; or how the two felt that President Nixon had been framed; and last but not least, how some "teenage hoodlums" stole that "cute" little cast-iron jockey off the lawn in front of their suburban manor (it was a valuable antique, Ruth assured me). Everything was proceeding nicely until Mrs. Zartler sadly stated that their on-flight movie had burned up just prior to the final scene. There the whole flight was waiting for the cinematic conclusion when suddenly the screen filled with the bubbling and crackling visage of burned celluloid. I inquired as to the film's identity, and learned it was *The Shootist*, starring John Wayne and Lauren Bacall.

Realizing that this was all that was needed to cement our new friendship, I turned to her and said, "Mom, you're in luck 'cause I've seen the film." Her husband was now erect with anticipation. "Well, tell us, how did it end?"

I answered, "Harry, to put it succinctly, John Wayne gets gun-shot, and Ronnie Howard avenges his death." Suddenly old Zartler was beside himself—"You expect me to believe that?" and he shouted, "Hey, here's a laugh, this fellow says John Wayne dies at the end, and that the kid who used to be Opie on *The Andy Griffith Show* kills the gunfighters." Total group intimidation . . . rejection . . . alienation . . . all of the "Your Man Tour" was now on my case.

Christ, why did I ever get involved anyway? At least we were landing in Honolulu and I would never have to see any of their stinking China-white faces again. I knew why they hated me; I had dared to challenge all that they believed in. As I ran down the airport corridor, I could hear Harry chiding me—"Duke Wayne NEVER dies . . . NEVER."

At the customs declaration area, the official hands me a form asking if I have any plants, animals, micro-organisms, objects manufactured of vegetal material, firearms, foreign currency, machine tools, etc., to declare. I give him the list back, and tell him no. Now I look up and see two crew-cut men in tan leisure suits with 45s bulging under their coats and carrying walkie-talkies across the disembarkation area. It is obvious that they are cops; who else would be wearing coats on an 80-degree day? Having already surpassed my paranoia quota on the journey from Hilo, I figure that there can be no way they're looking for me.

However . . . they keep relentlessly advancing, and finally the one with the greasy fenders on his flat top flashes a D.E.A. badge and states: "Mind if we search your person and baggage?" Meanwhile, Ruth, Harry and the Your Man entourage are watching with suspician, wondering if they will ever learn to never trust anyone under thirty. While the one D.E.A. is feverishly scrutinizing every article of my luggage, the other carries on the inquisition—"Where's your passport?" My less than brilliant retort was something to the effect that Kahoolawe was still part of America. Q—"What were you doing on Kahoolawe?" A—"Visiting my grandmother." Numerous Q's and A's follow until the agent of the law grabs me and yells "Look, boy, nobody ever comes from Kahoolawe; besides, your plane came in through Hilo." The guy's right, and I'm really beginning to wish that I'd never left. Here I am getting the shit hassled out of me in town by these ominous haole D.E.A.s, and all I can think of is how pleasant it used to be living in this very same locale during territorial days. (Of course, before statehood, any place in Hawaii was a nice place.)

Now, more pissed than amused, I give the government man a terse lecture on Island history and the spirit of aloha. His cohort, having thoroughly examined everything down to my dirty underpants, is now considering the possibilities for concealment in the 12-foot-long surfboard I'm transporting. He reckons this must be it . . . it's got to be, nothing else remains, so he holds it up to a wall-mounted fluorescent light fixture, and . . . FLASH . . . they can't see anything. "Of course you can't see through it; it's made of wiliwili wood." I further try to explain that the board is a sacred palo-olo, several hundred years old, and so leaded with mana (accumulated powers) that they had better not mess with it or me anymore 'cause we've both run out of patience. This falls on deaf ears, since even the Drug Reinforcement Agency knows that surfboards are all short in length and made from plastic foam (which is precisely why they hold surfboards up to the light to see if there are any telltale contraband shadows inside their volumes).

Now I'm being loaded into this Gestapo-looking van, with cops on all four sides of me, and the palo-olo forlornly laying on the floor. This one guy is trying to tell me my rights, and I'm telling him that if I had any rights, I wouldn't be going through all of this.

At airport security headquarters, the boys are Pavloviantly salivating in anticipation of another endless-summer hashish surfboard bust. I'm sitting there with the magic surf craft that undoubtedly belonged to an ancient Hawaiian King, wondering just what sort of kapu these people are going to bring down on us all. Up walks the man with a saw, and I'm screaming, trying to warn them, "Don't cut this surfboard; you're messing with powers so heavy that this entire island might be destroyed. You may have taken it too far already." The head guy looks over and says, "Look, son, don't give us any trouble." To which I replied, "I'm not, you guys are the trouble here." Now the leader is calling for some doctors with some psychiatric restraints. Incredible, I'm being taken involuntarily to a mental hospital, and the retribution these infidels are going to incur is awesome, for like it or not, the ancient Island Gods still reign supreme. A local gentleman in a sweat-stained straw hat comes over and advises them that what I've been saying could well be true. "It's quite possible this is a valuable historical artifact; I suggest you call the Bishop Museum for confirmation," he clearheadedly imparted.

Suddenly their demeanor changed, perhaps the kamaaina's advice has swayed them . . . but no, they're drooling again in preparation for another kill. Over at the contraband illuminarium they are inspecting an Australian's surfboard, and there are these strange opaque cavities deep within its plastic heart. The foreigner informs them that he is a professional surf rider, and that this is a Dick Van Stralen chambered surfboard inserted with ping-pong balls for added buoyancy—"it's the compressed air, mate."

Viewing his plight, I know two things for certain: (1) They will shortly dissect his surfboard, and (2) they are doing him a big favor, whether he realizes it or not, because ain't nobody gonna ride big Sunset on a raft of ping-pong balls.

The sputtering rose-colored neon light in the airport bar aptly underscored the situation; it kept blinking ALOHA-HA, ALOHA-HA, ALOHA-HA.

The Last Soul Surfer

By Phil Jarratt · SURFER Vol. 20 No. 8 · August 1979

In 1979 Pipeline master Gerry Lopez turned 30—the dreaded age at which surfers are put out to pasture. Yet, while his performances at Pipeline were finally being challenged, nobody could touch Lopez's legacy. Pipeline and Gerry Lopez were the sport's first Bogart and Bacall. By the time other surf stars mounted any serious threat, Lopez had already moved on, parlaying his fame into business successes that would pave the way for an entire surf industry. SURFER's editorial menu was also changing with the times: While travel was still the central theme, writers like Phil Jarratt began filing more in-depth profiles of renowned surfers. In this piece, Jarratt resists the urge to fawn and asks what we all wanted to know: Where do our surf heroes go when they kick out? Here we find that Lopez seemed to be making all the right calls, offering one of the first real blueprints for the Surfer Over Thirty set.

Gerry had been out there two hours or more without exactly setting the Pipe on fire and the gallery in Fat Paul's backyard was getting restless. "He's gotten old," said Fat Paul, by way of explanation. "Anybody want some more beer?"

A new pack of Heinekens was broken open and half-consumed before the familiar figure appeared, paddling away from the others towards a slightly wider peak. Lopez stood up and drove a straight line through the eye of a monster. Simple and dramatic, and with a touch of class that no one—not the backside brigade, not Russell, Dunn or Crawford, not one of the new wave Pipe aficionados—has yet been able to emulate.

A few minutes later he was back at Fat Paul's trading jokes with Flippy Hoffman about the onset of middle age, mingling with the people who knew him before he became an industry. A small, elegant and friendly man who plainly couldn't give a damn that this was the day before the Pipeline Masters, that he'd just had a bad session, and that young hopefuls all along the beach were already spreading the word that Lopez couldn't cut it anymore. At 30 Lopez is used to that sort of speculation. "I was trying like hell out there but I couldn't catch anything," he joked. "I'm not going to take off on anything where there's a possibility I might not make it. Hey, I'm past that, I can afford to let the 50/50 deals go by. I'm kind of a chicken at heart, and I don't have anything to prove, that's for sure." Later in the month, Lopez the Chickenheart finished in the top six in the Masters, playing a starring role for the cameras on the Pipe's best days and headed back to Maui safe in the knowledge that his North Shore performance would keep Lightning Bolt sales figures alive in '79.

Only those who have watched people watching Gerry Lopez surf the Pipeline will understand just what a drawcard he is. His agility and funky cool in terrifying circumstances are the very essence of surfing's attraction to the masses. Take a kid from Detroit and show him ten waves of some hot rat tearing up a beachbreak. Hmm, he'll say, that's clever. Now show him one wave of Lopez blasting out of the horrible bowels of a Pipeline monster in a casual arch. He'll gasp. He'll scream. He'll holler. He'll go mad. He'll go apeshit on surf lust. He'll run from the theater frothing at the mouth and he'll buy, buy, buy . . . he'll buy three Lightning Bolt surfboards, four T-shirts, two pairs of Bolt boardshorts, a neck chain and at least a dozen color posters of the Great God of Pure Source. He'll understand at last what this thing called surfing is all about.

Ironically the Pipeline antics of Lopez and his macho soul brothers represent only a very small part of the surfing experience, but it's a highly visible and influential part. The Evel Knievel element if you like, but there's much more to it than that. Great beauty enhanced by the smell of death. And the danger is very real, even to great surfers. Jeff Crawford went close to death two winters ago. I've watched Michael Peterson fall out of the top and miraculously escape serious injury. He ran up the beach shaking and close to tears. Gerry Lopez rarely gets hurt, but he's not infallible. His average is simply better than the rest. There are few Pipeline watchers who would take odds on the master getting nailed and many who wait for his re-emergence even when the wave has disintegrated on the shore. As Lopez and his business associates know only too well, this is the stuff of which legends and sales figures are made.

Like most modern Hawaiians, Gerry Lopez is a racial casserole rather than a direct descendant of the Alii. His Spanish-American father had lived in New York and settled in Honolulu after serving in the Pacific in World War II. Lopez Senior married a local lady from Kauai and Gerry was born in November 1948. He was thrown into the ocean at an early age and learned to love it. By the time high school came around he was getting hot. He became Hawaiian junior champ and talked surf incessantly with his schoolmates at Punahou. Kindred spirits were all around him. Jeff Hakman was a class below, Fred Hemmings a class above. Paul Strauch was a year above Hemmings and Jimmy Blears was in Hakman's class. But there was no skipping lessons to go surfing. Punahou wasn't—and still isn't—that kind of school. Established last century by the haole missionaries as a haven for white man's learning and Calvinistic discipline, it became a recruiting ground for Yale. As the missionary influence declined, the doors were opened wider to locals, but when young Lopez and his hedonistic buddies arrived there was still no doubt in anybody's mind that Punahou boys were destined for college on the Mainland. So it came as no surprise to anyone in Honolulu that while Nat Young was taking out the World Title in San Diego in '66, Gerry Lopez was up the road enrolling at Whittier College, an establishment famous for teaching Richard Nixon some early tricks.

Gerry took his surfboard to California but his heart wasn't in it. Punahou had had the desired effect and he was enthusiastic about majoring in architectural engineering. But this was Southern California in the middle '60s, Nuuhiwa was god, Jan and Dean had a firm grip on the soundtrack controls and boardbuilders were giving away team colors and free surfboards to anyone who could stand up. Punahou got blitzed by the surf monkey. Gerry found good waves in Mexico and did not top his class. The following year he was back in the Islands, feigning interest in his studies at the University of Hawaii and establishing his credentials at the Pipeline. In his third year he dropped out of UH and fell in with Jack Shipley, a beefy local surf shop domo and boardbuilder who loved to sit in Fat Paul's backyard and watch Gerry do it at the Pipe.

Lightning Bolt surfboards were an immediate success. These days they're what Hawaiian surfing is all about and they rely on a large team of experts to keep ahead of the pack, but back at the start it was just Gerry and Jack. Gerry rode the Pipeline and Jack signed the checks. Occasionally they'd get fatherly advice from Duke Boyd, the man who first flashed that surfing and sportswear had a lot to offer each other. Boyd had, among other things, helped to create the Hang Ten, OP and Golden Breed labels. He saw that the Lopez charisma had a lot more going for it than gimmickry and he talked to Gerry and Shipley about forming a corporation.

In the four years or so since Bolt expanded its horizons, Gerry Lopez has gone from cult hero to corporation figurehead. Duke Boyd might be president, Jack Shipley might run the board business, Dick Graham might control Pacific operations, numerous functionaries might supervise Bolt business in little corners all over the world, but every customer is buying a piece of Gerry Lopez. He's a kind of surfing monarch. He signs pieces of paper, he shakes hands, he talks to kids in stores and he rides the Pipeline. Most of all he rides the Pipeline. Unlike others at the top of the surfing totem pole, Lopez has never been much of a contest surfer. He says he never had the right temperament for contest success. "You have to think about where I'm from. In Hawaii contests don't have the same connotations. For us, for a long time, contests were a fun thing. You won, you lost, it didn't matter. Now I'm kind of apathetic about the whole competitive thing."

While others bathe in the competitive spotlight Lopez is usually in the shade of the Pipeline lip. His earnings from this exercise are more indirect but the press coverage is probably greater. Cameras might not have made him what he is but they have shown the world what he can do. Very few surfing movies have been made that don't feature at least one Lopez ride. This in itself doesn't make him a rich man, but it does make him a very saleable commodity for Lightning Bolt, and it follows that he is anything but hard-line on the question of commercial rights for surfers. In short he thinks it is easier to let people take pictures of him and do what they will with them than it is to hassle for payment. "If I hassle them and they use someone else and don't pay him either, what have I achieved? I might as well get the Lighting Bolt symbol in there and maybe sell a few more boards." In the past he has taken issue with filmmakers using him on a grand scale to put bums on cinema seats but for the most part he's prepared to let it slide for the mythical "percentage of net." He says: "Percentage of net doesn't mean anything. It's just a bunch of shit, but if the filmmaker isn't making much either it makes me feel good to think I can help out. I mean they're busting their asses to shoot the thing and I'm just out there having fun."

Lopez has always given the impression that he's out there having fun. True, he's locked into an international corporate master plan and Duke Boyd may well fancy himself as the Führer of Fabric and Lopez probably does lick his lips as the Lightning Bolt tentacles embrace the world, but his personal goals are pleasantly simple. For the past four years he has lived on Maui in a hilltop house he built himself. He commutes by plane rather than live closer to the action in Honolulu. "There are a million people in Hawaii," he says, "and 800,000 of them live in Honolulu. I had to get out of there." The house on Maui means a great deal to Gerry. He built the basics, with the help of a friend, in six weeks while he was out of the surf with torn ligaments, but he sees it as a 20- or 30-year project. He sometimes gets the urge to build on a room, or rip down a wall. Lopez enjoys his life on Maui. "I'll tell ya real simply," he says. "I get up in the morning and the first thing I do is I look out my window and see what the surf's doing. If there's even a remote chance of surfing I'm down there." There are, of course, other things. Lately Gerry's been getting into guns. GUNS? "Yeah, guns. Actually I'm a right-wing zealot and although I may not look it I'm also a racist. I've always been fascinated by guns and hanging around with someone like John Milius—who's holding onto close to a million dollars worth of guns—I guess something rubbed off. There's something about guns, I don't know what it is but I like to shoot them and suddenly I've got a whole bunch of money so I thought, what the hell, I'll buy some guns."

I'd always suspected there was a touch of the Burt Reynolds in Lopez. All that running in the heat of the tropical day, eating all those durians, yoga, trail riding. Macho, macho man. But guns were another matter. I took the questioning further. What do you shoot at?

"I don't shoot any animals. I just kind of have them, and I don't really have any use for them. Just iron. In fact they're kinda a pain in the ass because I gotta clean them all the time or they rust, and bullets are so goddamn expensive." It's a very macho kind of hobby, isn't it?

"Well, in a way. What it really comes down to is guns are bitchen, they're a neat thing. There's nothing quite so satisfying . . . " What do you mean they're a neat thing? They kill people.

"No, guns don't do that, it's people who pull the trigger. But guns are tools for killing."

"Bullshit, guns are for shooting bullets." And bullets kill.

"No, people kill each other. I don't think I'll ever kill anybody with my guns. I kind of feel bad after I kill a pheasant, you know, because it really doesn't taste that good and I'd rather go down to the store and buy a chicken that's already plucked. I don't know Phil, I guess it's kind of silly that I have all these guns, but there's nothing quite as satisfying as having blazing Colt .45 automatics in each hand."

No, I don't believe you're saying this. This is all a bad dream, isn't it? Have you got any other strange obsessions you'd like to talk about?

(Laughing) "No man, that's it. All I got is my surfshorts."

Gerry can get away with a bit of eccentricity. He is, after all, a surfing legend and a Hawaiian institution. Cecilio and Kapono wrote a song about him. You touch down at Honolulu in the middle of the night and grab a cab. The driver says as he stashes your board in the back: "Surfin', huh? Hey, my brudda, he know Gerry Lopez, yeah?" No other surfer enjoys fame like this. In Bali the kids cut each other's hair in poor imitations of the Lopez pageboy look. They even copy his mannerisms. In Australia not so long ago I was with Gerry at a launching party for Lightning Bolt sportswear. A woman approached somewhat hesitantly and blurted out: "Do you actually come from Hawaii do you ride inside the waves or on top of them my brother took me to a surfing movie once and I nearly fainted does it hurt when you fall off are you scared are there any sharks over there?" Lopez just stroked the bristles of his moustache, grinned like a politician on polling day and said: "Well, yes and no."

Gerry is well aware of his exalted position in the surfing culture and it sometimes embarrasses him a little. He stares out at the world from the back cover of this magazine most months (often he's on the front cover too) and he is recognized everywhere he goes. It's a mixed blessing. His cameo appearance in *Big Wednesday* played up the legend, and while it seemed to me to be a pretty fair representation of what the man has meant to a whole generation of surfers, Lopez thought it was "a little silly." It was "too hokey, too serious. I sometime wonder how all this happened, you know? All I did was go surfing and it happened all around me. I don't think I've ever pushed this image thing, not even with Lightning Bolt. It's just a business I play a part in. I don't think we're ripping anyone off, and I gotta make a living somehow."

And not a bad living at that. Gerry says he's "as comfortable as I ever imagined I would be. I've got all the material possessions I could possibly use—probably too many—but I don't have all that much really because I don't need much. My surfboards, my shorts, my wax, my car. That's all that's primary in my life because surfing is where I get most of my fun, most of my energy. The rest of the stuff is incidental. I got a motorcycle but I don't really need it. I don't need a fancy car because all I do is I throw the surfboard into it and the dog rides in it and it just gets beat to shit anyway, so I've got a pickup truck." What's far and away more important to Lopez is his health. We'd been sitting on the sofa in Fat Paul's for quite a while and Gerry was getting a little jumpy. Craning his neck to check the indicator sets, touching his toes and lapsing offhandedly into deep breathing exercises. Far too polite to suggest we terminate the proceedings but plainly toey for action. This, after all, was the second time in a year that I'd waylaid him in a room and pestered him. I decided to be merciful and let him go get healthy, but first, one last shot. Gerry, I said, OK, you're fit right now but you're also 30. How long can you keep it up?

Lopez thought for a moment because fitness really is his trip. Healthy mind, healthy body, take your pick. Gerry Lopez has gone for the body. He said: "I don't buy the idea that age takes it away from you. I really feel that physical conditioning is a belief system. Look at these old Zen priests. Their whole life is geared toward sharpening all the way to the end. As for me, I feel in better shape than I've ever been. I go through a whole series of daily exercises and people who don't do them just can't believe I'm doing this stuff. They go, are you nuts? But you get to a point where what is pain to one person is in fact pleasurable to you. Like getting down there with my rope and my gut wheel at six in the morning and getting my heart pumping. I love it. I've done more yoga this past year than I have in the previous four or five. Hey, I'm having a great time. I enjoy myself, and it all comes back to surfing. I can go out there and catch waves and I'm not choking my ass to make it over the ledge. It comes easy, and it's just as well that it does because you get to a point in your surfing where you think you know enough to cover all possibilities. At a place like Pipeline you never know that much. Each wave is a whole new deal and I want to know I'm ready for it."

And with that, Gerry Lopez—possibly the last soul surfer, possibly the most artistic tuberider surfing will ever see, possibly just a good Punahou boy, possibly a whole lot of things—walked out the door to work up a sweat and draw yet another thin line between pleasure and pain. 🏄

The Tropic of Cancer?
Is California surfing terminally ill or just ...?
By John Witzig · SURFER Vol. 22 No. 1 · January 1981

Is Richards Unstoppable?

In the summer of 1980, Australian writer John Witzig made his first visit to the Golden State in more than a decade. Spending several weeks traveling the coast from San Diego to Santa Cruz and beyond, he shared wax, rides, beers, and stories with a wide variety of Californian surfers, and found they had essentially become strangers to one another—to say nothing of the rest of the surfing world—during the dark age of '70s localism. Witzig's chronicles appeared as a three-part series in *SURFER* that remains the richest portrait ever produced of the California surf scene.

Witzig couldn't have picked a better time to make such a journey. Isolationism was giving way to international influences, talent was growing in a few hidden hothouses, and there was even talk of an emerging Californian renaissance. As you read, keep track of how many Witzig predictions came true.

Chapter One: It's Been Very Nice to Know Me

This is just another California story. Despite what the editors will try to tell you. It *isn't* the definitive article on surfing in that diverse state. They couldn't find a local that was stupid enough to generalize to the degree desired . . . up shot my hand . . . "Me sir! Me! I'll say anything." Well, I spent the better part of a month wandering around the coast. It was pretty much fun, and it was at the magazine's expense.

By way of some sort of introduction, it seems sensible to declare my interests. The first is that I happen to like California. A high (or low) point of my idiot youth was to pen an article in the mid-sixties that made some extravagant and fairly amusing claims about Australian surfing being the best in the world. Actually, I didn't really say that, but it was what everyone reckoned I'd said, and I've grown to live with it. They all noticed the extravagance, and none of them saw any of the humor. I've also come to accept that.

But the upshot of the article was a torrent of abuse that kept the letters column buzzing for a year (mainly with my detractors . . . there was a letter from my auntie who said that it was a very nice story . . . but I digress). It kept me in a vague position of contributor with this magazine in the hope that just maybe I'd do it again. Well I'm afraid that I'm going to disappoint them. It took ten years before I was game to come back after that article, and I'd prefer an earlier return this time. So I suppose cowardice in the face of an opportunity to offend is another interest I'd better declare.

And so this, while I remember it, is a necessarily limited view. I'm not sure I'd disagree with someone who'd say that it's dumb to try and gather an overview of a place like California in a month. I feel like adding an "Errors & Omissions Excepted" paragraph to the end. If you're a hottie at the local spot and you're reading to see if you got a mention, then I can probably save you the energy. There were times when I was told whole lists of who had been, might've been, and probably was, good. I even wrote them down a couple of times, but I'm afraid that they're boring for everyone except the people on them and their mothers.

I'm in no way apologizing for the people who I *have* written about. Nor for the omission of the fourteen or so million that I didn't get to mention. I hope that I've been pushed in the right directions, and that I've selected in such a way to paint a broad canvas. That, at least, is the intention.

And before I descend into seriousness . . . and feel free to interject should it happen again, may I allow myself a parting shot at the most current of the California expressions . . . *everyone* that I met, people I'd barely exchanged three words with, their brothers and their dogs, they all, *without exception*, assured me that "it was very nice to meet me." Well how would they *know*? I barely resisted rudeness in the end. And this article, if nothing much else, is an attempt to show them all that they were probably wrong.

Chapter Two: North County

North County is where there's a whole heap of hot kids . . . it's the home of a unique American cultural event . . . and it's also where my friend Orchid lives.

Orchid is a reactionary. Nothing that's happened in the past five years in surfing has meant anything to him. Well, nothing positive, anyway. California, he says, "has withdrawn from the field of battle as the field grows more and more ridiculous." And California, he insists, had *made* its contribution . . . "it's like having a full tank and saying you haven't put any gas in for a week . . . there are no contributions. The path is downhill."

He compares the decline of surfing to that of the U.S. as a superpower . . . acknowledges that professionalism is the main influence, and accepts that California has had no part in it. Orchid states, unequivocally, that surfing doesn't lend itself to competition. "It's like a guy who's a good f--- becoming a gigolo . . . it doesn't mean it's a sport . . . just something natural." He supposes that the connection between "surfing" and "competition" was originally made by Fred Hemmings' mother.

Orchid reckons that the object of surfing is *not* to "win." That it never has been and never will be. He says that no matter how good Shaun Tomson looks, he will never look as good as a wave without him . . . and supposes that the only professional surfer with any class is Gerry Lopez . . . "he doesn't try to win." For Orchid, the object of professional surfing should be spectacular wipeouts . . . preferably causing injury and/or death.

He offers his Pro Surfing Quiz (choose one answer only):

A man becomes a pro surfer because:
>(a) he is tired of washing dishes at the Chart House
>(b) he wants to lay dumb girls
>(c) he needs gas money to get to the beach

The smaller the board:
>(a) The smaller the brain
>(b) the smaller the organ
>(c) The bigger the asshole

The only valid contest, says Orchid, is when there are no rules other than sitting 'round arguing who won . . . what, he says, people used to do when they were too tired to surf. It's of *no* interest to anyone else.

My friend Orchid would not, I think, be one to claim that his views represented anyone else. The fact remains, though, that North County remains a holdout of sorts for the Organic School of surfing. And it coexists happily enough with the latest collection of kids for whom the concerns of the sixties are not even a memory. They simply have no experiences of the laid-back hippy trip. Being cool is uncool. The period seems to be past, to quote Jeff Divine, when "even if you weren't stoned, you acted like it." The emerging kids are competitive. In junior high, to use the vernacular, it's "sooo baaaad" to be on a surf team. In North County, that might be the Nectar team, or Donald Takayama's. These days, it's certainly socially acceptable. The kids want to shred like all the rest of the world.

In a way, North County contains the paradox of California surfing. The organic-hippy thing had such a strong influence. Being mellow went into every level. As Divine put it, the biggest respect was to surf unreal and have everybody like you. But the interest is quickening in competition. *All* the hotties are into it. The young guys are concerned about *losing*. It's what Ian Cairns says has to happen if they are to win anything. And it's part of the paradox that one of the really fascinating contests in California surfing is held each year at Stone Steps.

As I understand it, all the competitors have to drink a pitcher of beer before they go in their heats. Whoever makes it through to the next round repeats the process. Whoever can stand up wins the final. The spectators keep drinking the whole time.

For some reason, they never switched over to joints or more recently to the more exotic drugs. (It *would* lend new dimension to the term "lineup.") Beer it is, and stays. I find the whole idea immensely pleasing. Totally a waste of time, and consequently terrifically important.

Chapter Three: Cottons with Corky Carroll

The best thing about hanging 'round with Corky is that you tend to have a lot of fun. He has a habit of outrage that's hardly mellowed by the passing years. He is going to be an international affairs advisor to Ronald Reagan . . . "You know what we should've done when Russia moved into Afghanistan? Boycotting the Olympics . . . what a shitty idea . . . we should've taken over Mexico. It's true, you know."

Corky takes us surfing. He says that he has an obligation to do the surfing for the rest of the people at the magazine . . . (*this* magazine). He will pretend that he will look at other places, but every time you end up at Cottons. He can do head-dips there without anyone taking any notice.

If you could have a number of quintessential surfing experiences in California . . . and since the word means *most* essential, then I suppose that you can't . . . but if you *could*, then surfing at Cottons would be one of them. I have the pass stuck into my journal to remind me of what it was like. The pass says that on Tuesday, the Cyprus Shore Community Association will allow C. C. and two friends in, so long as they park in front of lot #24. At the gate, there's the guard in his little house and those delightful spikes that stick up out of the roadway and will rip the shit out of your tires if you decided that you were going in without permission.

I *know* that you get used to such displays of privilege . . . and I *know* that the recent coastal protection proposition means that there won't be anymore unrestricted development . . . and that access will be gained where it's practical . . . but *still* I find it offensive. A bloke that I ran into north of San Francisco said, in referring to land on the coast, that "it's not for *people*. It's for *rich people*."

But I've got diverted . . . and never one to notice that he's being a hypocrite . . . or arguing that in fact he must *see* the situation in order to mount a criticism . . . this reporter happily went surfing at one of the bastions of liberty and freedom . . . *"free"* provided you have a quarter million dollars to buy a lot. It was pretty much fun.

Chapter Four: The Loss of Influence

There hasn't been a California surfer of influence for ten years. Rolf Aurness was the last one in 1970. After the World Contest in Victoria, he and others dropped out of competition, and the kids followed. Competition itself was fairly discredited by the Me Generation.

Now this may well be a healthy thing. I'm reminded of a comment I read about Gerald Ford . . . "The country counts it a blessing that Jerry Ford is psychologically secure enough not to need to be president." It went on to say that it was a pity he didn't know what to do with it since he had it . . . irrelevant to the point I'm trying to make, but a good line. Perhaps it *doesn't* matter that there hasn't been a surfer of eminence on the pro tour, or on the North Shore. *Does* anyone give a shit anyway?

Kempton and others talk about the California "dilemma." They say it in such a way that you assume they're articulating the feelings of the beach, but are they? Buried deep in what Corky Carroll calls the world's surf ghetto, Huntington Beach, Ian Cairns reckons that "they don't even know there's an international surfing scene."

Michael Tomson has written that the surfing psyche is still locked in the sixties. Both he and Kampion have talked of the New Wave . . . an emergence of enthusiasm and competitive style that will mark the next generation of Californians. Whether they speak from observation or optimism seems to this reporter to be a matter of some debate.

I find myself quite ambivalent about this whole issue. I've never much enjoyed the excesses of competitive zeal that seem so often to accompany success. Too often it seems to distort the value of achievement. In California, surfing fits far more into a broader lifestyle . . . which, in passing, is remarkable for its hedonism, narcissism and straight wealth. I ask my friend Jack Shipley, who is as acute an observer as anyone I know, why he thinks that the Australians, Hawaiians and South Africans have dominated the pro pack. He draws in the scope of the question to compare the West Coast and Australia. In California, he says, there are so many things that you can do. "In Australia, you can become an electrician or a pro surfer. Which one would *you* choose?"

The success of Cheyne Horan in the last couple of years is in many ways straight out of the how-to-do-it manual . . . well, the Australian edition. This particular overnight success went through at least ten thousand club, schoolboys, state and national championships. Plus every trial and two-bob professional contest known to man. He is a very good competitive surfer and a totally seasoned professional. He's nineteen. Any comparative kid in California who thinks he's going to make the break into competitive stardom can fairly much forget it. He's five years too late. And he hasn't got a competitive structure to give him the start.

The WSA seems to be having dying pains, and the fledgling NSSA isn't even trying to provide regular contests for those outside the school system. Ian Cairns, NSSA coach, says that the organization *will* provide a competitive base, but he has no illusions about how long it will take. "Five years."

Ian, P. T. and Greg Hodges have formed a company called Sports and Media Services. They act as the executive directors of the NSSA for a fee of $12,000 a year. The irony of Australians occupying the position isn't lost either on them or their critics. There are few people, international, with more experience. The Bronzed Aussies and their corporate child are headquartered in suburban Huntington Beach. For P.T., it's his home break and he surfs it every day. "You've just got to lower your standards," he says of the waves.

Huntington is a remarkable place. Few surfing locales stick in your mind as it does. It has been fourteen years since I'd been there. The beach area seemed like it'd had some attention in the intervening years . . . the pier much the same, but the buildings around the back of the beach had a new gloss of a kind.

Main Street is, I imagine, the same as it's always been. Well, since surfing arrived to dominate the lower end of it. It's not a beautiful place, but it certainly has character. It was here that I first saw David Nuuhiwa in the sixties . . . during the period that he dominated the surfing landscape of the United States with feline grace. His demise, when a rough kid from Australia arrived with a board called Sam and rewrote the rules, that moment, in many ways, signaled the end of the beginning. And with it, the end of the domination of California . . . and it *had* been total.

After David, there was only Rolf . . . and he's more a glorious individual effort than representative of a school. It is surprising that there haven't been others like him. The standouts from the general social style. If you can understand why the prevailing attitudes have precluded the development of an intense group of competition-oriented surfers, then it remains a mystery why there weren't individuals who either didn't understand, or ignored the social norms.

Chapter Five: The Hill & the Flatlands

The South Bay ends at the Hill. It's where the endless stretch of lifeguard towers and power stations, parking areas and fairly featureless landscape gives way to the Palos Verdes peninsula. The elevation of the hill puts you above the smog line . . . or that's how it looks. From it you look down on the sweep of the "beaches" . . . all the way to Santa Monica. I once heard a theory about the differing characteristics of flatland people and hill people. I don't remember it too well, but recollect that the flatland people, of whom I was one at the time, didn't come out of it too well. It seemed to ascribe to the hill people desirable characteristics. I doubt the elevated elite of Palos Verdes would quarrel with the description.

There *are* ways in which landscape directly affects the style of the lives that are led in it. You feel differently about a break that you clamber down a cliff to reach. It's more personal than driving to a car park cluttered with mechanical and human debris. You have to care more to bother. It tends to induce a more aggressive defense (if you'll excuse that contradiction in terms).

Palos Verdes is defensive about its surf areas. Maybe too much so, Tuzo Jerger feels. His Kanoa Surf Shop is supporting a couple of the B's . . . the current crop of professional hopefuls, so many of whose names seem to start with B. In Tuzo's case, it's Barela and Benavidez. His endorsement of "professionalism" has brought him into some conflict with the mood prevailing on the hill. He hasn't, he says with wry humor, had a widow broken in four months.

Some of the surfers on the hill mightn't like what Tuzo's up to, but undeniably they are influenced by it. Surfboards have dropped a foot in length in the early months of 1980. Partly that's been influenced by local surfers traveling, and partly by the exchange of ideas and experience induced by Kanoa.

Everyone says the P. V. is an intense surf area. It's been more of a black-wetsuit, down-the-line style, while the beaches opted for the bright-red-shred approach. It seems like the latter might've been having too much fun. Anyway, the rigid barriers are falling.

Tuzo offers an assessment of the current influences. He says that Australian ascendancy may have maxed, and uses as a measure the sale of decals in his shop. And Australia, he says, was last year.

Tuzo, his brother Kip and Greg Bowman all seemed to agree that enthusiasm was on the rise. In the competitive sense, they think it'll be only a couple of years till there are some dominant Californians. That's optimistic, perhaps, but they are closer to the subjects than most.

They concur, too, about the isolationism . . . "They're not concerned with anything outside themselves," and sense the contradictions that are at present contained in the California surfing body . . . "They want to hang onto the 'soul' and still cop the bucks." Tuzo says that it's difficult for the kids to get any sort of financial support to go on the pro tour, but there is really no difference between Australia, Hawaii or any place on that one. It's not much of an investment anywhere.

The reporter ran into the 14-year-old surf team back in 1976. At the time he was on the authentic search for an American Surf Hero. They couldn't help.

Lincoln Fowler is one member of what's now the grown-up 14-year-old surf team. He represented a contact with the beach scene without stars or promoters. The kid-on-the-beach opinion, if you like. He lives at Manhattan . . . an environment his mother encouraged him to leave for a while so he'd see a world where alligators weren't sewn onto everyone's left breast.

Linc has just graduated from high school, and he's hanging around the beach. I prowl around trying to find him without what you'd actually call success. But I see Manhattan Beach. It's a nice environment. Relaxed and approachable to someone without the letter of introduction that friends in a foreign place give you. I feel comfortable there. It doesn't *look* like it's the world's greatest surf spot. The kids around the back of the beach look like they're having fun. Cruising for the summer.

Benavidez and Barela came from Hermosa, says Lincoln. There weren't too many surf stars living in. He nominates M.R. and Dane as the heroes of the beach . . . Shaun, he says, has faded. The interest in professional contests is muted. Sure, he'd gone and had a look at the Katin contest, but "personally, I think that's just about enough."

He says that California surfers are territorial because of the lack of quality and consistency in the surf. "Good waves are such a rarity . . . you don't want to share them with someone you don't know." Lincoln is practical about the influx of Australian surf product . . . "I don't know anyone who doesn't have a pair of Quicksilvers . . . they're good shorts." He doesn't see any bias one way or another about the Australian influence. No one, he says, is jealous of them.

For this part of the grown-up surf team, nothing much has changed. In fact, if he has to nominate a characteristic of the time, then it's just that . . . lack of change.

Part II: Hotel California
SURFER Vol. 22 No. 2 · February 1981

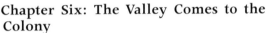

Chapter Six: The Valley Comes to the Colony

It's hard not to feel an outsider in Malibu. Privilege, position, wealth . . . they all conspire to make the place look immensely appealing, and to prevent you from being any part of it. And if you're a "valley," the exclusion isn't even a passive one. The assumed air of belonging, that means you don't, is replaced by messages sprayed on street signs that tell the valleys just where they can put their lowriders. The only gesture I saw that was in any way welcoming was an optimistic sign painted on a construction site . . . "COME BY," it shouted, "AND SHOW US YOUR TITS." Socially, Malibu is about exclusivity. I read in the *L.A. Times* about a tour you can do in Hollywood that takes you 'round all the homes of the stars. It's hardly necessary. Everyone you meet points them out while assuring you that *really*, "they" are just like any other neighbor. I gather that on the public tour, the odd one comes out to wave. That didn't happen on the private ones.

Surfwise, Malibu has always been one of the great places. Partly that was the quality of the surf, and partly the quality of the eccentrics who seemed to grow there. That superb article of Stecyk's a few years ago painted the picture. These days, Mike Perry, shaper, traveler, good drunk, is part of it. He takes us one morning to "the office." If "check-ing Trestles" is a euphemism for a tea break around the *SURFER* office, then going to "the office" with Perry means that you go to Zuma Beach. He regales us with tales of mayhem as the Valley invades. Of how we will witness weird cultural rites and, hopefully, violence.

When we arrive, there are still some surfers around, but even then they are starting to leave. Place by place, the lowriders took their park-ing spots . . . Kenny arrives on his moped and places it strategically so that later he could sell the spot for $5. Even this early the breeze onshore from the north and cool . . . only the desperates are in the water. The early arrivals amongst the valleys leap, with more vigor than the surfers have, into their Frisbee throwing. One group tries a variation on the standard cultural experience that's called "bury the cooler."

Finally, someone asks if we own the yellow Chevy occupying two parking spaces . . . and after negotiation on the value of one of them . . . "that sucks," I relent amidst jeering and moving it up. The surf talk that morning wasn't too different to anyplace. Tales of murder and violent car crashes . . . reminiscences of the best swells of the winter . . . all the usual stuff. It even gets esoteric, and the group decides that the only val-ues in L.A. are money and beauty. And on that note of great significance . . . not a drunken brawl in sight (Perry lying again) we leave.

In the absence of international stars, California has had a whole collec-tion of regional heroes, who, if they're good enough and experienced enough, can gain a grudging respect from outside their area. J. Riddle is.

Up to 1970, he says, the USSA, and particularly the WSA, was mov-ing towards professionalism. He blames, rather than a prevailing social mood, a series of mishaps that hurt the competitive sport. There was bad organization and contests run poorly. Surfers felt that they might as well stick in their own ideas . . . "and make a local stand." But Riddle corrects himself . . . he is nothing if not a supporter of the competitive ethic . . . they did, he says, "stagnate in their own areas." There was a slump, with no one really progressing.

J. credits P.T. and Ian for helping to establish a competitive structure for the kids. It's been there, but it fell by the wayside . . . and with it the opportunities for communication, for display of equipment and its riding, for the stimulation of the exchange of ideas. And with its going, came a reinforcement of the retreat into individual local areas. California was denied information. J. doesn't think it was the better off for it.

But a change, J. feels, is coming. There have been some hiccups along the way. The Robert Hart fiasco, and the poorly handled 1979 Stubbies California trial, where places were traded for shorts sales with as much style and finesse as an el-cheapo used car deal. The push now, says J., is coming from down south . . . "but it'll be a kid four years down the road."

He cites the acceptance of the Malibu Pro as part of the change. The contest will be IPS rated this year. Last year, he says, the sand was solid people . . . that there were cars two miles in each direction. Describing his own Pro Series Junior Contest, he captures as well as anyone this part of the mood of California. The sentiment is diametrically opposed to that of my friend Orchid. The forcefulness is its equal . . . Riddle wants to "have them out there fighting for cash and new boards and wetsuits . . . get them into what they're reading about."

Kevin Roberts is quietly impressive. He blames the absence of influence on an equal absence of waves. In many ways, the obvious thought is a right one. California is less well off than many other places in the world . . . for average, consistent waves day after day. Ten years ago, Mickey Dora made the observation that there wouldn't be any more good surfers out of California because there weren't enough waves. What sufficed for the beginnings may not be enough for the zip-zap of performance surfing in the seventies and eighties.

There is not the single-minded obsession with surfing in California that you tend to find in Australia. It seems more to fit as a segment into people's lives. Kevin reckons that he's not surfing as much as he used to. But he's building and playing music; living with his girlfriend at his parents' home. It's a beautiful place . . . the essential Malibu for the reporter . . . right on the beach a way from the point. Kevin is 23 looking at 18. Down at the Natural Progression Surf Shop he's reminded that someone pegged him as "Angelea's younger brother." He smiles. We are recited tales of Australian atrocities . . . with American variations. It induces a bit of cultural cringe, but the bloke running the shop didn't notice. It pleases him immensely how Australians treat their women. Badly.

In the Surf Punks' record, there is a parody (or so I'm assured) of how surfers treat one another. In a wonderful track that is, I think, called "My Wave," the chorus, with a certain economy, repeats the lines "my beach, my wave, f__k off" . . . or something like that. Kevin, who is responsible for my introduction to this terrific stuff, points to a resurgence of a kind in surfing music. If it's in any way a repeat of the sixties, perhaps the Golden Age of California is coming back?

Chapter Seven: Don't Mention Oxnard

When I'm setting off on this journey, someone says to me that Santa Barbara and the Ventura/Oxnard areas are far closer in style than either one would be prepared to accept. What one protected with money, the other did with a clenched fist.

Oxnard in particular is not an easy place to approach, and the value of the correct introduction is inestimable. Happily, I got it. It didn't come without warnings and exhortations of caution. I'd asked a friend in Santa Barbara if he knew anyone that would talk to me in Oxnard. "I didn't know," he replied, "that there were any human beings in Oxnard." He's wrong, but such is the reputation of the place.

Ventura, says Paul Alary, is getting over its image. Eight years ago, it was radical. Cars were burnt; guys had their heads caved in with rocks. "We're the younger generation . . . we're paying for it."

It's 8:15 in the morning. The wind is in and we're looking at California Street . . . "the mushiest surf spot in the world . . . it gets good at ten feet. That's once every five years." Alary is a smart-arse . . . in the best sense of the word. He's clever, and keeps the reporter constantly amused with one-liners. He's working as a carpenter . . . well, about 20 hours a week. He doesn't know what to do with all the money he's been earning.

He is obsessed with surfing . . . "I can't go to sleep without thinking about surfing . . . now I've got my little board I'm going crazy." There are a few hundred surfers in Ventura . . . which has a population of 74,000 people. How many are good? "Ten." Paul surfs every day. "It has to be awfully, awfully bad for me not to surf."

At 22, he's had six trips to the Islands. And eight to Mexico. It's been four years since he was in Hawaii. "My parents got tired of sending me off on a dream." He says that he does a hell of a lot of driving around California. He remarks how "zoned" the surfers are. And how terrible the surf is . . . "I can't believe these waves . . . it's like this every day now." He supposes that in the summer there is swell every two weeks . . . a four day swell is a long one. The offshore islands block the south and it has to wrap in. "The Pipe's bigger than this . . . I'm wondering if it was a tanker going past."

Paul has lived in Ventura for eighteen years. For sixteen of those he's been surfing. He's been trying to get into the pro thing for so long . . . "I've put a lot of hours in . . . it's my job." He says that it's difficult to gain acceptance when you live in Ventura . . . that the reputation hurts. It's not so much the mythical money that attracts him; he's keen to gain the recognition of his abilities. "I've seen all those guys surf. I don't feel that I'm far ahead or that far behind. Actually," he adds, "I'm the best." Paul Alary is funny; he's self-deprecatory, but he's also confident.

There are no contests at Ventura. It's difficult for the would-be. Especially if he'd rather surf eight-foot waves than have a thousand dollars. Paul isn't too interested in the "tour" but he'd like to score some sponsors. "I'm open to offers." For the sons of wealth, the priorities are a little different.

We drive past a primary school, and Paul gets a wave from the playground. That, says the reporter, is surf-star recognition in Ventura. Do you have a black wetsuit? "No way." It's a full suit . . . red and blue. Do you want to see it? No. "You've got your sunglasses on . . . it's cool." He warns of the giant killer piranha dogs in Oxnard, and the fire-bombing cats . . . gets serious for a moment and says that the violence is real at Hollywood by the Sea. "A bunch of assholes with nowhere to go. The guys who behave like that aren't the serious surfers. There are some good surfers down there."

We are looking at the Pipe . . . or Derelict Point as Paul calls it. It wraps, he says, "you have to duck sometimes." He talks about his favorite surfers . . . Emilio Garcia, Davie Smith . . . "we push each other, Steve North, and Buttons" . . . and then of the surf (which hasn't got any better), "you know I'm going to have to go out here a little bit later."

Usually, when you're doing a piece like this, it's left to the writer to ask the questions and supply the interpretation that will turn the answers into a picture of sorts. Such was the explanation of why-Oxnard's-like-Oxnard-is that this reporter was given, that he simply sat, scribbling, barely interrupting. It was unusual, I said later, that no one had described the place before in the way I'd just heard it. "Well," replied my informant, "people from magazines haven't actually been welcome here."

Localism in Oxnard, he said, was compounded by the fact that most surfers came from in town . . . a lot were Mexican and were very territorial. And here the term "barrio" came to embody an understanding of this singular area. (I'd heard earlier two definitions of the term. In their prejudice, they too offer some insight. *Barrio*, I was told, in Spanish means a neighborhood or a district. In English, *barrio* was translated as meaning a Mexican slum.)

In Oxnard, you fought for the barrio. It wasn't just in surfing. It happened after baseball matches. And after the exodus to the coast . . . after development, the beach area became a barrio of its own . . . drawn together by the commonality of surfing interest.

Ten years ago, Oxnard was barely surfed. In the early seventies, there was some media attention to the quality of its waves . . . the channel is deep off Oxnard, and the power is up . . . and some of the hotties of the day caught good surf after a contest. These factors, combined with rapid residential development, meant that there was a huge influx of surfers. "The barrio was threatened." There was a lot of fighting, a lot of vandalism. As it was described, the change was almost overnight after a 4A contest. "The war began."

The waves at Oxnard, ignored during the long-board years, were better suited to short boards and leashes. As tube riding became the vogue, the uncrowded beach break peaks became very crowded indeed. The result? "This is probably the most violent beach you'll hit in California."

There is a changing of the guard . . . and a more general and subtle alteration occurring too. The population is becoming more transient, the local grouping not so tight. But to some extent the new arrivals, looking for peer respect, are still jumping on the localism bandwagon. But even three or four years ago, taking off in front of someone was taboo. Now there is fighting even amongst the locals. "It's just a matter of time for Oxnard."

Each spot has become so crowded that the barrio has become a whole series of them. It's okay for the older guys who have a broader respect, but not so for the kids . . . "guys will assume that you are a 'souther,' and jump on your back and drag you into the water."

There are only two ways to reach the beach . . . "you can come through the middle of town and never come out." People don't know how to find the surf. And yet they still come. They brave the violence, and they brave the drive from L.A. Perhaps the behavior is becoming more diverse, but it only needs a handful to carry on the traditions. In the north, I'd heard of the SSL, the patrol of the Silver Strands Locals, who, I was told, actually wear black armbands of wetsuit rubber. Maybe memories are short, or maybe, in an age when you can have a punk band called the Dead Kennedys, nothing can offend.

Summer is quiet in Oxnard . . . "we don't have waves. Come fall, I could show it to you." Photographers aren't welcome. "A lot of guys have lost equipment . . . teeth." The locals know that photos are the quickest way to push a difficult crowd situation toward the impossible. It is allowable to take photos there, but only with the right introductions, and the rights come equipped with severe attendant responsibilities that are ignored at risk.

One of the contradictions that is contained in Oxnard is that the barrio that produces the unacceptable violence also provides a sense of community that seems desirable. Familial ties are still strong. And while that may be under challenge by the rapid increase in population . . . and it has doubled in ten years . . . it is still very much in evidence. The barrio may transcend even wealth. The McGrath kids surf with the Mexicans, and have acceptance.

Oxnard is a tough place. Its waves are strong. It's hard to get out at the beach breaks. But it's harder to get a view into the barrio. Maybe that's impenetrable to the outsider. It's the only place the lowriders come to the beach with surfboard racks. They get out of their tight jeans and silk shirts, into shorts, and they rip. Oxnard surfers are not travelers. The guys who fight a lot can't go anywhere else.

Occasionally people come to challenge. The "I'll surf it and let someone tell me to get out of the water" style. One gathers that they seldom go away disappointed. You don't gain a reputation like Oxnard's simply on talk. But there exists the possibility still, brought into the water as a guest, for visitors to surf here, and to be able to appreciate relatively uncrowded waves. It's something I'd like to do. But, as even one of its friends said about the place, one might choose to live somewhere "more desirable."

Chapter Eight: 2002s, 320i's and 530s

The reporter wanted to see the Ranch again, but there was some difficulty. None of the rich trendies will let me in, I was complaining to a bloke I met in a party in Montecito. Why don't we walk in, he said? I have this sneaky suspicion that the question wasn't looking for an affirmative answer. (There was no sign of swell.) Always an idiot, I agreed. That was a bit before midnight.

By about 1 a.m., there was a small expeditionary force of Sam and Matt George, Tommy Curren, and two Australians assembled. Sam and Matt are actually two quite different people. One talks more, and laughs louder. But somehow it's difficult to think of them as other than a complementary pair. Both bubble with an enthusiasm that is happily contagious, and both are good surfers.

Tommy Curren is a hot surfer. He's fourteen or fifteen (I forgot to ask), and while I hate to put a jinx on him, if anyone I saw in California is likely to do a Rolf Aurness, then I'd imagine it'd be Tommy. Whether he wants to or not, even he's not sure yet. He seems to suppose so. He tells some funny dirty stories.

By 1 a.m., we had borrowed food and clothes, packs to stuff them in. The enthusiasm was undiminished. When we got to Gaviota in Old Yeller, there was no swell. Still, we told each other, remember that time when it looked flat and whatitsname was four feet at dawn. We were undeterred even by a crew who'd been in by boat and said it was quite flat. They, we figured, were probably valleys who wouldn't recognize a wave if they fell over it.

And so we walked in. Not after some agonizing about the right way that this should be accomplished. The beach-and-rocks route was ruled out by purely practical considerations. It was high tide and you'd have had a difficult enough time trying had it been broad daylight. On a dark night it was ridiculous. Besides, we like the idea of staying dry. We might, we thought, have to cut down by the cliffs to get past the guard posts, but reckoned that the railway line provided the straightest, driest, and altogether quite the most simple way in.

We thought that we were pretty clever as we sneaked past the guard by keeping in the shadow of the inland cutting. We did it one by one. Good war games. Exciting even. On the way back we just wandered through as a group. No one took the faintest notice.

By 2 a.m., we're approaching Razorblades where we've agreed we'll decide if it's worth going any further. It really was flat. It was barely bothering to break. So we sat down at the northern end of that trestle bridge, and we had an early breakfast of bananas and some disgusting cake that tasted terrific, and we passed the water bottle around. The spirit of camaraderie that had accompanied us thus far didn't desert now.

Sam or Matt had an idea. There would almost certainly be waves at Jalama. If we walked back (there really being no reason at all to go on), we could drive to Jalama and be there about dawn. And since going back to Santa Barbara without having got in the water would be an admission of defeat of the worst kind, it was agreed.

If the meal at Razorblades had been memorable, then the landscape near Jalama, pre-dawn, was equally so. It is a most beautiful bit of country.

I think it was perhaps the first time that I've seen forests of those black-green oaks that remind so much of Spain. There had been a lot of rain, but in the early summer the hills were already browning. The contrast between it and the trees is at once subtle and spectacular.

There were waves at Jamala. It was also very bloody cold. I wanted to wait at least till the sun had cleared the hills behind us. Nothing would deter the enthusiastic Sam. He said that 56 degrees was warm. I didn't, of course, accept the argument until he came in and I used it to convince him that he didn't need his booties. Matt said that it was our "duty." Everyone hit the water eventually, quick, with an excellent wave sense. Sam was next. I brought up a long last. But in the spirit of the occasion, Sam and Matt might just about have granted me "water-man" status for the day (had they thought about it).

Santa Barbara has been described as the "heartland of California regression." Unfortunately, I can't remember by whom. It is also (well, Montecito in particular) one of the most spectacular . . . in its own sub-dued fashion . . . elitest areas that I've ever seen. And while I know that its mere presence means that someone, somewhere, is getting screwed, I can't help but admire the quality of the product. It really is very beautiful.

Greg Huglin lives in Montecito. He describes the surfers' cars there. "If you're fifteen, you have a 2002, at twenty-one a 320i, and at twenty-five a 530." Such is the style of the place that he didn't mention that they are BMWs.

Mexico doesn't present itself as the "escape" here, as it tends to in the south. Guys have boats and head to the Ranch and the islands. Santa Barbara, home to some of the best quality surf in California, and some excellent surfers, has rarely produced competitive surfers. Margo Oberg is a classic standout from the pack. And if Palos Verdes lays some claim to the black-wetsuit approach, then Santa Barbara is sure that it was born and bred there.

"I still get irritated by colored wetsuits," says Chris Kunze. "The kids that you see them on are just seventeen-year-old blond heads who think they're the tops . . . you need that down south to establish an identity. You don't need it here." To this reporter, it seems pretty funny. That Chris is serious makes it more so. In this most modern state, with every form of communication thrust upon you, the relative isolation of the surfing communities is a curious phenomenon.

Huglin, commenting on the defensive sort of insularity into which surfing has drawn through the seventies, says that in Santa Barbara you don't want to go south because "Everyone hates L.A. . . . and you wouldn't want to come from the Valley. P.V. hates the South Bay; Ventura hates Oxnard, and Oxnard hates everyone."

Maybe because it's summer . . . though the memories of an excellent winter are not left far behind . . . but again and again people say that there is simply not enough surf. And, though they will tend to agree that in fact it hasn't generally got worse in the past ten years, they will blame the crowds. Davy Smith, star of a short feature that Greg Huglin is running with Fantasea, says . . . "It's been so long since I just surfed with me or a few friends that I'd almost forgotten what the feeling was like."

Part III: Spirit of the Place
SURFER Vol. 22 No. 4 · April 1981

Chapter Nine: A Cutback Company Town

Everywhere in California has a Valley. In Santa Cruz, it's referred to as "over the hill."

There are rougher names for its inhabitants. And each weekend, and all the summer, they head along the line of least resistance into what is their recreational suburb. Out along Highway 17 from San Jose, winding through the trees, and then Santa Cruz is spread out in front of you. It's a surfing town, cut off from the sprawling population to the east by the geographical barrier of the hills, and for reasons that evade me still, by rural splendor to the north.

It's a surfing town, but it's a cold surfing town. In the winter, the water is generally between 45 degrees and 48 degrees. In summer, it will reach 60, but there may be no waves for months. Still, there is consistent surf within reach. And "reach" in Santa Cruzian terms is long by Californian standards. The enthusiasts may cover 80 miles.

Santa Cruz has always given the impression of being a "serious" surfing area. That the level of ability and dedication is high. The area doesn't seek and has never received much publicity . . . well, not since the early years. The surf is crowded and the water situation pushy. *Everyone* agrees that there are some hot kids there.

There's been a gap, though. The retreat into insularity was as pronounced there as anywhere, but it was heightened by the cream of the earlier crop moving to Hawaii. Increasingly now, there's more internationals consciousness . . . the movement is back into the mainstream. The place from which the "discovery" of Hawaii stemmed to a large degree seems to be on the resurgence.

O'Neill will probably make the break with a major competition in the next year. In a way, Santa Cruz is a company town. There is not much that happens that isn't influenced by them. If in boards, Doug Haut's shop is the leading economic force, then it's O'Neill all the way on wetsuits . . . "nobody likes to be cold." They are seen as a major drive behind surfing in the town. But if they do make their move, it won't be without opposition. Santa Cruz is also home to the arch-reactionary school. John Scott is hardly a passive observer of commercialism in surfing.

Ernie Oliveras works in the O'Neill shop. He says that the whole town transforms when there's waves. That the sport is public and influential. He describes how the town divides into the East and the West sides: who's hot in each; who shapes for each; what the major breaks are. He says that the relative lack of exposure has meant that there are lots of "underground" surfers. And that there are a *lot* of surfers.

The bay in Santa Cruz faces south, the prevailing wind offshore. Climatically it receives more sun . . . in a cold area it's reason enough to attract surfers. Ernie says that they come from the east, from the south, and that they come from San Jose. And that they get a lot of shit from younger guys.

Ernie is part of the "Team O'Neill." He supposes that it's kinda a position of prestige. But, he says, "it's no biggie."

Steve Coletta is identified as one of the leading shapers for the Eastsiders. (Joey Tomas is the Westsider, and Haut's shop has enough prestige to cover both.) Steve has been in Santa Cruz through the seventies. He attributes to cords and better wetsuits the fact that there are more people to catch the available waves. He says that if you can handle pressure, you can surf anywhere. He doesn't particularly blame the media for overcrowding. He doesn't seem to be sorry that the magazines are situated in the south . . . and feels that their influence in determining styles is rather a case of the tail wagging the dog.

Steve says he's noticed that the kids seem more outgoing these days. The "drug hangover" from the sixties and seventies seems to be passing. He observes that photographers attract surfers rather than the other way 'round, and sees it happening in Santa Cruz. He nominates K-East and K-West (in the style of Off-the-Wall as Kodak Reef) as Insides and Stockton Avenue.

He agrees that Santa Cruz is a pretty intense surf area. Says that there's a lot of waves in the winter . . . "Long duration swells" . . . and that even though the climate is fair for this far north, the cold means that "you've gotta be keen. It lends itself to rough and tough individuals." Temperature and the hard reef waves have meant that the influence of the cord is amplified. Last winter, he says, he surfed nearly every day. It was a *good* year. He is a traveler . . . 150-mile round trip as a max. For some of the kids on the beaches, he says, it's 500 yards.

Like other places, board length has dropped. Coletta the shaper is turning out everything from 5'10" to 6'8" at the moment. The drop in size has not been without its consequence . . . there is "a lot of wiggle-butt action around." Santa Cruz is, he says, "a real cutback-oriented town."

Brad Asmus has produced six issues of the tabloid *Santa Cruz Surf Line*. He describes the town as a semi-rural island surrounded by population. He adds to the Eastside/Westside definitions by describing "Purgatory" . . . the area between the wharf and the river entrance. When there's swell, he says, there's lots of surf within bike-riding distance.

But it's not the kids so much that attract his attention. He admits that some of them *are* hot, but says that most of the good Santa Cruz surfers are older . . . fitting surfing into broader lives, and he observes that this isn't the way to build a reputation . . . but that it doesn't seem to matter to the older guys if they have a reputation or not.

In the cool climate, there is less of a beach scene, which means less of a tight community amongst the surfers . . . and possibly less of the cult of personality. Even the stars, Brad says, go to the beach for a surf and then get on with the rest of their lives. Elsewhere you've heard that Santa Cruz tends not to see Mexico as one of its escapes. That Hawaii is the nirvana, and the inclination is to jump on a plane. Brad disagrees. He's been, he says, at Puerto Escondido and it looked like "Puerto Santa Cruz."

Doug Haut echoes the special relationship between the town and Hawaii. Santa Cruz surfers, he says, do good there. They're used to power. He feels that there has never been a competitive feeling in the area . . . and that it hasn't changed much. There is, he says, no push from the kids . . . that basically they just want to surf. And yet, he has on his hands one of the kids who has a growing respect from all sides of the town, and who is thinking of making a try for the pro scene . . . Richard Schmidt. Doug will probably help him, but he's not sure he likes what he sees.

Even the surfers, he says, know that there isn't any money in it. And the hype . . . he equates the south with the magazines and the false hype. And he's sick of reading about Australia.

There is a sign at Stockton Avenue that says "BE PREPARED TO FIGHT." Richard Schmidt doesn't have to do that, but he admits that he gets bad vibes kind-of when people see photos of him in the mags. That mood, he says, is staying pretty strong. "People are so protective about their area . . . it blows me out."

What sort of a place is Santa Cruz to surf? "Cold," he answers. "In winter you can still find a lot of places on your own if you're early and you're on top of the swell. It takes so much more time to make a living . . . it seems people have less time to surf." In winter it's dark till after seven and before five . . . so there are short hours of sunlight when there's surf. It makes it hard for surfers who work.

Richard went to Hawaii last winter. It was his first time. He was impressed. "I felt that I had as much ability as anyone, but not the experience . . . and Hawaii is the place to work on it. The power is always there. Here you have to wait for it." There is an impressive sequence of photos of Richard in the Haut shop that evidence the ability. Photos can exaggerate, but plainly the kid can surf.

Next winter, Richard will make his try at the pro class trials in Hawaii. But he has his doubts. "It's a long road, and you've got to aim at the top. If I got to travel to a few places, I'd be happy . . . that's what I want out of surfing." He doesn't mention any of the other advantages of surf stardom. Owl Chapman, who is at the house, reminds him that he and Charlie had ten girls around the other night . . . "if your mother knew . . . "

Why, asks the reporter, do you think that there are no California surf heroes? "Because," interjects Owl with the definitive statement, "they're all dead, or in jail, or rich."

Richard doesn't know. Supposes that someone has to do it and then it'll be easier. At the moment there is no one to follow. He didn't feel that there was any prejudice *against* California in the pro ranks . . . *or* that the current crop of hopefuls from the south were standing out. He had been impressed by Joey Buran at Pipeline, but reckoned that "the Californian wiggle doesn't look too good on the power."

Owl talks about Mark Richards . . . "It's rare to find anyone who dominates anything. Jack Nicklaus just won the U.S. Open . . . but he didn't dominate anything." He's impressed by Richard Schmidt. Along with everyone you speak to in Santa Cruz. The kid is quiet, reserved, raw maybe. Says Owl . . . "he doesn't know what he's got. Real class."

Chapter Ten: B.W.C. Rule. OK?

I first met the Bolinas Wave Crew one morning at half past nine outside Ed's Superette at Stinson Beach. In my journal, I have a firsthand report as to how I was feeling. "I have a headache. I also have a bad cold. Actually I feel terrible."

I made a caffeine-assisted recovery. First cup at Donna's where we were staying. Then one at the Bolinas bakery . . . Then one at Jonathan's place. He makes one of the best cups of coffee in America. I consider myself an expert on atrocious American coffee. It's grasshopper piss.

Jonathan is one of the B.W.C. For those not used to acronyms (though I don't see how you could live in America and *not* be), that stands for Bolinas Wave Crew. Someone up north called them that and they liked it. It's sprayed on various gutters and the like. I'd met Richard down in Santa Cruz. He said that he'd get a few of the boys together for me to have a talk to.

So there I was, outside Ed's, feeling fragile. There was Richard and Jonathan, and Hayden. "We're the crowd right here," they said. Later I met Kirby Ferris, who has the surf shop at Stinson, and Mark, whose grandfather invented TV. "My grandfather ruined the world. He never watched it."

The surf 'round Stinson is inconsistent in the summer. In winter it's cold. There's no work around there, so most people have to drive "over the hill" to work. It's the last real surf outpost before you get into the country. There are surfers living up there though. I asked Kirby how I'd find one of his friends . . . I was to go to the gate; I was to make a lot of noise; I had to shout out what I wanted and who I was and then I was to hit the ground. Fast. He said people were a little touchy about outsiders in that part of the country.

I had a lot of fun with the B.W.C. that morning. They took me around and showed me the local breaks. They gave me a guided tour of Bolinas and its burn-outs. They had an engaging enthusiasm. "The most crowded day of the year," explained Jonathan, "and twelve guys out." "And none of them," said Hayden, "can surf." Whatever problems they have up there with the surf, overcrowding isn't one of them.

They said that there used to be more surfers around. "A good ten guys . . . it was hard to get waves." Nowadays there's generally four or so out. A half of Bolinas lives on Maui, and half of Stinson on the North Shore.

It *does* get cold there. Mid-forties in the winter, anywhere in the fifties in summer. You need a *full* suit. Booties and gloves and a hood once in a while. The Japan Current, which is the supply of warm water, can be thirty miles out in the morning and one mile in the arvo. On the 23rd of June, we were at a fishing port a hundred or so miles to the north. The water temperature was 44 degrees.

Bolinas used to have a surf shop some twelve years ago. It was in a remarkable building in a town that has quite a collection of them. About a year ago, or maybe it was April '78, Kirby couldn't quite remember, he'd opened the Live Water shop in Stinson. Mark had been shaping boards for the shop during the past year and a half. He does it down at the Haut shop in Santa Cruz.

One of the businesses that is thriving on the north coast is dope grow-ing. The government at various levels is trying (without marked success) to discourage this free-enterprise activity. It's not so much that they don't like the enterprise, but perhaps it's a bit free for them. Or maybe the other way around? Anyway, as part of the scheme to stamp out this subversive behavior, they have overflights of the country to pinpoint crops. Add to this the fact that the dope growers have their own to see if theirs is visible . . . and that there are third parties looking to see what they might just be able to sneak with . . . as a friend of Kirby's said to him . . . "there's so many planes around it's like a scene out of *Tora! Tora! Tora!*"

The North Coast is a superb bit of country. Physically reminiscent in so many ways of Australia. The psychic distance between it and L.A. is almost impossible to travel. It amazes me that it continues to exist. I don't really understand why it hasn't been raped and pillaged years ago. It remains as the frontier surfing area in California, no less significant because it's seldom surfed. If you should have the good fortune to run into Kirby or the Bolinas Wave Crew, you will find that the spirit still thrives.

Chapter Eleven: Pardon the Noise . . .

San Diego is a military town. It's more than that, but when you're at the airport there, you could be forgiven for forgetting. If you can't remember what *short* hair is like, just head out there for a while. And there is this wonderful sign near one of the Navy airfields. "Pardon the noise," it says, "but these are sounds of freedom." If you can excuse a certain note of amazement, there is not another nation on Earth who could have put up a sign like that.

San Diego is a beautiful place. A magnificent harbor, a city not so large as to have swallowed its inhabitants, and some excellent surf. Jeff Divine (of "sleeping through the best morning of the year at Pipeline" fame) was this reporter's guide.

Wealthy though it certainly is, it's a democratic coastline. There is not much that is private. Most of it, if you want to take the trouble to hike in, is accessible. The exception is the La Jolla Beach and Tennis Club. They have a sign above the door . . . "Tennis stairway to fame." Poor old Vitas Gerulaitis thinking he had it made growing up in New York . . .

South past Cardiff, you come to Blacks. There, you can forget you're in suburban California. It gets crowded now. Lots of UCSD surfers. For a while it was a nudist beach. Divine says that there used to be 20,000 people down there looking at each other . . . but he's lied about other things.

And then to La Jolla. It went from small town to super elite in fifteen years. When Highway 5 was built in '64, its million-bucks-a-mile pavement made *everywhere* accessible. It had been a rich small town, but now at La Jolla Shores, you couldn't buy a garage for less than $250,000. There are, says Divine, bulk chicks. "They can go and hang in bars and get picked up by guys with lots of money."

In the summer, it can be pretty flat for weeks. Even in winter La Jolla Cove is rare, but it's one of the big-wave spots. Lots of roots of California's surfing came from La Jolla . . . Grigg, Curren, Diffenderfer, Van Artsdalen . . . the old-time crew. The reef experience gave them an advantage to the Islands. The breaks that they pioneered are now set amongst an incredibly privileged residential area.

The palm-thatched hut at Windansea is a relic of the Hawaiian influence in the '50s and '60s. On the reef beyond it, this reporter sees some of the best waves he's seen in a month in California. Windansea is a significant area in so many respects. There are good waves and good surfers from the area; there is a wide diversity in age and style in the water on any day; the famous "pump house" of Tom Wolf fame is sitting there, undistinguished otherwise, between Windansea and Big Rock. There is a sign on a pipe: "Tourists Go Home," it says, "Locals Only." After Oxnard it seems restrained.

Windansea is renowned for its drinkers . . . but the kids are super into their surfing. There are bunches of them down on the cliffs every day. Divine, trying to live down a vicious rumor that I'd started about his having a torrid affair with a guy, comments again about the beautiful chicks . . . "wealthy and high class," he says. It's transparent overcompensation I say to him . . . "you ought to assume that no one believed what I said." Divine ignores me and talks about Raquel Welch, whose real name was Tejada and whose brother was a glasser for Nelson Ekstrom. No one needs to know that, I say to him. Stop changing the subject.

If Orchid was a reactionary, then Divine is a jingoist. I was going to say that he was xenophobe, but I couldn't spell it. Basically, like all good Americans, he dislikes foreigners. Australians in particular. He says that there are hot kids in California. "They're there . . . they just haven't been put out there." In California, he insists, there is more of a spread of talent. It's not as condensed as Durban or Newport . . . no one sees the push. "It really blows my mind that the f__kin' Aussies can come over here and start up businesses. It's ludicrous. You've got to be more nationalistic."

Pacific, Mission, and Ocean beaches are the low-rent area of San Diego coastline. Which means that they're not half-million-dollar houses. Skip Frye is still an influence around P.B. But in boards . . . even Divine, the ultra nationalist, mentions Cheyne, Dane, and Tommy Carroll as the surfers the kids are emulating. Not a Californian in sight. He insists it's "insulting" to have Californian kids influenced by the Aussies. But then he'll say that his friends have gone to Australia and been "blown away" by the number of hot kids. "We should have that."

Sunset Cliffs starts at Pt. Loma Avenue. There are about eight miles of reef breaks . . . "some of the best waves in California . . . except the Ranch." It's one of the heaviest zones for outsiders. The surfers are heavy on one another.

There are a series of breaks. Of secluded beaches sheltered by low cliffs. The road runs 'round the cliffs for the first mile or so. After that you have to walk in. Each spot has its crew . . . mostly of older guys. There are fights, but the workovers are verbal mostly. And apparently effective. They walk in with backpacks. It fits the older "hippy" image of what surfing is/was all about. Further out to Pt. Loma, you really have to hike in. At the very point, there are dolphins on one side and Polaris submarines on the other. It seems symbolic in some way. Despite this reporter's inability to pinpoint why.

Divine is back on his tack . . . California, he says, must fight back. But what, you ask, about the U.S. companies who have been exploiting Australia for decades? "That's different. That's corporate ripoff. This is more personal." The surfboard, he says, is the base line. "The Newbreak crew would stone a McCoy crew if they arrived."

J.D. doesn't really know why there isn't a California crew like the Aussies. He supposes that it simply runs in cycles. He says that the kids haven't been touched as much by the media; that they are more naïve; that maybe it's starting. "We made them (the Australians) out to be the hottest thing on wheels." He acknowledges that the media blitz on the Aussies has had its effect. "Four years of Rabbit, Cheyne, Shaun, P.T., etc., has had its influence. The kids are a product of it." But there is nothing that the competitive California surfer would like more than to clean up in Australia. It's not exactly a revolutionary idea you say. It's just a rerun. It's a new thing, he insists, for California now.

Surfing contests, says Divine, are a macho contest . . . and the South Africans, Australians, and Hawaiians have been best at it. In a country never exceeded in its ability to create images . . . even, I'm assured, the California palm tree was a product of Hollywood in the thirties . . . it's ironic indeed for the Hot New Product that everyone is on . . . that it should be Australian. Divine is disgusted.

Chapter Twelve: The Conclusion

"We do not see things as they are
We see things as we are."
                —The Talmud

I really can't read all this again to sum it up. It's too long. Random thoughts that have surfaced during and since will have to do.

What an amazing place California is. It's at the forefront of an astonishing experiment. Heaps of money, people and automobiles all chucked together. No real rules. Nobody has done it quite like that before. And like everyone else, I don't know where it's going.

The place is an amalgam of lots of different attitudes and approaches. Steve Sakamoto told me that it was an insult to nutshell it, and I'd have to agree. What I've seen has been a series of scenes, of incidents, and, most importantly, of the people in them. As a matter of personal pride, I hope that I've done justice to their description. But I notice that I have no peculiar pearl, no revelation to expose to the world. Sorry about that.

Things do seem to be changing. Quite of their own volition. It may be simply change for change's sake, or it may be that in the end, intercourse is more interesting than insularity . . . that it's more fun to swap ideas on style and equipment . . . and just to share. And that's not threatening when you're feeling tolerably confident about what you're doing.

There were quite a few times that I was told how the kids don't care too much about the lack of a California influence . . . that essentially there is only one pier in California . . . my pier. The state of surfing there is tribal. And, like the Indians who preceded them, characterized by diversity. Far more so than comparative places I've seen. I'd have to admit that I don't really understand why that's so. But perhaps that's changing too.

The kids, especially around L.A., don't know about uncrowded days. They've been bred in the competitiveness of beaches that owe nothing to soul surfing. And they are amped by the energy of punk music. There is a positive response at last to professional surfing. But this California Renaissance, should it come, will embrace an increasingly vulnerable professionalism. Will it be gone before they get there?

I had a very good time in California. The generosity and hospitality were remarkable. I'm quite unsure that I behave as well to visitors in Australia. But thanks. ▧

Morocco: Surf Madness and 1001 Moorish Days and Nightmares
By Bruce Valuzzi · SURFER Vol. 23 No. 8 · Aug. 1982

Uppermost in the code of the surf traveler is that he should blend in as much as possible with the local culture, yet we all frequently violate this sacred tenet. The truth is that many surfers simply lack the desire or patience to play chameleon, and often our clumsy tromping leads to serious cultural faux pas. Case in point: see what results when Oahu's North Shore "pleasure hound" Rory Russell and his East Coast counterpart, writer Bruce Valuzzi, decide to plunder the shores of Morocco with photographer Art Brewer in tow. The consequences, however hilarious, do not entirely erase the birthmark of American ugliness. Some twenty years later, we're probably still paying the tab for this one.

White Trash Run Amok on Foreign Shores

A sarcastic wind ruffled the bay and rude noises annoyed the dawn as traffic jostled aboard the boat in Algeciras. Our tickets said "Africa Flash." How true. The passengers were a collection of seedy men in rumpled suits, hooded Arabs, German skinheads, some overripe goat farmers (the fragrance told the tale), truck drivers, assorted creeps, weirdos and of course, us. Standard fare on the boat to Morocco. *Maroc* is French for Morocco and "us" was Team Maroc: Art Brewer, Rory Russell and I. Brewer, you may remember, is the large and fearless "Don" of surf photography, easily given to thundering tantrums, who thinks Helmut Newton is a pussy-whipped choirboy. Russell is the Pipeline Tubemaster whose game is audio/visual entertainment for the Bolt Corporation but who, once out of Big Duke's sight, clutching an expense check, becomes a demented pleasure hound hell-bent on sniffing out every willing wench and sleazy beer joint from Laguna Beach to Marrakesh.

In Lisbon five days earlier these two stumbled off the plane from New York at 7 a.m., swilling the dregs of a quart of Jack Daniels. Rory tried to hustle the stewardesses while he flashed the grin of a convicted sex offender . . . I sensed trouble. The plan was to drive to Morocco, shoot an article for *SURFER* magazine, then hook up with a film crew from ABC-TV's *American Sportsman*. They had just won an Emmy for their piece on surfing in Indonesia and were ready for a sequel. Our trip was a modular enterprise organized independently of them that plugged neatly into their "exotic locale" format. Management hoped the dual tasks would squelch the ludicrous tendencies inherent in a trio of notorious screw-ups. After hanging around Portugal a few days hoping the 15-foot storm surf would clean up (it didn't), it was obvious their worst fears were justified. This was to be another episode out there with the lunatic fringe. We trespassed all boundaries of social outrage, lechery, drunkenness and bad breath. In short, we were on a surf trip.

I was relieved to be on the boat, off the Iberian peninsula. Surely it was just a matter of time before the Guardia Civil closed in for the kill, leading a horde of irate villagers waving axes who remembered us from "The Sweet Garden of Maria," a roadhouse in our recent past. A covey of truck drivers was drinking quietly when we blundered in the place sometime after midnight, fired up the jukebox and demanded beer and espresso. The commotion awoke Maria, the barman's daughter who wandered out of the back room in her nightshirt, a real cutie. It was lust at first sight and Brewer sprang into action. He focused his fish-eye in on her young cleavage and while his motordrive was blasting away assured everybody in the place it was all perfectly proper. He was, he explained, on personal assignment from King Juan Carlos, a geologic survey you understand, and this was some terrain the King just had to see. The jukebox was blaring Rod Stewart's "Passion" ("everybody needs some") but the Spanish truckers weren't going for it. The mood turned mean and an ugly crowd formed around Brewer. Things looked grim so I lobbed a flaming roll of toilet paper into their midst, grabbed a CO_2 extinguisher off the wall and gassed the mob, screaming, "FIRE! FIRE! RUN FOR YOUR LIVES!" Blinded by the fumes, the truckers crushed each other's toes as they tried to stomp the flames out with their hobnail boots and fistfights erupted. Everybody was yelling, then furniture started flying. Team Maroc slipped out in the clouds and coughing and confusion.

We were on the boat, but wouldn't be safe until the line was cast off. If they caught us, we could expect special vengeance from the parents of the shepherd girl who had stumbled on me guzzling a beer and peeing simultaneously. She was traumatized, her sense of digestion distorted forever.

Ancient Aeromatic Fuels and Arrogant New Fools

The arid north of Africa has been called various names over the centuries: the Egyptian Empire, the Roman Empire, the Kingdom of Morocco, etc. The desert's origins are subject to wide speculation. One theory is the Flood, brought to you in Christianity as the fable of Noah's Ark, but contained in creation myths the world over. This version has a sudden tilt in the Earth's axis causing the oceans to slosh out of their beds like sodden drunks at a beachside camp.

The Sahara is extremely harsh on any life, but in the northwest corner the Atlas Mountains affect a change. There, some of the highest peaks in Africa leap up to gouge moisture from the clouds, like hungry teeth cleave meat from an artichoke leaf. The flowing mountain waters irrigate high plateaus and wide Atlantic coastal plains, making Morocco a pleasant, temperate place. Good crops grow under the abundant African sun but the soil is thin and rocky, and cultivation is very, very laborious. It's a hard life, but it beats wandering around the desert collecting camel turds to fuel campfires, which is what the Moroccan farmers' nomadic ancestors did. In good years Morocco produces 10 percent of the vegetables exported in the world, yet is still very poor, like Egypt, an Arab nation with no oil.

Arrival by air is a painless affair, where visitors breeze through the bureaucratic functions. Unfortunately, Morocco's welcoming committee for land travelers is a gang of querulous cranky thugs in military-looking outfits who seem to thrive on the hassles they create. While Art and Rory hid behind the language barrier, I fenced with a strutting little 5'2" pile of sullen egotism who had a fresh black eye behind his cheap aviator shades. He extorted a $600 "refundable deposit" on our five surfboards. A shabby welcome.

Mickey Takes a Licking and Keeps on Ticking

Shortly after our arrival, pilot error struck hard. Blazing down a dirt road on surf patrol miles from nowhere, Rory managed to hit a big rock that wrecked the front end. It felt like an anti-tank mine. WHAMM!! The beer in my hand hit the roof then fell back to soak my crotch in warm foam. I swooned . . . the closest thing to total pleasure in Far Too Long. The dashboard had big knee dents from restraining my catapult exit through the windshield and my Mickey Mouse watch crystal was broken. Rory was already kneeling in front of the car, moaning. "Oh cripes, the suspension's wasted." "FORGET THE CAR!" I snarled. "It's a rental. MICKEY'S WOUNDED! We need a watch repairman or a veterinarian, quick!"

Brewer was reeling. Cameras and lenses littered the back seat like a swarm of dead bats. His lap was also drenched in beer and a grimace of bliss played across his lips. On these foreign excursions you must take your pleasure where you find it and in this case the suds hit home. Then he saw his equipment and started screaming. "YOU DRUNKEN IDIOT!! YOU HIT THE ONLY ROCK FOR MILES IN ANY DIRECTION!" Rory, of course, claimed the rock jumped out and bit him. Crashed in the tullies, limping back to town was the only avenue. While Brewer muttered threats of dismemberment, I begged Mickey not to die and Rory recited the common litany of the premature lover, "I am sorry. Oh I am sorry. So sorry. Geee, I'm sorry."

Gerry's Shadow and the Geometric Disease

Checking into a hotel in a coastal city one evening, the young man behind the desk looked at Rory and asked if he were Gerry Lopez. That was how we met Madani. Camaraderie and curiosity form a natural bond for surfers in much of the world and Madani is a member of the embryonic community of Moroccan surfers, friendly and eager for progressive news on anything surf-related. Moroccan hospitality, when genuine, is very gracious and this fine charismatic young surfer was the first of many people in the country to extend to us every possible warmth and courtesy. A few days later we met Hammid, who supplies tidbits to the Surf Report, and dined at his parents' stylish home. Hammid and his chums are caught in the wild, thrashing throes of terminal surf-stoke. It's all they think or talk about. His mother hates it. His schoolwork is shot to hell, she claims, and when he sees a parabolic curve in geometry class, to him it represents a wave. Introducing the friend who started Hammid surfing she said, "This is the one who gave my son the sickness of surf." World Motherhood seems unanimous on the subject.

Serious Abuse, the Demise of Dry Land and Four Camel Waves

Wintertime surf in Morocco is often a dangerous seething violence. Far more than just ripples undulating across the sea surface, it is a liquid conspiracy involving the whole ocean in a concerted assault against the minority ingredient of the globe: land. Massive storms marshal their forces in the North Atlantic and rampage down, disciplining the seas across a great fetch. Undiluted by island or reef, the swells barge in with organized, elemental malice. On a Moroccan cliff above the raging but strangely ordered confrontation between the old rivals, wet and dry, one is glad to have the continental mass of Africa standing behind. It seems inevitable that Earth will become a planet of oceans. The sea level is perceptively raised by the fantastic power of the surge and doubt is valid about any permanent resistance to such a force.

Lacking a suicidal surfer for on-site inspection in giant surf we tried to gauge the size of the waves against animals grazing in the foreground. The practice began with small surf, when the waves were a sheep-and-a-half, maybe two sheep high. Things get serious when you start talking camels and many days had three- and four-camel surf.

The winter sea is frequently too turbulent to ride. You surf the swell in ascent or descent or find somewhere sheltered. The best wave in the country, ranking as a world-class surf break, is just such a sheltered configuration. Surfing "Islam's Window of the Atlantic" is a dangerous proposition. Nowhere is constantly big, of course, and myriad surf spots exist, all with a common component: Cruel and Radical Rocks. Morocco's rugged coast is geologically youthful, unlike California and Australia where eons of oceanic abuse have humbled the boulders into roundness.

Several places have potentially perfect setups but either the wave-forming shelf is too shallow beneath the surface or impudent crags insult the contour. With a bit more erosion they will become excellent surfing waves. It won't be long, a mere tick of the geological clock. Say, a couple of thousand years.

Few of the quality waves that do exist have sand beaches, much less sand bottoms. You leap off the rocks to get out and scramble up the rocks to get in. Misjudging either move can be very costly. Of absolute necessity are leashes, obviously, and wetsuit boots. Not because the water is so cold (although it is) but without them the barnacle-encrusted rocks will grind your tootsies to hamburger.

Live Fast, Die Young and Make a Good Looking Corpse

We named our white car Nellybelle. She was a zippy little unit crammed with three crazies and enough knives, cameras, wine, surfboards, wetsuits, maps, binoculars and suspicious materials to incriminate a herd of nuns. Art had a bulletproof equipment case secured in the trunk with stainless-steel cables that would confound a military demolition team. When the boys were blazing in the Full-Tilt-Boogie mode smoke clouds puffed out the windows like a little albino choo-choo chanting, "I think I can, I think I can . . . but why bother?" In short, a four-wheeled multiple felony hurtling over the potholes just this side of slobbering chaos, constituting a continuous mobile breach of the peace.

Brewer was banned from driving because of his old-lady style at the wheel. Good surfers are notoriously wild drivers. This is natural. Good surfing is aggressive motion pushed to the limits, waffling on the knife edge between control and catastrophe. A car is a moving vessel subject to the same laws of physics, the same speed, distance and timing principles as a surfboard. In the hands of a wild-eyed surfer under the right influences (insufficient sex, LOUD rock 'n' roll and beers for breakfast, for example) road travel is just another medium for aggressive motion. Four-wheel drifts through merry-go-round intersections are like full-rail power-on roundhouse cutbacks. Playing chicken with dump trucks on single-file blacktops can rival shoulder-hopping thick mokes at Ala Moana. But for sheer no-tomorrow craziness it's hard to top passing buses on mountain curves at night. This was Rory's specialty. The trick is to see the dust in the air illuminated by the oncoming lights before the vehicles themselves actually round the bend for a head-on hello. The intensity of illumination tells how tight it is. For a surfer in the "vessel-in-motion" frame of mind, winding mountain roads have a flow like pointbreak waves. Oil that flow with a few attitude adjustments and buses become sections in the wave, tricky but makeable. A darkdust pass needed no comment but lit air would evoke "could be tight, guys" from the pilot. One night, hell-bent for an early grave, Rory was passing a bus and started with "could be tight, guys!" Suddenly the dust in the air was very bright. "Could be REAL TIGHT, boys!" and this huge mastodon of a truck whipped around the turn trumpeting as he charged, "OH NO! TOO TIGHT!! TOO TIGHT!!" The bus horn started blaring, people inside hung out the windows screaming and we plowed off to the left shoulder, catatonic with panic and gratitude there had actually been a road shoulder instead of the usual sheer cliff. After a second of dead silence Art asked nobody in particular, "How's the drop?" I glanced over the edge into the black abyss. "Perfect. If we go over we'll plummet, not roll, so our bodies will be more easily identifiable." Outraged at the foreign devils endangering his life, the truck driver screeched to a halt beside us and climbed down waving a crowbar. We left with no goodbyes.

A Baseball Substitute, Greedy Tides and Improving Memories

Violent crime is rare in Morocco. The locals are into more subtle varieties. Thievery is a time-honored tradition, so popular it could be called the national sport. Not all Moroccans are thieves. Far from it. It's just that the honorable people are definitely in the minority, almost an endangered species. Corruption rages like fire in a coal mine, ardent, sinuous, unquenchable. When smoldering bureaucratic greed is fanned by popular need, the burn victims are legion. Nothing of consequence can occur without official participation, unofficially of course. Tourists, for the most part, are viewed not as people but as a resource to be exploited, gouged like fleshy mounds bloated with silver.

Nowhere is worse than the area around the country's premier surf break. Some distance from any town with police, a virtual state of war exists between the campers, mostly surfers, and the young punks that case the place by day and return for their marks at night. The locks on car doors and trunks are useless. In the dark they quietly slice the rubber windshield seals, remove the glass and scavenge the trunk from the back seat. One couple told of awakening to find a Moroccan, his head and arms leaning through the hole he slit in their tent, trying to steal a necklace off the girl's neck as she slept. Another guy was asleep in his station wagon when a boulder crashed through the window to land on his chest. Then a hand reached in, grabbed the cassette player next to him and disappeared. Some English guys had their surfboards stolen, a fatal blow to any surf trip.

There is still justice in the world, however. After being ripped off twice, some Australian surfers sought revenge. They left their tent one night, knowing the thieving bastards were lurking nearby, then doubled around to stake out their own camp. Sure enough, after a while three Moroccans crept up to rifle the tent. The Auzzies pounced. Two guys escaped but they caught one and gleefully proceeded to beat the living crap out of the guy. Then they tied him to a tree all night. In the morning they took him to the police station and when the cops heard the story they all jumped the guy and wailed on him again. As the Australians left, the cops had the guy's fingers wired up and were plugging in their "memory enhancer" to help him recall his cohorts' names.

Ventilated Victims of Noisy Jaws and the Last Laugh

Retaining refuse for proper disposal is practiced erratically by industrialized societies and generally ignored in underdeveloped countries. In the sad fashion of the third world, Moroccans trash their own country with abandon. But Team Maroc was loath to litter and three gluttonous surf dogs generate a lot of garbage. Nellybelle's belly clattered with beer bottles over every bumpy kilometer, along with candy wrappers, sticky yogurt cups, rancid cheese, evil-smelling towels, the foulest socks known to man and all manner of vile debris sloshing around ankle deep, breeding unimaginable stench and vermin. Your basic surfmobile. This good citizenship was not without hazard.

Decelerating for a police roadblock outside Tiznit (they're everywhere), a beer bottle rolled forward and jammed the gas pedal. With the clutch in, we were breaking to a respectable stop but the motor was roaring full blast. When the cop in the road heard the pistons blazing and saw a carload of white trash bearing down, he was seized by abject terror and lunged off to scramble up the side of his van, as though Nellybelle was a snarling Land Shark he could evade by reaching higher ground. We thought that was hilarious but our giggles changed his fear to rage and the gendarme began raving in Arabic, which brought his military buddies running.

Suddenly Team Maroc was about to have its ticket perforated by six machine guns. It was a Delicate Moment. We just played dumb tourists and the soldiers, absent for the original event, thought their comrade, scarlet-faced, sputtering and drooling on himself, was suffering from some kind of seizure. They helped him out of the sun and we rattled on intact, more or less.

Dirty Diapers and Drowning Rodents

As a veteran traveler in the third world and areas of marginal sanity, I am accustomed to the personal irregularities one endures and the bizarre behavior among the natives one encounters. I mean, you expect slovenliness from Ubangis, Aborigines or people that surf Sebastian Inlet, you know, the real primitives. But not among your own travel companions. Art and Rory eat with all the slurpy slobbering daintiness of fat-lipped cannibals masticating missionaries in the Borneo wilds. My subtle hints went unheeded, muffled by their grunts. Across the table from me, morning after morning, day in and day out, wads of food bobbed in their mouths visibly, like the heads of tiny gophers struggling in flooded holes but finally going down.

Eventually, at one especially obnoxious feeding I made some pointed remarks about their table manners. Rory jerked his face out of his plate and angrily told me that they knew how to act around people but this was just us so there was no need to be civilized. As he spoke the shredded mutton on his chin flaked off like a dandruff-ridden goatee. What could I say? Social defectives are immune to reason. I closed my eyes, screwed wine corks into my ears and got on with it, dining in braille.

Imprudent Moves and Scarred Prospects

Surfing under friendly skies in familiar waters, I was disrespectful of the danger. There is no beach. Every set slams into the point and rakes across raw rocks that bristle with barnacles, mussels and urchins. Leaving the water is tricky, but I have lunged across these rocks, surfboard in tow, countless times before. It's all in the timing. Floating with one arm around your board, you wash up the rocks on a rolling swell then cling fast at the height of the heave so the ebb won't suck you back. A bad mistake in big surf and you'll be keelhauled. Incautious with enthusiasm from several deep tuberides, I misjudged my exit. Half-in half-out, the most vulnerable place, the wave behind blasted me and I bounced across the rocks like a side of beef tumbling out of a speeding meat truck. My hand shrieked with the pain of a vicious tear. The tiny yellow globules of fat that puff the palm curled back like the curdled lips of an ugly sneer, baring the muscle and spewing a stream of scarlet insults about my ineptitude. Awash with red blood, the whole forearm of my blue wetsuit was purple, and the stain quickly bloomed all down the front. Love of the sea and third-world charm falter during a drive to the hospital, when visions of native incompetence grin sadistically, but the kind French doctor, Madame Gabrielle, assigned three interns to attendance.

After the trauma of a 2-inch novocaine needle snaking through the wound, numbness set in and the boys gathered round. Hunched over my hand with their foreheads almost touching, they seemed a team of fortune tellers pondering my palm and I looked on while, with needle and thread, they sought to salvage my mutilated future.

Obsession, Violence and Ruin, All in Good Fun

Rory is a genuine world-class talent who surfs hot in all conditions, surpassing most surfers whose acclaim flows from the Pipeline. He has also completely embraced the persona of a Party Animal on a Rigid Pleasure Program. Although versed on practical subjects from clothing design to sexual aberration, he refuses serious pursuits. When the mood wanders he interrupts impatiently, like a hedonistic sheepdog herding wooly thoughts back to pleasurable pastures.

Brewer is generally mild-mannered but when a frown, like a cloud, darkens his brow, near bystanders must beware the thunder of a large angry man capable of great destruction. (There's a fisthole in the wall at *SURFER* Mag's offices where Brewer vented his displeasure on the plasterboard instead of an offender's face.) After becoming one of the world's best surf photographers, he wedged his way into the photographic mainstream. Except for weddings and baby portraits, which he classes right down there with herpes, he'll work anywhere on anything, with a personal preference for the really sick and deranged. Which is why he agreed to come on this trip.

An expedition with these two was like traveling in parentheses. Rory sought to have things gratifying and Brewer was prepared to kill if they weren't.

The *American Sportsman* crew were relaxed travel vets who've seen everything at least twice before in some guise or other. Casual professionalism is the trademark of network television production and anyone obsessed with posing, on either side of the camera, won't fit the program for long. With seasoned tolerance they endured rain, fog, dust storms, fraud, police intervention, flat tires, finicky talent and erratic surf, not to mention incoherent consultants and felonious travel advisors. When the dust settled, they got what they came for. The piece on surfing in Morocco should air sometime in the spring of '83.

After the ABC-TV crew left, Team Maroc hung around a while longer to be certain we had left no scandal untried, no chastity untempted in the quest to thoroughly burn out our welcome. Nellybelle was almost 6,000 miles the worse for wear when we finally dumped her like a soiled young damsel violated, ruined and abandoned by vicious surf nazis abusing one more pleasure-source far beyond rational limits. ▩

You Wouldn't Read About It . . .

By Ben Marcus · SURFER Vol. 29 No. 1 · January 1988

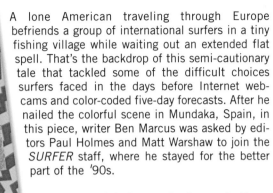

A lone American traveling through Europe befriends a group of international surfers in a tiny fishing village while waiting out an extended flat spell. That's the backdrop of this semi-cautionary tale that tackled some of the difficult choices surfers faced in the days before Internet web-cams and color-coded five-day forecasts. After he nailed the colorful scene in Mundaka, Spain, in this piece, writer Ben Marcus was asked by editors Paul Holmes and Matt Warshaw to join the *SURFER* staff, where he stayed for the better part of the '90s.

"You wouldn't read about it!" An Australian uses this exclamation to express frustration or exasperation when Fate, the Odds, or some other supernatural force has turned against him. You will hear it muttered or shouted at horse races, in sudden rainstorms and after elections. You will also hear it said around the ocean.

I'm from California. I first heard that expression as I was leaving Biarritz to travel south with the Australian Odd Couple. We rounded a corner near Napoleon's summer place, when the boards flew off the roof of the Renault, almost nailed a guy on a motorcycle, then crashed onto the pavement.

"Shit! The boards!" said Oscar.

"You wouldn't read about it," said Felix. "Stop the car!"

Two days later I heard the expression again. We had just left the terrorist city, after stumbling upon surf where we didn't expect it. We were halfway through a highway tunnel when the car started bumping.

"Aw, you wouldn't read about it," said the Odd Couple in unison. We fixed the flat, continued south, and pulled into the fishing village in the evening.

I lived in the fishing village, and surfed the Point for two months. Life there was full of surprises, and I had occasion to use that expression a number of times myself.

To give you an idea of how perfect the Point was, I got the best tube of my life there. It was a fluke—a happy accident.

There was no surf for the first three days of our stay at the fishing village. The swell came up the morning after a huge fiesta: *Todos Santos*. The fiesta took place at the town Picasso made famous. It was a full-throttle rage, and I was up drinking and dancing all night. I had to wait until sunrise to take the train back to the fishing village after Oscar head-butted a local guy, and the Odd Couple drove home without me.

"You wouldn't read about it! Bastards bail out without me!" I mumbled, as I rode the train home.

At six in the morning I got off the train, and straight into the surf on a borrowed board—with a hangover and no sleep. I blew every wave for the first hour. Then I stood up on a medium-sized insider.

I got to my feet shakily, and barely made it to the bottom. I came off the bottom off balance and in big trouble. I am only capable of standing in a half crouch, but that was all I needed. The wave threw out oily-smooth over my head. I heard that roar, and saw the wave funnel down and turn the corner. A Frenchman paddling out was peering into the tube and hooting. I shot out of the tube and fell off, wasting 200 more yards and the inside bowl. Oscar was paddling out and trying not to smile. He rewarded me with the ultimate Australian superlative.

"That was bullshit," said Oscar, trying not to look proud that he was traveling with such a hot Seppo surfer.

I was touched, but I blew the rest of my waves, crawled home, and slept until sunset. That night in the pub the impossible happened again: An Australian gave a compliment to a Seppo.

"Aw, you got a classy barrel today, mate," said the Australian from the Green Slime (his lime-colored Volkswagen Bus).

Yep. I shouted everyone a beer, and decided to stick around.

The surf went flat. Oscar and Felix headed south, looking for waves to surf and drunken locals to head-butt. I was supposed to go with them, but I dissolved our week-old partnership.

"You wouldn't read about a guy like that," said Felix. "Seppo bails out on us already!"

I wanted to surf the fishing village some more, and the Australian Odd Couple were impossible to live with.

While the majority left for places north and south, I settled into the fishing village with a dozen other internationals. We were gambling that a sudden swell would leave the Point full of waves and empty of people. Hog heaven.

When the surf went flat there was little to do in the fishing village, but the town had a hypnotic effect on certain people. There was little to do, but we never got tired of doing it.

We watched the soccer highlight on one of the two television channels. We drank countless mugs of *cafe con leche*. For laughs, we ordered Fockink Gin by name. We listened to the shark and war stories that all South Africans have. We watched the weather maps for low-pressure systems. Two hundred Marines died in Lebanon, and we read about that. We got sick. To justify the risk of waiting, we watched Super-8 movies of perfect point waves at the Otra Bar. We recorded lewd songs and played them on the stereo in the bars. We read old surf magazines.

We sat in the sun on the benches that overlooked the Point and watched for a sign, a ripple. Nothing for two weeks.

We played pelota—a ballgame played with wooden paddles. Every town in the province had a Catholic church, and every church provided a wall for pelota.

"Inside for the mind, outside for the body," is how the church saw it.

As the flat spell continued, many of the internationals became very good pelota players. The best was a swarthy Frenchman from Marseilles, Bertrand, who looked and spoke exactly like Inspector Clouseau. Americans who met him for the first time would burst out laughing when he said hello. He had never seen a *Pink Panther* movie, and didn't understand. I felt sorry for Bertrand—until I challenged him at pelota.

Bertrand was due to enter the French army for his mandatory service. He was in the fishing village surfing, getting blasted on legal hash and blasting anyone who dared challenge him at pelota. Bertrand was an amazing pelota player. This became important toward the second week of that flat spell. The internationals took out their pent-up surf energy on the walls of the church. Bertrand would take on the two best players in town and beat them single-handed.

The pelota court was within 10 yards of the cliffs that overlooked the Point. We never let the ocean out of our sight. We were ready for action. We weren't getting it.

The fishing village overlooked a wide bay rimmed by mountains and capped by an island. The view from the cliffs over the bay could cure leprosy. The internationals weren't the only ones who were entranced by the peace and ease of the town. Citizens escaped the grimed and dirty air of industrial cities to breathe the salt air and stroll about the town. The citizens watched the placid ocean as intently as the internationals, but for different reasons.

The *surfistas extranjeros* added to the mystique of the town. When the surf was cracking, the citizens would line the cliffs to watch the show. Paddling out, you knew how a matador felt in the ring.

The influx of people on the weekends gave the small town a raging nightlife. Local girls would come from all around to mingle with the *rubios*. This arrangement worked well for everyone.

The local girls had the jet-black hair and flashing eyes for which the women of their country are famous, but the girls in this area had something extra. It's hard to explain; they were a mysterious bunch. They had a bemused, sensuous reserve that was like the smile on the Mona Lisa. They loved to drink, dance and talk until well past the witching hour.

The custom on weekends was to eat dinner very late in the evening. The local girls would leave their houses ready to party when many Anglos are ready to call it a night. The only weekend night we went to sleep before four in the morning was Christmas Eve. It fell on a Saturday, which ruined it.

"You wouldn't read about it," grumbled Alto Bill, who let a recurrence of malaria spoil his Christmas cheer. Just as the Catholic church was the dominant building in the fishing village, so was the Church the dominant structure in the mores and manners of the girls.

"Inside for the mind, inside for the body," was how the frustrated internationals saw it.

It may not have been solely because of religion, but the girls in this province and town were infamous for their unwillingness to screw around. They knew that we knew what the score was. They knew we didn't like it, but we learned to. After that the internationals and the local girls mixed well, and had a hell of a good time together.

Many of the local girls were shy, coy or disinterested. The Englishman came up with nicknames for the girls whose names we didn't know or couldn't pronounce: "The Girl from the Flat," "Motorcycle Suzie," "The Hash Queen," "Filthy Barrel," "The Translator."

I fell for "The Bootmaker's Daughter." I suppose I'm a romantic. Why else would I be enjoying perfect surf and easy continental living while the rest of the United States was at home earning their MBAs? The girl I fell for lived in a house along the main street of the fishing village. Her father worked in a shoe shop below the house. The Bootmaker's Daughter was tall, gorgeous and very dignified. Many of the internationals had taken a run at her and been stonewalled. She must have thought I was harmless, as we became good friends on the first night we met. Almost made an enemy out of Doug Wombat because of that.

On weekdays, the Bootmaker's Daughter taught kindergarten at another fishing village up the coast. On a Saturday night, one week into the flat spell, the Bootmaker's Daughter invited me to accompany the Translator to visit her during the week. She had seen me playing soccer with some of the schoolkids in the fishing village, and guessed correctly that I liked rug rats. The plan was for me to attend her classes, spend the night at her apartment and return to the fishing village the next day.

Well, why not? I wanted to go. But I knew that if I left, the surf would come up. Guaranteed. I KNEW this would happen. That's the way my luck goes sometimes. Visiting the Bootmaker's Daughter was a unique opportunity, but a potentially disastrous decision.

I studied the ocean and debated the decision for three days. I unwisely leaked word of my dilemma to the internationals, who were becoming increasingly tense from the lack of surf. They urged me to go. They were all seasoned travelers who'd been burned making similarly stupid decisions.

"I don't care what you do, as long as the surf comes up," said the South African Who Had the Place Wired.

"Go for it, mate. It's only for a day—you won't miss anything," lied the Australians. Serge and Eddie were mates, who'd just returned from South Africa. They had each other's names: Eddie was usually surging, while Serge was lethargic.

The Englishman shook his head. "If you go, you'll blow it. But I know you'll go because you're stupid, and the Bootmaker's Daughter's beautiful."

The Inspector said, through hash-lidded eyes, "Don't go for a cheek! You vill miss ze vaves. Plenty of cheeks! No vaves for dayz!" He looked at the flat ocean. "Pelota, anyone?"

Never turn your back on the ocean. It can work you over without getting you wet. I knew I was risking a supernatural pummeling by leaving town during a flat spell. I also knew that if I stayed, the ocean would stay flat. If I left, the surf would come up. The ocean demanded a sacrifice. It works that way.

The day came when I had to make my decision. We had to telephone the Bootmaker's Daughter that evening to tell her whether or not we'd arrive the next day. I watched the ocean nervously from dawn to dusk. Nothing. I looked at the weather maps. Nothing. I watched the weather news. Nothing. I asked the fishermen. No way the swell would come up that fast.

I showed myself to be a heel by laying my priorities bare to the girls. "*Olas grandes, amigas,*" I explained. "*No quiero perder las olas.*" The girls shook their heads, but they understood. Priorities. *Surfistas locos.*

It wasn't very gallant of me, but anyone who has traveled 6,000 miles to surf knows how important a day of good waves becomes. You don't want to risk missing a good day, because you might not get another. I wanted to visit the Bootmaker's Daughter. I had left the town twice during the flat spell, and had returned to find I'd missed nothing. I wanted to go, but I had a bad feeling about this time.

At 8 p.m. I looked at the ocean one last time. Not a ripple. Flat. A nice sunset, but no surf. I walked to the phone booth and made my decision. I was committed. We finished the call to the Bootmaker's Daughter, and the Translator walked home shaking her head. I walked to the pub to tell the internationals what I had done. They gave me three cheers, and we all walked to the Atalaya to watch the swell jump.

And it jumped! You had to see it to believe it. The tide was low at 10 p.m., so I walked down with the Englishman. The surf was pumping. The wind was blowing fast through the river valley, and straight offshore. There was enough light to see whitewater folding over and bounding for hundreds of yards down the line. It was perfect.

A hard-core surfer would have bailed out on the commitment. I figured that if I stayed to surf I would cause a hurricane, or onshores, at least. After checking the surf early in the morning and seeing tons of lonely swell, I boarded a bus with the Translator and headed north.

Two hours later I got another look at the Point, as the bus traveled north along the other side of the bay. I saw less than a dozen black dots riding more than a dozen 6-foot waves.

"You wouldn't read about it," I muttered to myself.

"*¿Que quieres a leer?*" asked the Translator.

"*Nada*," I said, as the bus turned the corner and headed for the other fishing village.

The Bootmaker's Daughter had control of a roomful of brown-eyed kids who worshipped her. The kids considered it a great novelty to have a tall, antic *rubio* in the classroom. I managed to disrupt an entire day's instruction. That's always worth doing.

I was treated to lunch at a small restaurant near the harbor. The girls ordered for me. I trusted them, and my trust got me a bowl of black goo with bits of raw squid swimming in it. *Calamari con tinta*—squid in its own ink. I like calamari, but I like it cooked. I don't like eating substances that have the color and consistency of crude oil. Neither did the Translator, so I wasn't too embarrassed.

Serge and Eddie had told me to keep my eyes peeled for surf. I didn't see any.

That evening we sat in a café near the harbor, drank coffee and talked. The girls cooked dinner.

That night I slept in a separate room from the Bootmaker's Daughter. You wouldn't read about that. But I wasn't as aggravated about missing the surf. I'd had a fun day, and there was always tomorrow . . .

The next morning we rushed back to the fishing village. There was still some swell left, but it was clear that I'd missed a CLASSIC day. The internationals had that look of fatigued satisfaction. I knew they weren't exaggerating as they raved about the waves I'd missed.

Watching performances by the South African Who Had the Place Wired was almost as much fun as surfing the Point, and I had missed one of his exceptional displays of tuberiding. The internationals were yakking about it for months.

As the internationals ridiculed me for missing the surf, they were also aware that I had spent the night with the Bootmaker's Daughter. As they laughed at me, they searched my expression for a clue as to what had happened the previous night. I let them see nothing—I had to save face.

So I missed one day of perfect waves. It could have been disastrous, but it turned out that my five months in Europe were full of waves. I was lucky to catch one of the best seasons in years. I got so many days of good waves in France, Spain and Portugal that they blend together.

The day that stands out, however, was the one I spent with the Bootmaker's Daughter at the other fishing village, trying to forget about the surf long enough to enjoy myself.

At the time, I was in pain. I knew how a Volcano Virgin feels on the eve of the plunge. I had made myself the laughingstock of the internationals by setting myself up to miss a day of waves. They thanked me for being the sacrifice. Martyrdom sucks. You wouldn't read about it. ▨

Cheyne Horan's Rainbow Bridge

By Matt George · SURFER Vol. 29 No. 4 · April 1988

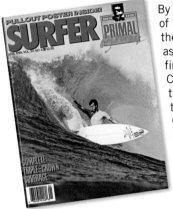

By the mid-'80s, American Tom Curren's dominance of professional surfing signaled a shift away from the perennial dominance of Australia and Hawaii as the primary hotbeds of surfing talent. For the first time since Phil Edwards was King of the Coast, U.S. mainlanders seemed to be leading the way, and California writer Matt George was there as *SURFER* magazine's preeminent profiler. Grouped with his landmark profiles of Kelly Slater and Tom Curren is this piercing study of Australian Cheyne Horan, who, at 26 years old, was the embattled veteran of the world tour, a long way from his promising days as surfing's Boy Wonder. Plagued by bizarre equipment choices and a mysterious alternative lifestyle, Horan's career seemed to augur ever deeper into failure, and George was there to provide an unflinching record of its decaying orbit.

I awoke with a start—soaking wet, chest heaving, completely disoriented. The room eventually stopped spinning enough for me to realize it had only been a bad dream—I was still alive. I focused slowly. It was dawn. I was lying on a soft Indian rug beneath two batik blankets, waking up on the floor of the house where Cheyne Horan lives. I was surrounded by sleeping dogs. One's warm flank served as my pillow, another was at my feet staring at me, puzzled by my stirring. I smiled at him, he smiled back, then we both lay our heads back down; him to sleep . . . me to think some things out.

I had arrived the previous morning at the Coolangatta Airport; jet-lagged, exhausted and with a lot on my mind. Mostly Cheyne. He and I had been acquainted since 1980, and on occasion—as is true with all who fall into the currents and eddies of the Pro Tour—had actually had times of common camaraderie and friendship. Yes, I thought as I stepped off the plane, Cheyne was a friend of mine.

Having heard the rumors and accusations about his so-called descent into weirdness, I was curious to see what the real story was. I had intended to find out by coming to live with him for a while. After all he had contributed to surfing and, I dare say, to a lot of our lives, he deserved to have his say—to be understood. He deserved that much, surely.

I could smell Cheyne before I could see him. I turned from the baggage carousel and there he stood, barefoot, wearing sweatpants, no shirt, and carrying a burning stick of cherrywood incense. We embraced. It seemed a perfectly natural thing to do. The physical power and girth of the muscle on his body was staggering.

We loaded my board and luggage into his car and took off, headed south out of the Gold Coast toward a place called Goonengerry. We caught up on some memories—some glory days: South Africa, Brazil, early Stubbies, Bells and a funny little excursion that Dave Parmenter once took us on out to Rottnest Island, off Western Australia. At one point I mentioned that I was really beat, so he offered me some rainwater he had collected in a bike bottle. He said it would help. It was lukewarm and tasted like plastic. Out of courtesy, I drank deeply.

Slowly, carefully, he drove through town. Cheyne seemed at peace with everything. It wasn't until we crossed the border into New South Wales that the change came over him. He had some room to move now, as the roads became rural on the outskirts of Tweed Heads. He told me we would take the back way to Byron; it was faster.

That must have contributed to my nightmare: Shedding his tranquility like a snake's skin, Cheyne drove like a fiend, hunched over the wheel. We averaged 90 mph, sometimes more. Things just got quiet between us. He was intent on the gravel backroads that spun below us like some live video game. On one particularly long straightaway, we had the white-knuckled composure to discuss what he felt about the public's opinion that his time was over. A bygone era.

He sped up. "Mate, like I'm 26 right? Twenty-six! A lot of people do put me in that era with MR and Shaun and Bugs. But when those guys were actually happening, I was still a grommet reading about them at school. I've never felt a part of that era, but I feel like I got dragged into it. When everyone saw MR fading out, they figured I had to go with him, since I dueled with him for so long. And I've had to handle that. I mean, I can see why MR has faded out—he drinks f—kin' Coca-Cola and hangs out in a coal mine. I'm into health and fitness. I reckon I'm in the Tommy Carroll era. He and I have been competing against each other since Day One . . . I'm not through."

At that particular moment, I was sure we were both through. The curve up ahead was way too much at this speed, and even if we pulled it, I was convinced the panel van tottering toward us in the opposite direction would surely finish the job. Cheyne hunched forward, downshifted, threw it into a slide half off the road, stiffened his arms to control the pull of the boggy shoulder, threw up a 6-foot rooster of mud and grass, missed a fence, rocketed by the van and swung it back on track just before a drainage ditch.

My heart hadn't even begun beating again before he chuckled nervously, gained some speed, and said, "That was *heavy*, mate . . . " This was the Cheyne I remembered. The boy wonder with the heavy moves . . .

I sat up, still groggy. The place was silent and sparse. No one was up yet. Cheyne still lived with the friends most of us had heard so much about. I'd met two of them the night before: Kerry, early 40s, tall and thin, with baleful eyes and curly-haired, graying temples. He didn't really fit the description of the evil Svengali he'd been painted as. And Brad, about 20, a dark, beautiful child, with piercing blue eyes and a simple countenance. The third, Paul, was down in Sydney doing . . . well, that was all I knew . . . he was down in Sydney. It had been explained to me that they'd named their compound "Solarfarm" due to their latest interest in the possibilities of manufacturing futuristic, solar habitats, and that the four of them and the dogs—Matilda, Jock and Astro—were a "group" committed to yoga, health and "Global Enchantment."

I was too tired to ask. I figured we'd get into all that later. After a homegrown meal of tofu and greens, I collapsed on the floor where Cheyne had made up a place for me. I had fallen asleep, feeling tucked in.

I stood up, stretched, then tugged on my jeans. I was experiencing that clandestine feeling one always has when awake and alone in a stranger's house. I took a look around. This house was isolated, all right—tucked right up on top of one of the rolling green foothills behind Byron Bay. It was a simple structure: three bedrooms, two ranch-style porches, and an open, chalet-style living room. Picture windows were everywhere, each framing bush country views like realist paintings. The kitchen was one of the larger rooms, a veritable nest of vegetables, fruit, grains and battered cooking hardware. I stepped up to the overstuffed bookcase and fingered some of its reads: *Seven Pillars of Ancient Wisdom, Secret Teachings of All Ages, Jesus: The Evidence, Esoteric Astrology, The Penguin Book of Homosexual Verse, The Underworld Initiation*, and then—seemingly out of place—dog-eared copies of *The Warrior Athlete* and *The Warrior's Way*. On the top shelf was Cheyne's certificate of merit from the Australian Surfing Hall of Fame, for "The Development of the Winged Star-Fin Concept with Ben Lexcen." It was dog-eared too.

Posters were up: here, one of Buddha and the 16 arhats, there, a Gotcha contest poster. One unicorn motif, and over by the weight set and press bench in the corner, torn from the pages of some magazine, was a kind of shrine to assorted musclemen and rippling bodybuilders. There was no furniture, just rugs and pillows, except for a desk that held a bizarrely incongruent personal computer—"to plug into the global brain," I was told. The stereo was high-tech, as well—compact disc, and all that. The TV was a nice color job. And in the center of this communal room, on the floor, was all the "enchantment" paraphernalia, neatly arranged. It formed a sort of center of things . . . like a fire ring in a tepee.

I stepped out onto the porch and breathed the morning in. The sun had yet to burn the horizon. Diaphanous folds of tule fog had filled in all of the valleys below, leaving only a rank of lime-green humps that marched off to the sea. The ocean was black in the distance, and the Byron Headlands' Lighthouse was still washing the countryside at intervals—a quickly dimming radar of white light. The few birds starting their day only added to the pressing quiet. I watched it all for a while, feeling a long way from home. Just standing there, arms crossed, gazing upon an awakening world from the porch of Cheyne Horan's Mount Olympus . . .

Dusk. Same spot. Two days later. Up to now, Brad, Cheyne and I had been spending our days surfing Lennox and Broken Head: two classic Australian points, which were suffering from not-so-classic conditions at the moment. Brad would just ride whichever board Cheyne wasn't using that day. Cheyne referred to his sessions here as nirvanic; a soothing balm for the bruises gained while on the Pro Tour. Yet he also considered his "sanctuary surfing" as a heavy R&D and training period. Every time we paddled out involved at least three mock heats, which Cheyne would attack with a vengeance, although Brad and I were his only available adversaries. His onslaught would be relentless. Every time he took off it was as if the wave was sucking all the energy it could muster out of him, and expending him with its own; transforming him into a surfing . . . instrument, forcing him to charge. It was a mad, almost violent union, despite the mellowness he may convey on land.

This was an indication of an emerging dichotomy I had observed in Cheyne's behavior: driving like a maniac one moment, then quiet and reserved at home the next; fiercely competitive during a game of sand-lot cricket, then later passively agreeing with a peaceful doctrine of the group. Speaking of improving his relationships with some people on the Pro Tour one minute, then vehemently explaining how to mash his competition during the heat. I found myself a little confused by it. I could only imagine how he felt.

In town and out in the surf, Cheyne is clearly regarded with awe. In a region that is considered an official national preserve of alternative lifestyles, Cheyne's commitment has gained him deity status. With that shock of blond hair, the hot-pink wetsuits, the bizarre board and his powerful animal aura, he's impossible to miss wherever he goes. But I didn't see one other shortboard with a keel in it, though every single longboard in the lineup sported one. I brought this up to Cheyne. He just smiled and said, "Yeah . . . they're unreal for noseriding." And that was that.

In the afternoons after the blow-out, the three of us would head back to Solarfarm with the day's fresh vegetables. Everyone would pitch in to fix the evening meal. It was an incredibly involved process, with everything made from scratch. The pressing, grinding, shredding, chopping and eventual presentation of this macrobiotic fare would take about two hours and the daily activity was treated with much warmth and fun. It obviously brought this nuclear family of men together. Like most secluded cadres, there was a tribal bond and love shared between them all. What it was based on was rather hazy to me—mostly yoga, I imagined. But what the hell, I'd seen a lot of unhappier households in my time, so I just relaxed and gave them their sphere. Kerry, certainly the leader of this outfit, seemed to spend his days reading and pondering—he doesn't surf. And Paul, who had arrived sometime during the first night, having hitchhiked all the way up from Sydney, just slept a lot. Cheyne was the only one employed. The rest of them were on welfare. And each day there had a great deal of what the group referred to as "Herbal Enchantment." A *great* deal.

It was handled ritualistically and with reverence. It was explained to me by Kerry, with a wave of his hand: "These herbs are the key to all that we're doing here . . . it opens all the doors . . . "

By this time, I was ready to open a few doors myself, so I came in off the porch and sat down with Cheyne for an on-the-record interview. After spending a few days surfing with him, and after they had screened Cheyne's movie for me, *Scream in Blue* (a startlingly well-crafted and brutally honest documentary of Cheyne's worst year ever on the World Tour), and after hearing some vaguely outlined interests the group had in things like solar shelters, environmental protection and making this cruel world a better place . . . I just wanted to talk to the man.

We weren't to be alone. All nine of us (including their band of vegetarian dogs) sat in a circle. The group waited patiently for Kerry to properly prepare the herbs, slip in a Van Morrison CD and then begin the enchantment ritual. Then, and only then, did I begin.

I started by asking Cheyne just what the underlying purpose of his lifestyle was. What was the message he was trying to get across to the common man through his surfing? There was an eruption of opinions from everyone but Cheyne. Kerry said it was a holistic message of unification. Paul said something about it being bits and pieces that can be singled out and made whole. And Brad said Cheyne was a disciple of health whom others could emulate. I hadn't taken my eyes off Cheyne. Again, I asked him what he thought. He just smiled softly, and replied, "I reckon all that is right."

Well, I asked, if you are trying to set an example of what a lifestyle like yours can achieve, what about all the competition failures you're experiencing? Didn't that hurt your cause?

He said, quietly, "Yeah . . . but . . . " (pause).

There was another eruption at this, but after a few moments, Cheyne just stared his friends down. He'd handle this one. "I try not to get caught up in all that stuff; the winning and the losing . . . " I wasn't buying it, and he knew it. He continued. "Well, I mean, I'm still going out trying my best moves and trying to win, right? But I'm not that attached to winning anymore. If you're attached to winning, you feel down if you lose. And if you win, you feel elated. They're each as bad as the other . . . " When Cheyne speaks, there are murmurs of encouragement from the group. It reminds me of a Martin Luther King speech. Brad piped up with, "Someone has to set that example for other people—winning and losing aren't everything. You don't have to jump off a cliff or become a heroin addict if you lose, you know . . . Maybe people will see how to modify themselves in losing . . . "

More enchantment all around after this. I wait. And then I say, simply: Cheyne? You hate losing.

Before he answers, there's just the music for a bit. "Yeah . . . I know it . . . but I'm changing. You gotta change. You gotta become a better person. You gotta evolve—you can't stay a leaf all your life, or a stem . . . you have to grow into a flower, or the best thing you can be . . . "

What is the best thing you can be? I asked.

He sighed, and smiled. "Happy, peaceful . . . content." (silence) A CD change. Joe Cocker: greatest hits. Cheyne begins again, "Yeah . . . you know mate, I'm still just working on credibility with the judges. I think the whole way they judge competitions should be reviewed." This gets Kerry going. His voice rises at the end of each sentence, making it sound like each statement is a question. "Well, I think what it is, is that there is something new developing here. In surfing. And surfing is part of it. I reckon we should be careful not to squeeze it into the old bottles and shove it into the old trips. Especially when we adopt the American way; what they inherited from Europe: capitalism and commercials, and all that stuff. That's where I reckon they've made a mistake in surfing. Like, it was growing OK, you know what I mean? Then they said, 'Aww, now let's go back to America and do it their way. Get an American champion and get money for the sport, and then it will really grow.' I reckon they're wrong . . . "

I asked Kerry just who "they" were.

He replied, "The magazines! The clothing companies! It's a conspiracy . . . !"

I wasn't going to touch that one with a 10-foot pole. Instead, I changed the subject. I asked Cheyne what the ultimate success of the group would be. Kerry answered: "Self-transformation. Like, if the group could devise the way for people to transform themselves. That's the original yoga goal. As a group, maybe we could transform society a little bit; transform the planet within the time that we live. But, it starts with yourself: If you fix yourself up a bit first, you can fix up others—and then the world."

Kerry, Brad and Paul are all hugging their knees at this point, staring into the center of our circle. Cheyne sits cross-legged, bolt upright. More enchantment is needed; Cocker is singing "Feeling Alright." I asked Cheyne what he would transform the world into. What exactly needed this "fixing up."

"What needs fixing up?" he asked, surprised that I didn't know the answer. "Well . . . people are starving; we've got a nuclear threat hanging over our heads every day—there's paranoia. There's f—kin' shit in the ocean . . . and after all that is fixed up, that'll clean up the vibration, and then the relationships between leaders can be fixed up . . . "

What kind of fixing up do these relationships need, Cheyne?

He takes a breath and comes down a bit. "I reckon just harmony, basically . . . "

Kerry is on it now. "It's like . . . yoga is sort of an integration. You know that in the body there are seven centers?"

No, I replied I didn't know that.

"Well," he explained, "the Kundalini, which is the yoga we practice, is sort of a male/female bond of that multistructure. And the idea is to awaken it and pierce all those centers in the middle of your body until it hits your head. Enlightenment, and all that sort of stuff." Kerry went on to explain that everyone is split into two polarities: male and female. The problem is that no one has this figured out, really. The answer is to seek a way to even out these male and female polarities—the yin and the yang—so they can cancel each other out, and transform the individual into a more complete, balanced person. We gotta fix this up first.

Does this fixing up require a bisexual lifestyle, then? I asked. Dead silence. The music had stopped. Everyone was waiting for Kerry to field that one.

He eventually does. "OK, we're a yoga group. And at the moment we're a celibate yoga group. Everyone has to handle their sexuality in their own way. But we're a Tantra Yoga group eventually, too. Tantra Yoga involves centering yourself through touch. It's actually through touching or using sexuality as an engine to find the Kundalini centers. It's a high and advanced yoga . . . "

I ponder this. Everyone is pondering this. I turn to Cheyne and look him in the eyes. Cheyne? I ask, in the quiet. Is that the way you feel about all this, too?

By this time, the peripheral effects of all the enchantment going on had made me about as high as a kite. Paul had just dozed off, and Brad lay on his back, tapping his hands against his chest to the beat of a song in his head. Kerry had begun explaining just how easy it would be for the world to be harmonized through "Global Enchantment," and Cheyne? Cheyne remained cross-legged, still bolt upright, staring deeply into a full-length mirror that was propped up over by the barbells. His posture was so intent, so wise, yet the look on his face as he peered into his own eyes seemed so naïve. Twenty-six years old, I thought. Twenty-six. It made me wonder just what he was seeing . . .

Cheyne and I were sitting up on the chimney rock that overlooks the pass; Byron Bay's famous point. He was in the process of dropping me off in town. It was time for both of us to start thinking about getting down to Bells. We'd decided to check the surf first. It was sparkling in at 2 feet, pipedream perfect, with a raft of silhouette figures moving about in the lineup's diamond field reflections. We were flanked by the enormous, verdant headland. The utter beauty of the scene right there, right then, was astounding. We were alone. I could tell Cheyne had something to say for himself.

He got to it. "I'm not a homosexual. That's not the way it is . . . " I just nodded. He continued. "A lot of this prejudice I get on the Tour is just people and their assumptions. I've been treated as a homosexual, but that's not me. I love women . . . I'm just into modifying my sincerity right now, learning about myself. That's why I'm celibate. Because, when I choose someone to love, it will be because I am complete, and able to touch and share with purity. (pause) I know people get uptight about my trip—my yoga, my friends, my ideas. I just take that as it comes . . . No one really knows me. My mystique is there though, because I'm still out there battling on the front lines; still surfing against the best in the world on my own terms, and I just won't go away."

A bigger set moved through. We watched it tumble in—the whole thing. When it was over, I mentioned that maybe there had been a lot of assumptions because Kerry sometimes did a lot of talking for him.

Cheyne said, "No . . . no. He makes things a lot clearer than I can make them for people. I'm practicing the stuff. I'm in an initiation stage, and he's the leader of the group. I have my own voice, but it's an internal voice. It's not a struggle, either—it's like an understanding. And one of the things I understand is that I don't care what people think of me. I know me, my friends know me . . . that's enough for me, I think."

I asked him what was coming up for him, short term.

"Well, my . . . extremism has got me on the edge with my sponsors right now. If that doesn't get any better, I won't have any backing. You can't do anything without backing. I'll be a . . . Look, I love pro surfing, mate. I wish I could be mentally and physically able to compete until I was 46."

But, I had to mention, this year was the second year in a row that his Top 16 seed was seriously in question. What would happen, I asked, if he dropped out of the Top 16?

At this, he turned his head, brow furrowed, and stared down at his feet, picking at his toes. Another set moved through. He didn't watch this one. He just waited a bit, suddenly looked up at a seagull pinwheeling overhead, and replied, "I can't even think about that . . . "

Two weeks later, Bells Beach, Victoria.

This heat was going badly for Cheyne. Gary Green was plastering him. A cold wet drizzle, driven by a stormy onshore, had run almost everyone out of the parking lot contest area hours before. The PA had fizzled and stopped a while back. Except for the heat horns and officials in the double-decker bus, the place was basically a ghost town. I felt like the only one watching or even interested in this heat. It would just about decide Cheyne's year-end rating. One minute remained. He wasn't going to make it.

Outside, Cheyne took off on his fourth wave. He knew he was down—he poured it on. Like an aquatic dowser, he ferreted out some power spots on the funky wave face, and made some moves: a cutback, a bottom turn. During these moments his center, balance and strength would flash so purely that it was like watching a memory, like witnessing latent traces of his prodigious talent. Moments that not only reminded you he was once truly one of the greatest surfers on Earth, but also convinced you, for fleeting instants, that he most certainly still was. If only he . . . yes, if only . . .

The heat ended as Gary Green rode one to the beach, leaving Cheyne outside by himself. In these conditions, Cheyne looked adrift. I felt sad for my friend out there. For all the effort and commitment he's put into his personal journey—his search for meaning—he seemed to deserve so much more than this. In the '60s, an era from which Cheyne has embraced a number of beliefs, this kind of journey was known as one's "rainbow bridge": those personal inner attempts at mixing one's own energy and ideas with that of the cosmic forces of nature, to create a synergy that would leave the individual and the world enlightened, and in a better space. Out there in the water was an individual who had always had the guts and creative power to take his ideas to the end of the line— to make them really happen. Ideas like the laser-zap, the Star-Fin, and now his own visionary film, and an ambitious interest in solar shelters that could someday "fix up" the globe.

The trouble was, just as this contest site was abandoned and spectatorless, so did Cheyne seem to be losing his audience, and by slipping into the morass of the lower ranks, perhaps even himself.

From my vantage on that lonely, windswept cliff, it appeared as if Cheyne Horan's rainbow bridge was evolving into his own bridge of sighs . . . ▟

Sweet Konas:
Living and Surfing in Mokuleia
By Walt Novak · SURFER Vol. 30 No. 4 · April 1989

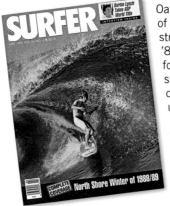

Oahu schoolteacher Walt Novak became a favorite of *SURFER* staff members and readers alike for his string of hilarious letters to the editor through the '80s. Eventually, the Hawaiian writer was recruited for larger assignments, such as this vivid snapshot of his home in Mokuleia, one of Oahu's hidden gems, with a reputation for being fickle and unpredictable—and that's just the neighbors.

I should probably tell you I don't feel guilty about "exposing" Mokuleia. It's such a fickle area that you pretty much have to live here to get it good. First of all, the tradewinds blow onshore at Mokuleia, and usually mush it up every day about 9:00. The only time it stays rideable all day is during Kona, or south winds. Last year we had just eight Kona days.

Also, with the notorious North Shore area only seven miles to the east—where conditions quite often stay clean throughout the day—few non-resident waveriders care to wander in this direction.

As I see it, an article about Mokuleia quickly turns into a story about people, not breaks. King Crustacean—or Ron Cleaver—is a good example. After dark King Crustacean takes a flashlight, swims out to the reefs and catches more lobsters than anyone. Subsequently, he tells more lobster tail tales than anyone. Ron's been known to pounce upon unsuspecting lobbies in between sets. Last year he brought one up, smashed it across the deck of his board, and shared the tail, sashimi-style, with me and two other amazed dudes in the lineup.

Ron pals around with wildman Tom Gunn. They blast across the Kaena Point motocross hills on their high-tech dune buggy on the flimsiest tip about a south swell. They surf Yokohama all summer, and usually return smiling. According to them, it's 6–8' and "heavy mojo" every time.

Ron and Tom haven't shaved for three days, no matter when you see them. They popularized the look around here way before Don Johnson did in Miami. Ron gets upset about it. "Hey, the networks ripped me off. I don't get no residuals, and I don't get no satisfaction."

One morning, as Ron detailed elaborate (but judicially abstract) plans to sue NBC, we strolled down to look at the surf. Across the lawn, through the palm trees, and there it was: Chances, in full-blown mode.

A good wave at Chances is all about pure velocity, and inspires few cutbacks as it jets across an alarmingly shallow runway. On a good Kona day you pull into the barrel on four-out-of-five waves. Some you make, some you don't. Either way, you're in there for long periods of time. Sounds a lot like Maalaea, doesn't it? Well, Chances is similar to Maalaea, except it's a left, and it's not on Maui. It's awesome when it's on, but extremely particular. Chances is almost never perfect, but when it is, it's almost impossible to exaggerate its perfection. Like Maalaea, the place has to be ridden to be believed.

Now, here's what happened that morning: Ron "King Crustacean" Cleaver and I paddled out. He was still blustering about "Miami Mice," and "no residuals . . . no satisfaction." As we finally approached the Chances lineup, I asked him why he kept sticking his big head under the water. "Checking for lobbies," was the obvious reply.

I got totally lucky on my first wave and streaked for well over 100 yards. Paddling back out I saw the darnedest thing. Ron Cleaver was riding a beautifully lined-up wall: He went square off the bottom, smack-a-whack off the top—then he suddenly dove off his board, straight for the reef.

I stopped paddling and watched. Ol' Ron was down there for a long time. At the end of its leash, Ron's board was bobbing around like a colorful cork. A nice set of waves came by. Ron did not surface. Ol' Ron was down there for a long, long time. I knew he wasn't dead, because every 30 seconds or so he'd cut loose a burst of bubbles.

At last he surfaced, talking a mile-a-minute. "I just had to chase it! Jeez! It was the biggest lobbie I ever saw!"

"So why didn't you grab it?" I asked.

King Crustacean slowly turned his dazed eyes upward. "Uh, uh, there was just no way on that one, Walt."

"Why not?"

"It was big, really big. It was so big I would have needed a saddle to ride him up to the beach!"

Did you ever hear that song by Johnny Cash that goes something like: "I've got a '51, '52, '53, '54, '55, '56, '57, '58, a '59 Cadillac./ I've got a '60, '61, '62, '63, '64, '65, '66, '67, a brand new '68 Cadillac."?

You never heard it? Well, I did the other day on the radio while I was driving to Mokuleia's number-one big-wave spot, Morning Star. Johnny was sounding as hillbilly as ever, twanging out that country-western classic like nobody's business. That was when the Epiphany of Truth came flashing though my rusty cruiser like a Tennessee breeze. See, Johnny was actually giving me the Day Star story right there in his twangy, melodious analogy! And it was being pumped conveniently through my FM just so I could tune in and log it down.

See, the song has this wacky plot about some Cadillac factory worker who steals one piece of Caddy per day, over 20 years. He steals a carburetor the first day, a bolt the next, then a hubcap, and on and on. After two decades of systematic pilfering, the guy has all the parts. And you can sure guess he assembles them in his garage, pronto. He proceeds to dangle his proud arm out the window, tilt his handsome head back without a sprinkling of modesty, and drive—totally stoked—down the main drag of town. That, of course, is when he sings the story.

And that is when I pulled my car under some ironwood trees and gazed upon a heavy set of big rights humping 200 yards from shore. Day Star—also know as The Boat—is one of the most impressive rights I've surfed in my 13 years in Oahu. The wave gets a solid 8–10', and resembles Sunset Beach at the peak. The rest of the ride, however, is totally different. Where Sunset gets super-thick and jacks insanely on the inside section, Day Star gets thinner and smaller as it peels down the line. It's sort of like combining an 8-10' Sunset peak with a 4–6' Laniakea wall.

The constant dilemma at Day Star is board length. Gauging by the peak, you'd ride a 7–8' just to get down the face. But you'll regret it for the remainder of the wave, as you dork along an immaculate-but-only-5' wall, totally overgunned.

Even more confusing to all the Day Star irregulars was the boat wreck on the beach—the darn thing kept getting bigger. Ten years ago we used to call the place the Boat because you lined up with a wrecked 40' boat on the beach. Then, one spring day we noticed the words "Day Star" had been recently painted in bright yellow on both sides. The Boat didn't break again until the following season, and, sure enough, the Boat had grown considerably during the interim. What we had on our hands was a mysterious wreck-in-reverse.

And, yessirree, it turns out that *Day Star*, the Boat, sits on the beach in front of a Pearl Harbor boatyard mechanic's house. I don't want to mention his name or get him fired, but if you listen closely to your local country-western station, you'll figure out that this Pearl Harbor boatyard mechanic is a heavy Johnny Cash fan.

So, if you're out Mokuleia way, looking for the big wrecked boat on the sand to figure out the Day Star lineup . . . well, you're liable to be disappointed. But listen carefully, and you might hear a healthy motor purring way off toward the horizon. And look way outside, and you might see a shiny 40-footer trolling for Pacific blue marlin. And if you happen to have a pair of binoculars handy, a quick glance might reveal a proud arm dangling aft, and a handsome head tilted back without a sprinkling of modesty.

Big D Williams is the most notorious skateboarder in Mokuleia. He and his considerable entourage are proud of the enormous half-pipe they've constructed across the street. It's tiled and painted blue, like a swimming pool. It draws enormous packs on weekends, was featured on a local TV show, hosted a pro contest, and is supposedly the largest in the state. Big D uses his skateboard to commute four miles to work, as well as doing grocery shopping. He prefers, however, to spend his hours going back and forth on the ramp. "You don't go anywhere," states Big D, "but it sure is fun getting there."

Big D used to weigh nearly 300 pounds back in his high school hockey days in icy Detroit. He was heavily into Snickers and Twix. Now, his mid-thirties midriff is straight out of Lean Cuisine. He is half his former self. He attributes it all to the glorious waves of Mokuleia. He claims that surfing is better for flattening the flab than push-ups or sit-ups. "Surfing is the absolute best exercise for fat stomachs. It keeps you away from the refrigerator for hours at a time."

Big D's favorite break is called Sugi's, a snappy little right with a nice wall in between two bowl sections. If it's glassy, Big D will paddle out his 5'8" quad-fin and wiggle it to pieces, even if the size is nearly non-existent. On one particularly miniscule day, Big D paddled in after almost four hours of hydraulic micro-surgery. I asked him how big the waves were. Big D's reply: "It's 8–10', with occasional sets up to 1'."

Speaking at length with Big D is an amazing experience. The ease with which he can change topics is not unlike the way a kaleidoscope changes colors. Speaking of colors, Big D colors surfboards and sailboards for a living. His logo says "Dinosaur Beach." He's kinda famous around here, and possibly a genius—but that's enough about Big D Williams.

This one surfer up the street really hates my dog, Trudy. My dog barks at people, but she's generally sweet. Still, this guy can't stand her.

This guy's got bushy hair and a grizzly mustache. He always wears shorts, sunglasses and no shirt. Every time he rides by on his bike, he gets off and puts the kickstand down. He growls and comes after Trudy. Then sweet Trudy freaks out and barks like crazy.

I got sick of it after several months, and walked outside. This guy had his kickstand down and his grizzled face was snarling. He barked when he saw me, "Hey, you should control your dog!"

I calmly explained to Grizzly Glasses that he should try to improve his relationship with Trudy. She is a sweet dog. She barks at bicycles because dogs do that. She barks at cats, too. Most bicyclists and cats pay her no heed and simply go on their way. Grizzly Glasses is the only one who stops his bike and kicks down the kickstand.

He snarled and grumbled.

Then I remind him of the time last week when he stopped his bike and chased Trudy away from the road, up the side of our lawn, around the house, back up the other side, through the front yard, then straight through the clothesline.

"Things are going too far, Grizzly," I stated matter-of-factly.

"You're not very nice," said Grizzly, "and I find that unusual, because most mental retards I've met were totally friendly."

After a few more pleasantries we parted friends, and I walked away secretly looking forward to the next episode of our little soap opera. Or, should I say, surf opera. Because this Mokuleia neighborhood is definitely a surf city. And Grizzly Glassess is a heavy local down the block at Slivered Rainbows.

I should probably tell you all about Slivered Rainbows, and how it bowls like Ala Moana. But, instead, I'll tell that Grizzly Glasses is nick-named "Tinkler," and he surfs the place totally naked . . . He growls people off the shoulder on crowded days. Nobody drops in.

Considering his macho-exhibitionist tendencies, you'd at least expect Tinkler to be well-hung. He ain't. But, then again, maybe it just shrivels and shrinks out there in that early morning water. I don't know.

Anyway, you probably shouldn't come down to Mokuleia looking for a bunch of great surf. All my neighbors will get mad at me and I'll have to move. And, more than likely, it'll be windy and junky any day you pick. This place is fickle, fickle, fickle. The surf is often good for 90 minutes, then terrible for the rest of the day. There aren't many great-and-consistent waves.

But Mokuleia sure is full of interesting people.

So maybe the thing to do is surf up the road along the North Shore, but come down here for the real interesting barbecues. It's possible that King Crustacean will have some fresh lobsters from the morning surf. 🦞

Alone:
A Trek to Namibia's Skeleton Coast
By Dave Parmenter · SURFER Vol. 35 No. 1 · Jan.1994

One of editor Steve Hawk's primary missions when he took the *SURFER* helm in 1990 was to tap a new wellspring of travel adventure stories for the new decade. His office map soon sprouted a crop of querying pushpins, and he searched high and low for surfers who could write. Dave Parmenter, a former Top 16 pro, quickly earned first right of refusal for travel assignments after establishing himself as an experienced writer. Parmenter usually turned the posh glamour trips down in favor of those that demanded a little less oversight and a little more fortitude. He preferred stretches of coastline that rarely, if ever, saw the footsteps of man. To hear Parmenter tell it, to be immersed in that sort of primeval solitude is akin to time travel. And so it was with the story of his 1993 trek along the ancient alluvial plains of Namibia's Skeleton Coast, which endeavors to form a bridge between the centuries on that desert coast.

Manuel spent his last dawn digging his own grave. The sandstorm had ended with an eerie suddenness late in the night, almost arbitrarily, as if a vengeful god had grown tired of that particular torture and was casting about for a new method. The jackals seemed closer then, their walls amplified by the empty ringing stillness. Finally, toward sunrise, the fog coasted in from the southwest and muffled their mournful retreat back into the hinterland behind the towering sand dunes.

Manuel drank of the fog by wringing the dampened square of canvas into his mouth. A pitiful few drops of brackish water, soaked up instantly by a bloodstream thick and sluggish after five days of unbearable thirst. But it was enough to keep his throat from fusing shut and a little strength seeped into his limbs. Strength to dig.

A lone castaway after his ship had torn its bottom to shreds on some fog-shrouded offshore reef, Manuel was just another of the growing ranks of doomed sailors cast up on the alien shores of southwestern Africa. As the Portuguese began pushing their barques south of the Horn of Africa in the mid-15th century, they ran into a welter of fog, wind and currents that seemed to work in malevolent collusion to strip timber from keels and flesh from bone.

Manuel dug and thought how it was odd what finally made man give up hope. Vanity. His arm had been lacerated on barnacles during the struggle ashore and now, days later, was streaked with angry, sup-purating sores. Gangrene. The realization struck him that even if by some miracle he was saved immediately, he would lose his arm, and the thought of being less than a whole man withered his resolve.

Not that there was any hope of being saved. The coast unspooled for hundreds of miles either way; a brutal empire of sand dunes and drifting fog, unrelieved by even the slightest trace of vegetation. The only water came from the morning fog each night once the daily sand-storms died. The beach was littered with seal skulls and mangled bits of pelt. At dusk, the jackals and hyenas would begin skulking out to the sea colony on the headland, and he would hear the horrifying cries of the seal pups being dragged away from their mothers, fol-lowed by the grunts and snuffling of the dogs as they set upon their prey. Manuel could hear the bones crunching in the oversize jaws, and he spent the nights shivering in a hollow at the base of a small dune, trying to drown out the slaughter by repeating prayers and psalms over and over, aloud, until his voice cracked or he shivered himself asleep.

Manuel had always been a devoutly religious man. For the first day or so as a castaway, he had brandished his childlike faith as one would hold a cross to a vampire. But now, with his gangrenous, evil-smelling arm drawing the jackals nearer and nearer in their death-vigil, he had a sudden and terrifying glimpse at the true workings of life, a lightning-flash illumination of a nightmarish charnel house that had lain hidden beneath the façade of incense and salvation and braying church organs.

He finished digging into the side of the dune. It was big enough to crouch in, and he had piled up the sand in a loose crest overhead so the wind would blow it over him. Not much time left. His throat had begun to glue shut, and he had heard when a man's eyes glim-mered with bright light it was over soon after. As long as the jackals didn't get to him, Manuel thought, anything but that. He crouched in the hole and hugged his knees, drained of his last energy, and waited for the lights to sear his vision. After a while the wind came up strong from the southwest, scraping away the fog and blasting curling wraiths of sand along the beach. The fine, powdery crest over Manuel showered down around his feet in little sprinkles at first, then mounds. By midafternoon, the little grotto was half-filled. The sand weighed against Manuel's chest, but he was far, far away in an impossibly green garden where water poured from fountains with the sweet tones of music. The sand blew all that night, and all through the next day.

I was sitting out in the lineup alone at a perfect left point on Namibia's Skeleton Coast, popping kelp bulbs and daydreaming between sets. The sun was going down and I was trying, with as much empathy as I could muster, to imagine what it must have been like to be suddenly flung onto these shores after some disaster at sea and to realize the utter hopelessness of it. I pondered the riddle of the "crouching skeleton," a man found buried alive very close to where I was surfing, hunched in a little womb-like grave. Most of the books dealing with the shipwreck lore of the Skeleton Coast found it to be a mystery. They concluded he must have been buried in a sandstorm while taking shelter in a hole. Just another riddle among hundreds on this coast.

Then I saw the jackal. He was on a little rise at the top of the point 30 yards away, just sitting on his haunches staring at me. At first I thought he was curious, with his pricked-up ears and comically serious stare. In our culture, generations removed from real wilderness, we anthropomorphize animals. Dogs "smile," lions wear crowns and bears are cute, cuddly things that bounce on our laundry.

It didn't take me long to understand that the jackal was sizing me up as potential prey, scanning through the predator checklist for some sign that I might fit the profile: old, young, weak, sick . . . alone? Even though there was absolutely no danger, it gave me a shiver to be considered as food, as well as a little insight into why a man might prefer premature burial to being jackal fodder like the countless torn seals that carpeted every square foot of shoreline for miles around the rookery at the cape.

Carnage is what the Skeleton Coast is all about. The name is derived from the profusion of bones strewn along a 400-mile swath on the northern coast of Namibia. From literally any random vantage point, some sort of pitiful remains can be seen, bleached whale ribs, broken-backed ships, piles of seal bones, and perhaps the tangled skeleton of some hapless castaway who made it ashore and died wishing he hadn't.

I was pretty keen on making it to shore myself. The last set of the day hit the outer indicator at Robbenspunt and filed down the half-mile point toward my lineup, the second perfect left point in a 2-mile stretch. With a rookery of 100,000 Cape fur seals just up the point, there's a pretty good chance of some sort of encounter with a white shark. Also, lions have been known, in years of drought, to sneak up on the seals as they sleep and have a little high-cholesterol snack. Most surfers live in a smug cocoon of invulnerability, and why not. With a good car in view, a jerrycan of water, a wetsuit, Swiss Army knife, duct tape and a little common sense, surfers are practically immortal. But with the sun all but gone, surfing alone without a leash, the nearest town 100 miles away, I began to feel the hair stand up on the back of my neck, and shivered to some involuntary primordial warning surging down my spine. A quarter-mile down the point, Lance had lit up the car as he packed away the gear—a cozy sphere of warmth and safety. I was tired of loitering in the food chain. The first wave of the set approached, a perfect 5-foot wall that roped down the point for 200 yards. I caught it, pulled my feet out of Triassic Park as I stood, and glided toward the 20th century.

"Puff Adder bites jogger three times!" screeched the bold headline. A "colored" newsboy stood in the median, one foot on his bundle of papers to keep them from blowing away in the Capetown gale. I'm in South Africa all right, I thought. Fresh off the plane from a mild-mannered summer in California, I couldn't reckon with this bizarre world where raging winter storms spun out of the southern ocean still tasting of Antarctica, and poisonous snakes still vented their reptilian angst on innocent joggers.

It had been five years since I had been to Capetown. Much had changed, and local surfer/photographer Lance Slabbert gave me the rundown as we tore through the gloom that creamed into the sloping sandstone cake layers of the famous Table Mountain. South Africa could well be the most beautiful country in the world, especially for a surfer. I fell in love with it long before I'd even been there, enchanted by Bruce Brown's voice-over in *Endless Summer*: "If you want to be alone in South Africa, you're welcome to do so." That and his vistas of empty highways, buzzing veldt and huge sand dunes hiding perfect pointbreaks in sphinx-like secrecy. When California was all about black beaver-tail wetsuits, circling the wagons against outsiders, buying the "right" to surf the Ranch, lifeguards and blackball, South Africa promised a new, adventurous melding of archetypes: Allan Quatermain crossed with Kevin Naughton, a fresh romantic offshoot from the tired old roots of Waikiki beach boys and Santa Monica misanthropes.

But now, South Africa seems to be in sad decline. And it's nothing like what you think, not nearly as simple as your "Free Mandela" bumper sticker on the ol' Volvo. Say what you will about apartheid, injustice and civil rights from your lofty American pulpit, but unless you've been there, you have no opinion. South Africa is an antipodean America, with common bloodlines. In both cases, whites migrated away from bureaucracy into native tribes with Bible-thumbing arrogance. The difference, and the real reason South Africa is in the international doghouse, is that our grim deeds were done long before CNN and bumper stickers.

Arm the Apaches with dirt-cheap AK-47s, waggle some Fervent Insurgency Dogma in front of them and, basically, you've got South Africa in 1993. Driving around the outskirts of a city like Capetown, snipers take occasional potshots at passing motorists. Bridges and overpasses are approached with dread, as terrorists have taken to hurling bricks into oncoming windshields. The N-2 freeway out to the airport has been dubbed "Hell Run," as it passes near a squatter camp with an apparently limitless quarry of bricks. It's Super Mario Capetown, with everyone zooming through the narrow, hilly lanes, dodging Koopas and Goombas, seemingly always in a manic rush to reach home—in most cases pastoral whitewashed Cape Dutch cottages that belie surveillance and alarm systems that would rival Fort Knox.

The second largest growth industry in South Africa is home protection: guns, alarms, video monitors, window bars. The largest is getting the hell out. The business sections of the newspapers are flooded with immigration ads entreating South Africa's best and brightest (and richest) to move overseas to more stable havens like Toronto, Sydney or Laguna Beach, where if a snake bit you it would probably be only once, and at least you could sue somebody or sell the screen rights.

Of course, there's always Namibia. Lots of people were moving up into that newly independent country, which was formerly a sort of territory of South Africa. I had stopped at Windhoek, Namibia's capital, on a flight years ago, leaving me with the impression that Namibia was 300,000 square miles of Bakersfield. But Lance had been up there on a surf trip recently, and his description of quaint colonial seaside towns, stately dunes and lonely left pointbreaks sounded much more sporting than the usual safari to J-Bay, which has become more and more a Surf City. I could picture Derek Hynd patrolling that fabled lava point, notebook in hand, wallowing in self-imposed exile, seeking his canine brethren. Also, Pro World was due to arrive soon, and that alone was a good reason to head off in the opposite direction.

Leaving Capetown and driving to the Skeleton Coast is the spiritual equivalent of going on safari from Dana Point to Vancouver . . . in 1936. The Namibian coastline is roughly the same length as that of California, but with twice the total area. Namibia means "land of no people," and even then most of the million or so inhabitants live in landlocked Windhoek or a narrow swale of arable land along the northern border near Angola. The coast is basically empty.

Just a few hours out of Capetown, the highway is deserted. Small towns are spaced farther and farther apart, finally giving way to forlorn, ramshackle settlements that seem to be nothing more than concessions to the shortcomings of the average gas tank. There are few towns on the coast from the cape all the way to Angola, as there are only a handful of decent harbors. Most can only be reached via a 50- or 100-mile sidetrack on a graded dirt road. Heading to the coast off the N-7, the main north-to-south highway, these secondary roads can be traveled hours without seeing another vehicle.

It seemed completely normal, then, when we pulled up at the legendary Elands Bay on a gorgeous, offshore, 6-foot morning and there was . . . no one out. There were a few guys camped next to their car, trying to work up a mojo next to a crude fire pit. They were in no rush. I got to fulfill a boyhood dream by surfing Elands as good as it gets for almost an hour, completely alone. It's a world-class left point often described as a flopped-negative cousin to Jeffreys Bay. But surfing in Atlantic waters on the west coast is a far cry from the comparative warmth of Jeffreys Bay 400 miles away in the more temperate Indian Ocean. At Elands, the water was like cold Santa Cruz, about 53 degrees. The icy Benguela Current socks a stiff upper-cut punch into the guts of southwest Africa, sweeping in chilled water from the Antarctic netherworld. The water temperature is rarely over 55 degrees. Thick and pulpy with upwelled plankton, the increased water density feels "faster," and the illusion of speed is increased as you fly through the tangle of bull kelp, the muscular bulbs flashing by like the blurred white lines on a highway.

There were 300 miles more of promising coastline before the Namibian border. On the map, the coast was kinked with the telltale squiggles of one left point after another. But three quarters of this coastline is the domain of the infamous De Beers Diamond Company, which invented localism 60 years before Dora first kicked his board as a kook wearing cutoffs. Security measures and treatment of trespassers is rumored to be harsh, sometimes beyond the law. All things being equal, I'd rather face some grumpy, walrusine "owner" at the Ranch than an X-ray and sigmoidoscope at gunpoint.

Here is the world's last great reserve of temperate climate surf, virtually untapped from Lambert's Bay to Walvis Bay. Seven hundred miles of points, reefs and beaches have been a *sperrgebiet* or "forbidden region" since Duke Kahanamoku was about 6 years old. The same antediluvian alchemy that made this the richest diamond field in the world also gave it limitless surf potential, with alluvial headlands and ancient, upthrust marine terraces forming a serrated coastline the length of Baja.

Lance had arranged for us to visit a 50-mile chunk of one of the mines. After filling out security-clearance forms and waiting around a few days, we were allowed to enter as "official visitors."

In one short afternoon, even with our limited access to the beaches, we catalogued a half-dozen world-class waves easily comparable to the Margaret River region of Western Australia. Headland points were spaced at regular intervals, often flanked by grinding reef peaks or wedging beachbreak—the Ranch if Wayne Lynch designed it. Toward evening, we surfed a right point that was like a high-voltage Supertubes. Eight to 10 feet and no way of knowing if it had been surfed before. In the middle of the bay was a gaping left that poured over a shallow web of sandstone reef. From talking to people in the area, we're fairly certain some lucky guys surf on this coast occasionally. If you don't mind surfing alone in the kind of chilly waters that scream "White shark!" like a berserk Ouija board, and if you don't object to the odd X-ray and personal body search, this place is for you.

The farther we got from Capetown, the deeper we plunged into Afrikaner territory. The accents grew thicker and thicker and the food more indigestible. Afrikaners are looked down upon as provincial rednecks by the English, but they really are the heart and soul of all that is good and bad in South Africa. The Afrikaans language sounds like variety show mimicry of Colonel Klink, a harsh-sounding derivative of Dutch and Flemish. "Thank you" sounds exactly like "buy a donkey," and "please," or "*assebleif*," sounds like some arcane gay password. And "*drankewinkle*," or "bottle shop," sounds like some monstrous derivative of the great Australian party trick "spitting the winkle," but let's not give them any ideas.

It was a Friday evening when we crossed the border into Namibia, and Afrikaner families were flooding over from their spartan farm towns, heading into the parks and reserves of Namibia like beleaguered *Norteamericanos* stumbling into Baja for a little Margaritaville respite.

Afrikaners are great carnivores. Waiting in line at the border for our passports to get stamped, I exchanged pleasantries with a family who had seen our surfboards on the car. I told them we were going up to the Skeleton Coast to do a little surfing, and they looked at me with that forced grin used around the world to tolerate eccentrics and crackpots. They were heading up to Windhoek on a pilgrimage to see "1,000 Meters-O-Meat," an attempt to cook the world's biggest shish kebab at a rugby stadium. A black day indeed for the slower cattle in the herd, and a red-letter day for Clark W. Griswolds everywhere.

Some will contend that man's greatest achievement is language or flight or the printing press. But on a bone-rattling, kidney-torquing journey into the Namibian outback, you'd swear that the pinnacle of human left-brain accomplishment is . . . duct tape. After 750 miles of jouncing along at 85 mph, everything not welded in place was working loose. Mysterious little bolts and screws littered the floorboard, tapes warbled and choked, and the peanut butter never had to be stirred. This was the Skeleton Road, a bitumen artery through the middle of Namibia, ramrod straight at times for hundreds of miles. Twice a day, a town would appear ahead, wavering in mirage, with osterizing dustdevils scraping across the flinty, rust-orange gravel plains. A gas station, some sad little plywood shanties and gaily painted donkey carts: a Baja fish camp plopped down in an artist's conception of Mars.

There are two strategies for occupants of the desert. Hole up and accept the worst, or migrate. The Namib Desert is the oldest desert in the world; its inhabitants have had some 80 million years to get their acts together. Ants lick the dew off one another's backs, lions scavenge dead whales along the littoral, and the weltwitschia, the bizarre "living fossil plant," lives up to 2,000 years on the wafting fog.

The few surfers in Namibia have had to adapt to a brutal environment that is a long, long way from Polynesia Idyll. The cold water creates a semipermanent canopy of fog, up to 340 days a year. The water is made colder by the prevailing southwesterly trades, a chill rasp of wind that churns up the cooler, nutrient-rich water from the deep, and gives the beaches a briny red-tide smell. The only surf not completely blown to rags by the southwesterlies are the twin left points of Robbenspunt, a hundred miles from the nearest population. Beachbreak, beachbreak everywhere, and not a peak to surf. One day, we scrutinized 50 miles of coast, and although it was a sunny, offshore, 4-foot day, and I applied the dogged search pattern used to survive 17 years of similar cruelty on California's Central Coast, we didn't find one decent peak.

By this time, Lance had imported his Performance Seals to add what magazine editors call "color contrast." I'm not a very colorful or even modern surfer. I have no tattoos, and if my fins slide out I feel a great shame. Our Performance Seals were very nice kids from Durban: Carl and Paul. Like almost all young South African surfers, they were polite, well-behaved gremmies who put their labels right where their sponsors told them and phoned home twice a week. They also had that unique adolescent ability to fold up and shut down like C-3PO and sleep anywhere at the slightest hint of downtime.

And we had plenty of downtime on the 100-mile drive up to Robbenspunt. Camping nearby was out of the question. Aside from the sandstorms and nightly jackal and hyena sorties, there was the biting, litterbox stench of 100,000 seals stewing in their own effluvia. Technically, it's illegal to surf the top point because the cape is a seal reserve, and the park wardens don't want the seals "startled." I don't see the sense in this, as seals are like cows: they're permanently startled. Anyway, the marine bovines have staked out the whole top of the point and swim through the lineup in such thick herds that the waves are literally warped into sagging ruin. A 6-foot wave will peel through this pinniped Ganges for hundreds of yards, finally elbowing its way into an uncontaminated final run down the point, which is still twice the length of a good Rincon wave.

Deeper into the bay is another point next to some settlement that appears to have been built piece by piece from shipwreck detritus. Until recently, an old German caretaker would sit out on the porch with a shotgun to keep away pesky surfers. When we arrived, the place was deserted. We didn't see another surfer in two weeks of surfing here. Four- to 5-foot lines peeled over the delicately ribbed sand bottom, translucent green in the settled calm of the inner bay. Not a gnarly Indonesian racetrack, but not some snail's-pace California point, either. Surfers have been hounding Scorpion Bay for 15 years without surf as good as it gets here monthly.

In the winter months, high-pressure areas fatten and bulge in the interior of southern Africa, occasionally steepening to form a hot, dry offshore wind not unlike the Santa Anas in California. This is the dreaded Namibian *ostwind*, an unnerving, grating rasp that scrapes up sand, melds into a gritty furnace blast and brings life to a standstill for days at a time. Temperatures can exceed 100 degrees, and the sandstorms are so thick that you often can't see 20 yards ahead. During *ostwinds*, a rime of fine dust covers every surface in even the most tightly sealed home. Cars have their number plates scoured to illegibility. Teeth take on an unpleasant abrasive sensation. Tempers flare at stoplights, and after a week under the Vulcan canopy, the suicide rate always soars.

Driving around in a sandstorm, we watched huge rooster tails of sand curling off the crests of giant dunes being torn into tornadic rotors. Flung instantly into the sea, they flailed into the spume of oncoming waves, blotching the white spray into a brown haze. Sea birds fluttered in awkward sideslip with grimaces of strained concentration. In town, Lance had to jerk the car out of the path of one stout old Germanic matron who had wobbled into the road from either heat-stroke or sand-blindness, walking with that erratic pattern that on the savanna says, "Fair game!"

In the desert, time is measured on a vaster scale than the clocks and calendars of man. Standing on the ridge of the highest dune for miles, my jacket and pants cracking in the wind like a luffing mainsheet, I watched a sandstorm swirl over thousands of acres of trackless dunes. Casting aside the measure of our pitiful 70 or so years on the planet, a deceitful benchmark, I could see this desert as a sort of antimatter ocean. Even on our day-to-day clock, dunes will crest and "break" like an ocean wave when they get to steep, sending out a roar. How would the desert appear from the vantage point of thousands of years of time-lapse photography? Wouldn't it appear to swell and crest in the ceaseless wind side by side with the Atlantic?

People from rich, green lands have always had to reconcile their mortality when confronted by the desert. Here a plant may live 2,000 years, diamonds are forever, and a man's tracks may last a thousand years on the delicate gravel plains. In the rain forest, things topple hourly and decay under a riot of growth and change, but here in the desert, the ebb and flow of an entire race of people is a mere second hand on the geologic clock that marks the passage of waterless eons and patient, creeping dunes.

The Bushmen of the nearby Kalahari Desert have acquired from their desolate origins a pragmatic grasp of mortality not unlike that learned on the Skeleton Coast amid the poking ribs of men and ships long dead. To them, there is no afterlife, no trumpets blaring at Pearly Gates. "When we die, we die," they shrug. "The wind blows away our footprints and that is the end of us."

While his predecessors at the *SURFER* helm wrote the lion's share of the features for the magazine, Steve Hawk spent more of his time as editor recruiting and orchestrating a diverse staff of in-house and in-the-field writers. His introduction of the monthly "Intro" column, two of which are included here, made him one of the most approachable and self-effacing editors in the magazine's history. Equal parts warm, witty, and authoritative, Hawk managed each month to coax his readers into an ideal reading repose, relying on personal experiences that frequently touched on larger surfing themes.

Getting Drilled

By Steve Hawk · SURFER Vol. 36 No. 11 · November 1995

I had to get my ear drilled a couple of months ago. Had a bad case of surfer's ear (or what insurance companies call exostosis). Surfer's ear is a stupid affliction—not because of the way you get it, but because the biological cause doesn't make sense. It's as if the Army Corps of Engineers had drawn up the ear's strategy for self-protection.

Surfer's ear works something like this: when you spend a lot of time in cold water, the body decides that the eardrum should be kept warm. Why? No one knows. Maybe it's tired of wearing Ugg boots. So, to keep the drum cozy, the bones that encircle the ear canal have this special feature that causes them to get stimulated by cold. You surf, they grow. Eventually, the bony growth seals off the canal, thus rendering the owner deaf and leaving the drum vulnerable to infection. It makes about as much sense as blocking a harbor entrance with rocks to keep the boats safe, and then suddenly realizing that the boats are now worthless.

Anyway, surfer's ear is no fun. Nor is the cure. They knock you out, the doctor carves away for a few hours, and you wake up wearing what appears to be a Wonderbra on your head.

Whenever I describe the operation to friends who don't surf, and tell them I'd already had both ears done 10 years ago, they look at me like I'm crazy—as if maybe I'm the kind of person who likes to wear a Wonderbra on his head.

"Why don't you wear ear plugs?" they say.

"Don't seem to help."

"Well, did you ever think that maybe you should just, you know, maybe . . . just, like, stop?"

"Stop surfing?"

"Yes."

"Get out of my house."

Insulting as it may be, that question is interesting to ponder—especially now that I've been out of the water for six weeks. How much am I willing to give up for surfing? For instance, if I knew for certain that surfing would cause me to go deaf in one ear, would I keep doing it? Of course. No question. What about both ears? Tough call. Maybe.

Over the past few days I've put the same question to several friends: If you knew that the only way you'd be able to surf again would be to voluntarily go deaf, would you do it? About half said yes—they'd rather surf than hear.

So I pushed it.

Would you give up an eye? Yes.

How about money? Would you quit for $100 million? The answer was unanimous: Get real. Who cares how much money you have if you can't surf?

Then it occurred to me that all serious surfers ponder such questions almost every day. From the moment the sport sucks us in, material and physical sacrifices are simply part of the program. We give up that shot at Little League All-Stars. We let our GPAs slip just a touch. We risk skin cancer. We lose girlfriends. We suffer chronic back pain. We turn down great job offers in Denver. We let doctors stick drills in our ears.

Of course, not all such sacrifices are necessary. We can study harder, stretch our backs each morning, and work overtime during flat spells. In my case, I can fork over money for custom-fit ear plugs. In fact, a friend of mine who should know about such things thinks it's possible to halt exostosis altogether. The theory is to keep the whole ear zone warm. He wears neoprene hoods year-round, and he's never had a problem.

Now *there's* a sacrifice. I mean, take my eye. Let me go deaf. But a squid lid? In July? Get real.

My Dad Never Surfed

By Steve Hawk · SURFER Vol 37 No. 2 · February 1996

Let me rephrase that: My dad never learned to surf. He tried it a couple of times in the early '60s, back when he and my mom owned a hamburger stand on the beach in San Diego. During one of Dad's first go-outs, his board smashed him in the face and shoved his lower front teeth clear through the skin below his lip so that it looked for a few ghastly hours like he had a second mouth. The accident left a modest scar, the kind that adds character rather than deforms, and when I was small I used to touch it sometimes and he'd tell me the story again, describing in detail how he'd shocked my mom and the nurses by sticking his tongue out the slit before the doctor stitched it up. He was proud of the prank, and I was always pretty stoked to hear about it.

Unfortunately, the accident chased him away from the sport, and though we would come to spend many hours together at the beach and in the ocean, it saddens me a bit now to think of how much closer we might have been if we'd both been surfers. We might have chased swells, split a few peaks, hooted for each other's barrels.

He died a couple of months ago, so this stuff is on my mind.

Although he didn't join me in the lineup, my dad was unwavering in his support of my obsession. When I was about 14, he gave me my first board. This was at the height of the shortboard revolution. Like a lot of people at the time, my dad bought a clunky, yellowing piece-of-crap longboard, chopped off the nose, reglassed it, and turned it into a clunky, yellowing piece-of-crap shortboard. A few waves into my first session, the board hit me in the face and bloodied my lip. Dad watched from shore and met me in the shallows. "Do me a favor," he said. "Don't tell your mother."

Later, he'd drive me to contests at daybreak and stand on the sand with a steaming coffee cup while I groveled through heats. In high school, he'd take me and my friends on camping trips to Baja, where he'd film us with a Super-8 movie camera. Through all of this, I don't remember him ever once suggesting that riding waves might be a waste of time.

Now that I have a son of my own, I realize that almost everything I need to know about fatherhood I learned from my father. But the single most memorable lesson has nothing to do with surfing—or maybe everything to do with surfing. It happened one hot September day when I was about 10. I was sitting in school, nursing a bad case of the post-summer-time blues, when I looked up to see my dad standing in the classroom doorway. He whispered something to the teacher, then motioned for me to follow him outside. I worried a lot as a kid, so I figured I was about to hear some terrible news.

"The yellowtail are biting," he finally said when we got to his car. "I thought we might go catch a few."

"Yellowtail? Fishing? What about school?"

He smiled. "I told the principal you had a doctor's appointment. Dr. Davy Jones."

And so we ditched school, my dad and I. We drove to Imperial Beach, boarded a party boat, and spent the afternoon hoisting tuna out of the sea.

I didn't see it at the time, but I realize now that that fishing trip forever altered my internal priority list. Although I went on to be a fairly reliable student, I also knew deep in my bones that school (and, by extension, my future career) was only part of the picture. For a long time, I assumed that the lesson from Dad was that doing what you love is as important as doing what you have to do to get by. But now I realize that the true message was much more basic, and much more potent. It was about family, about parents and children, father and son.

And while the tangible impact of that unspoken speech on my life will be impossible to chart, I do know that one day it will manifest itself in a very specific way. One day, maybe 10 or 12 years from now, a boy named Will Hawk will be sitting in class, bored, and look up in shock to see his father standing in the doorway. His father will tell the principal that Will has an appointment with a certain Dr. Jones. Then his father will take him surfing. We'll ditch school, my son and I. And if I'm lucky, my son will learn a lesson that he'll pass on someday to his own kids.

I heard you, old man. 🏄

Father, Son, Holy Spirit

By Bruce Jenkins · SURFER Vol. 36 No. 3 · March 1995

By 1995, Tom Curren's three world titles had transformed the United States into a surfing powerhouse. Although the 31-year-old surfer was nearly five years removed from full-time competition, and he typically played hard-to-get with the surf media, "Curren-mania" was as strong as ever. Those who remembered his father, 1950s big-wave legend Pat Curren, saw in Tom's reclusive behavior an uncanny father/son resemblance. Pat had long since faded from the view of the surf world, having left his family, destination unknown, when Tom was just 16 years old. Acting on a tip like a pursuing G-man, Bay Area sportswriter Bruce Jenkins hunted the elder Curren down in Mexico, hoping to unearth some insights into one of surfing's most intriguing families. This poignant family saga is the result of his persistence.

The road to Pat Curren's place leads to nowhere. It is the province of emaciated cows, soft-eyed burros and green iguanas, lurching to attention as the odd vehicle rolls by. It's a slice of the Old West, stark and remote near the southern tip of Baja, and the few people who live there find solace in the desolation.

Most of them are surfers, prominent names from the sport's glorious past. All of them crave the privacy that comes with a barren landscape, dirt roads and seldom-ridden pointbreaks. Not one of them, however, is as committed to the lifestyle as Pat Curren.

He lives in an old, beat-up trailer with his dog, his surfboards and a set of tools, because that's exactly how he likes it. Not even the incredible career of his son, Tom Curren, arguably the greatest surfer of all time, has brought the man out of the wilderness. The two haven't seen each other on Pat's turf in nine years. They both seem to fancy the idea, but the breakup of the Curren family left scars, and somehow the reunion just hasn't happened.

He is a full 30 years removed from his glory. From the fall of 1957 through the spring of 1962—the first five seasons of Waimea Bay's history—nobody rode the Bay bigger, better or with more calculated precision than Pat Curren. He also shaped the finest big-wave guns of his time. His legend is duly acknowledged by the likes of Greg Noll, Mike Doyle and Peter Cole, who said without hesitation, "Pat was the master, the king of Waimea. To this day, I've never seen anybody get bigger, cleaner waves or ride them so well."

The rewards? None, by his own choosing. Curren was always one to flee before a place got spoiled: Windansea, the North Shore, even Costa Rica—and he is found today in full retreat from civilization. He'll surface occasionally for a gathering of old-time surfers or the chance to shape some classic guns for discerning buyers. But mostly it's just Pat and his Jack Russell terrier in the wilds of Mexico, and everybody else be damned.

He is not easily reached, in any sense. I had the good fortune of tackling the washboard roads with Jim Hart, a transplanted South Bay surfer who has lived and worked in the Los Cabos area for eight years. He knew how to find Curren, and we approached him together on a sweltering August day. But we arrived with trepidation.

For one thing, Curren had sent a very direct message that he did not want to be interviewed. That came as no surprise to Noll, who said, "This guy hardly talks to people he knows. He's very quiet, and can be very intimidating. It's the first two minutes you gotta worry about, because this guy can spot bullshit from a mile away. You'll know within 30 seconds if you're an asshole."

"You're going down there?" said Tom Curren. "Well . . . good luck. Bring some beer. That might help."

We brought a case. Pat Curren had no idea what to do with his unexpected visitors, but the beer got his attention. We bought ourselves a minute or two as he stashed it in his refrigerator.

"Got a couple messages for you," I volunteered nervously. "Peter Cole says he's still mad at you for stealing his Thanksgiving dinner in 1959. And Greg Noll says you're the best chicken-stealing partner he ever had."

A thin smile of recollection crossed Curren's face as he cracked open a beer. Somehow, the three of us got seated in some old, creaky chairs, signifying progress. But I was still far from an actual interview. "Didn't you get the message I sent?" said Curren. "Because to tell you the truth, I don't want to do this."

Just on a lark, I mentioned Jose Angel, the great big-wave surfer from Curren's day. Another little light went on. "Jose was the best man at my wedding," he said, admiringly. "Toughest man I ever knew."

Thus began about an hour of conversation with one of surfing's most reclusive figures. Knowing I was walking the thin line of intrusion, I didn't even think of hauling out my notepad until Curren got up to take a leak. Right then, a little bit of the Curren mystique took hold. I had a little tape recorder in my bag, and while I intended to keep it there, I figured I'd just turn the thing on, maybe pick up a few choice sounds or comments.

It wouldn't work. Here was a tremendously reliable machine, never gave me a single problem before, and it worked beautifully that very same night. But I swear, it would not work on Pat Curren's property.

After a few minutes he asked, "You guys ready?" and I knew we had crossed the line. He was offering more beer. Hell, I said yes, and I wasn't even ready.

They were all crazy back then. Not modern-day crazy, with the gangs and the crack cocaine and the drive-by shootings, but innocent crazy. To be a La Jolla surfer in the '50s meant you never held back: in your drinking, your partying or especially your surfiing, where the test of skill was a double-overhead day at Windansea. Nobody savored that life, or typified it more, than Patrick King Curren.

Everyone took pride in his home area, but just as surely, everyone in California knew there was something different about the La Jolla guys: Curren, Mike Diffenderfer, Wayne Land, Al Nelson, the Eckstrom brothers, Ricky Naish, Buzzy Bent, Tiny Brain Thomas, Billy Graham, Butch Van Artsdalen. "The most rebellious group of people I ever met," said Fred Van Dyke, who came out of Santa Cruz. "I'm sure some of them came from rich families, but they rejected that kind of life, ridiculed it. If a guy made some money, he'd go out and buy everybody food and drink, and the next day he'd be scrounging for a cup of coffee. They were like wild animals."

With the Mexican border beckoning, groups of them would go on blind-drunk Tijuana rages for days, waking up on some roadside without a clue where they were. Pranks and daredevil stunts were the very essence of their lives.

They all surfed big Windansea—out of sheer determination, if not raw talent—and when the first films and still photos arrived with big-wave images of Hawaii, nearly all of them made the pilgrimage. Curren didn't even start surfing until 1950, the year he turned 18, but by 1955 he was among the first serious wave of California surfers to take on Makaha and Sunset.

"Nobody taught me," Curren said. "Does anybody teach anybody? It's kind of like learning how to ride a bike. Somebody gives you a push, then watches you crash into a pole."

Curren was a little older than the rest, and with his lifestyle honed by the La Jolla days, he set the tone for North Shore living. "He molded it into a state-of-the-art lifestyle," said Noll. "He had this terrible old '36 Plymouth, probably the shittiest car of all time, and the cops gave him a bunch of crap about having the front windshield knocked out. Pat always had this way about him, getting from Point A to B in the shortest distance, without getting real complicated. So he just jerked out one of the side windows and wedged it onto the driver's side, and he got away with that for a couple months. That was his idea of a windshield."

The North Shore was nothing but farmland back then, "and you basically had a bunch of local people growing food, raising pigs and chickens," said Noll. "When Pat and I went on patrol, there wasn't a chicken or a duck that was safe. I can still see us running down the beach at

Pupukea with a big fat chicken in each hand, calves burning in the soft sand with a couple of pit bulls on our ass. We'd barbecue 'em up later and have a hell of a dinner. Pat was also a pretty decent fisherman and a great diver. So between the ocean, the chickens and the ducks, he got along pretty good."

They lived out of cars and panel trucks, slept on the beach when all else failed, and occasionally got to rent an actual building. In a truly inspired moment, Curren created a surfer's palace that came to be known as Meade Hall. "It was mostly Pat and the La Jolla guys—maybe 10 guys altogether," said Van Dyke. "It was a three-bedroom, fully furnished place for $65 a month across from Ke Iki Road. Pat went in there like always, checked it out, didn't say anything. Then he lined up everybody for a meeting and the plan unfolded. Two days later, they had completely gutted the place. Just tore the insides out of it. With the leftover lumber they built surfboard racks along the side and a giant eating table down the middle. Pat got the Meade Hall idea from the old King Arthur books. That was the meeting place for all valiant gladiators."

Ricky Grigg said Curren would sit at the head of the table, often wearing a Viking hat, "and he'd pound on the table, going, 'Ahh! Eat! We hungry! Gotta surf big waves tomorrow! Take wife and pull her by hair into room!' Just totally joking around. I mean, the most Pat would ever say in a day was about eight words, and I just said all eight of 'em."

Needless to say, the landlord wasn't stoked. When he showed up a month later to collect the rent, Meade Hall died a tragic death.

Quite against his will, Curren was becoming legendary around the North Shore. Mike Doyle made his first trip in the fall of 1959, and in his book *Morning Glass* he captured the Curren mystique:

"From the way people talked about Pat Curren, I imagined him to be the greatest surfer in the world, a magnificent physical specimen, with an electrifying personality," Doyle wrote. "But when Curren finally arrived and we met him at the airport, I was disappointed. He was gaunt and pale, with a pointed chin, sunken cheeks and worried eyes. He had a military haircut, was real quiet and moody. On the drive back to the North Shore, he didn't say one word.

"Little by little, I learned more about Pat Curren: He made his living as a professional diver working the offshore oil platforms back in California. He was close to 30 years old, a bit of a loner, and I soon found out that Curren wasn't the dazzling surfer I had imagined. He had guts and rode the hell out of the biggest waves, but what really set Curren apart was that he made the most beautiful, streamlined boards any of us had ever seen. Each one of his boards was a cross between a work of art and a weapon, like some beautifully crafted spear."

There was nothing quite like the Curren touch. He had shaped for Dale Velzy back home, and by the late '50s, he was making the definitive boards for Waimea Bay. "Pat was putting rocker in his boards, which really set him apart," said Van Dyke. "If you needed a board in a day or two, he'd have it right there on your lawn, and he did all this with some really crude tools. If challenged, this guy could shape a redwood board with a draw knife."

"A lot of people don't realize that Pat and Diffenderfer were shaping way ahead of Dick Brewer," said Cole. "Pat was the first guy to produce the ultimate gun. Joe Quigg and Bob Shepherd were making nice boards for all-around surfing, but Pat made the stiletto, specifically for Waimea, where you go from Point A to Point B on the biggest wave that comes through."

"No question about it," Grigg concurred. "He was the best shaper. Number one. He had a real concept of the elephant gun. First guy to shape it, first guy to ride it. He was so respected, he had a cult following, kind of like David Koresh (laughs). He was a guru."

"He didn't want to be, though," said Cole. "That was the amazing thing. He did not want to be a leader. I think guys just gravitated to him."

They say Curren could easily go a full day without speaking—which was remarkable, for when it came to a pure sense of humor, he was an ace in any company. "He had that sly little grin, and almost everything he did had a taste of humor," said filmmaker Bruce Brown. "He's the kind of guy who would pour lighter fluid into his mouth, light a match and go, 'Hey, watch this' and poof! Big explosion. Then he'd give you that funny little grin and walk away. He'd be glassing surfboards in his kitchen, figuring you might sit there and watch for a while, and next thing you know, you're stuck to the floor. One time he showed up in Hawaii with nothing but a 10-pound sack of flour for making tortillas. That was his luggage."

In the words of virtually everyone interviewed, "There are a million Pat Curren stories." Here are a few:

Van Dyke: "Guys like Tommy Zahn, Buzzy Trent and I did a lot of training at Ala Moana—running, paddling, swimming, the whole thing. Tommy Zahn was a real fanatic. Curren didn't really care about training. So we're all down there one day and Pat's sort of standing around, smoking a cigarette with a beer in his hand. He says to Tommy, 'Race you the length of the Ala Moana channel.' Well, Tommy just starts laughing. 'You gotta be kidding,' he says. 'I'll be kicking in your face.' But everybody gathers around for this, knowing what Pat's capable of. Well, Curren just kills him. Leaves him in the dust. I thought Tommy was gonna commit suicide."

Grigg: "We were surfing a solid 25-foot day at Waimea one late afternoon, perfect conditions, sun going down, when we see this guy Jim Caldwell out there—bodysurfing! He was a collegiate swimmer at USC, and I guess he figured he'd get the feel of some big waves. A little before dark this huge set came in, so big that Jim couldn't get around it on the shoulder. He was in 60 feet of water and he still hit bottom. He ended up in mid-bay, screaming for help. Pat and I got over there, but the current was taking him so fast toward the rocks there was no way he could make it. Now it's just about dark. Pat and I talked him into going back out, full rotation, then coming in through the break. The three of us. It was terrifying. We were very lucky to get him in. He was so weak when we got him to the beach he just collapsed there, unable to move. Every now and then I see Jim Caldwell, and he always says the same thing: 'It's been a great life. Thanks to you and Pat Curren.'"

Brown: "In the early days, when Waimea was first being ridden, guys were real leery of the place. They felt a little better if Curren was around. One day it was just huge, and Pat was due in from the Mainland that afternoon, so everybody's going, 'We'll be on it. Pat's coming in. Wait until he gets here.' So Curren pulls up and they're all ready, waiting for the signal to just charge out there. Pat takes a look and says, 'Shit. Sure looks big when you haven't seen it for a while.' Walked off and left everybody standing there."

Noll: "Pat was really known for his diving. He'd free-dive down 60, 70 feet and wrestle huge turtles back to the surface, so guys loved to go out there with him. Neal Tobin told me he went on a diving trip with Curren, and Pat's totally quiet. Three days go by, and the guy's said maybe two words. Tobin finally grabbed him by the neck and screamed, 'I can't take this any longer! For God's sake, say something!'"

Mickey Munoz: "When the surf was flat, a bunch of us would hike up to Waimea Falls and dive off into the water. The normal jump is about 35, 40 feet, but if you go around the falls and up, there's a ledge people claimed was about 80 feet. Just getting up there was kind of dangerous, but Del Cannon and I climbed up and sat there, trying to psych ourselves into diving. So we're there about 45 minutes, hemming and hawing, finding all sorts of excuses not to go, when Pat Curren comes climbing up. This was around 1957, and I barely knew the guy. He takes kind of a nervous look over the edge and says, 'You guys are nuts. I would never do that.' And he kind of backs off the ledge and goes down below, where the rest of the guys are taking the regular dive. So Del and I go back to our psych job, and about 15 minutes later, Pat comes back up. Without saying a word, he crawls right between us and jumps. Everybody was just in shock. Couldn't believe what we had seen. That told me a lot about Pat: really a ballsy person, but understated. I just went, 'This guy's my hero.'"

Brown: "I heard Pat got bit by a moray eel one time, so I went over to Meade Hall to check it out. This is the conversation:

"Pat, I heard you got bit out there."
"Yup."
"Yeah, well, what happened?"
"I guess I scared him."
"Is it bad?"

"Umm . . . naw."

"All the while, Pat's holding his hand in his pocket," said Brown. "I asked if I could see it, and he begrudgingly pulls it out, just a piece of hamburger, covered with old tobacco and pocket lint, unbelievably bad. Diffenderfer and those guys tried to get him to a doctor, but Pat just sat and rocked in a chair for a couple of days. Finally he just fell out of the chair with blood poisoning. We had to drag him to the hospital."

Van Dyke: "I'm not sure anyone really knew Pat. I don't think anyone ever penetrated his depth. And that was sort of his charm. He was quiet, strong and silent, sort of a John Wayne type. He had an incredible effect on women; they'd be so impressed and nervous, they could hardly speak to him. They'd just fall apart. The image I'll always have is from Waimea one day in 25-foot surf. We're all standing around, waxing our boards, and there's Pat with a cigarette and a beer. He walks down to the shore, flips the beer over his head, kicks the cigarette into the ocean, paddles out and catches the wave of the day. He really was that way."

Countless surfers ride Waimea Bay. Only a few can truly claim it as their spot, their niche in the surfing world, at the kind of size that identifies the truly courageous. In a way, Pat Curren was the Darrick Doerner of his era: quietly going about his business, rarely mentioned with the really hot surfers, going virtually unnoticed in routine surf, then appearing on the biggest, nastiest, most hideous wave at Waimea and making it.

"Pat was the original," said Noll. "He was in a class of his own back then, the first guy to ride Waimea well and really examine the place. He was with us that day in '57 when it was surfed for the first time, and we all went on our ass. From that point on, he concentrated on making the right boards for Waimea, being patient, sitting outside and really tackling those big waves. And he rode the hell out of 'em. He does remind me of Doerner, come to think of it. And I'll tell you, to be honest, I tried to emulate Curren's better qualities as the years went by."

Van Dyke remembers feeling a sense of uneasiness when he saw Curren on big days. "I enjoyed surfing with him, but I didn't use him as a lineup. Wherever Pat was sitting, I didn't want to be. Because he'd be over on the other side of the peak, and Pat was probably the only guy who could make it from that position. He and Peter Cole used to push each other so far over, there was no place to go but left (laughs). He knew that lineup like nobody else. Even better than Greg."

His peers remember him as a quiet, brooding presence in the water, sitting by himself and waiting hours, if necessary, for the day's biggest wave. "But that's the essence of his reputation," said Cole. "To me, quantity means nothing at Waimea. If you get the biggest wave out there, you've won the day. And Pat had that over all of us. He never advertised it, either. Never had a media following. The rest of us were running around, you know, 'Did you get that picture?' while he's just sitting way outside, and all of a sudden the set of the day comes, and he's on the damn thing. Used to drive me insane. My first couple of winters out there, Pat gave me an inferiority complex."

Meanwhile, Curren had met the one woman who could steer his energy away from the North Shore. Pat and Jeanine Curren were married in 1961 and Tom, the first of their three children, was born three years later. As the Currens' family life began, Pat gave up Hawaii for good. "Knowing Pat, he just said the hell with it," said Van Dyke. "He had done what he wanted, he was the No. 1 Waimea rider, and he had nothing else to prove. It's funny, I saw him in Hawaii about 15 years later. I was driving down to Laniakea and Waimea was pretty big, maybe 18 feet plus, and when I drove up to the lookout spot, I saw Pat Curren standing there. I knew he hadn't been out there for years, and he was just reliving the whole scene. He looked so pensive, engrossed, you could almost see the memories come through his head. I didn't even disturb him. It was a really impressive and touching sight."

A look into the Curren family wouldn't be complete without the perspective of Sam George. He first met the Currens in 1977, when Tom was 13 and really starting to draw attention, and he lived in Santa Barbara for the next eight years. George was around in 1980, when Pat left the family and fled to Costa Rica, never to return. He has traveled the world with Tom in the dual role of journalist and friend. Now 38, George has a flood of memories and holds all of the Currens in the highest regard. In a recent conversation, these were some of Sam's thoughts:

"By the time I came around, Pat wasn't surfing much anymore. It was just too crowded for him. But he'd show up on big days at Rincon and he still had that really clean, trimming style. I remember being outraged when people dropped in on him. I just wanted to scream, 'Get out of his way! Don't you know who he is?'

"Pat had a detached way about him. Jeanine was totally involved with Tom, a real driving force in his career, but Pat was always off in the back, playing with his black Lab. He's always been really kind to animals, and if he went surfing, he'd make a little bowl out of foil, get some water, make sure the dog was OK. People rarely talked about Pat being the parent of this incredible surfer. It was always Jeanine.

"She has a photograph of their wedding day, at Maile Point on the West Side. The surf was pumping that day, and there's Pat standing behind an old woody, big guns sticking out the back of the car and he's leaning up against it, wearing Sammy Lee's tuxedo jacket—way too big for him—and smoking a cigar. The look on his face is so classic. It was like a treasure trove to me, just studying this portrait of self-assuredness. He's getting married, the surf's big, and he's leaning up against a board that he made. Jeanine told me that after they got married, they rushed back to the beach because the surf was big. She said, 'I spent my wedding day wondering if my husband was going to come back alive.'

"I was down at the office of a bodyboarding magazine one time, working on an article, when I came upon some old archival photos in a box. And I saw a picture so profound, I had to go home. It was an old black-and-white of Pat Curren, and it looked like it had been framed from a Douglas Fairbanks film. Pat had decided he was gonna sail home from Hawaii on a schooner one year, and there's Pat at the helm, with a beard, wearing a turban. You felt like you were looking at Sir Richard Burton, or Sinbad, and I thought to myself, 'My God, that's a surfer.' He wasn't flying back on Hawaiian Air, he was sailing home. The pride I saw in that photo, the sheer exuberance . . . I said, 'Look, guys, I'd love to help you out with Keith Sasaki drop-kneeing T-Street, but forget bodyboarding. I've got to go home now.'

"One thing I've always savored was a day at El Capitan when I saw Pat loading up his old gray pickup, and he had this board that looked like a replica of his old Waimea guns. I'm looking at the fin, and it seemed so inadequate—almost like a keel fin, not very high, with a real long base. So I summoned my courage and said, 'Pat'—I dared to call him that; 'Mr. Curren' seemed stupid—'you know, you didn't have a lot of fin on those boards.' And he sat there for a second, and all of a sudden he stopped tying his trucker's knot, because of course he wouldn't use surf racks. I'm thinking, 'Oh, God, I said a real stupid thing.' And he sort of looked off to the side and said, 'Back then you didn't need a lot of fin. All you needed was a lot of rail and a lot of guts.'

"A lot of people say Tommy's going to be like his dad. There are some parallels. Obviously they're both kind of quiet and speak mainly through their actions. They have the same walk. They look quite a bit alike. Pat had a major family breakup, and now Tommy's divorced, too, with kids of his own. Will he be a nomad like Pat? Hey, nobody can really say that. But I definitely think Tommy's a lot more driven than his dad. You can't become a five-time world champion—that includes two as an amateur—without loving the limelight. You might win one world title just on pure skill and verve, but you can't win five unless you really enjoy being a surf star and a champion. And Pat legitimately turned his back on all that kind of stuff.

"Tommy told me one time that his dad disapproved of what he does, being a pro and competitive surfer. It hadn't been spoken in words, but Tommy got the feeling his dad wasn't real stoked about the direction he went in surfing. Now that's a pretty tough thing to live with. You become the greatest surfer ever, and your dad, who was also a great surfer, doesn't approve of it? The last time Tom saw him, I think they reached some kind of resolution."

A Curren story was relayed to George: Apparently, a year or two ago, someone sent Pat a surf video that showed Tommy in full glory, ripping waves all over the world. Pat was reportedly so overwhelmed by the scope of his son's work, his eyes teared up.

"I don't know if that really happened," Sam George said. "But I hope it did."

The little Jack Russell terrier curled up and fell asleep as Pat Curren relaxed in his chair. They are incredibly sturdy dogs, tiny in stature but of a mind that they are large and can enforce. "He got into it with a couple of ranch dogs the other day," said Pat. "They beat him up pretty good."

The place looked totally disorganized, almost abandoned. Curren's layout consisted of a dirt floor, a five-board quiver, some tired and loose lumber, a propane refrigerator, well-worn coolers, some work benches, assorted tools and a handsome dune buggy for four-wheel travel. A simple palapa covered the trailer, and there were no screens on the windows. A midsummer rain had drenched southern Mexico the previous night, bringing great hordes of insects into everyone's life.

"Too hot with the screen," he said. "I sleep outside."

"That's hard-core," said my friend Jim Hart. "What about the bugs?"

"Just eat before dark," he said.

The interview progressed in that tone, Curren taking lengthy pauses before answering, usually thinking it over with a long hit off his beer. He didn't say much, but his comments were direct, right to the point and spiced with the inevitable Curren humor. We couldn't help but be impressed by the man's honesty, humility and light-hearted nature.

It went something like this:

* Looks like you've been glassing some boards.

"Well, it's a real good way to ruin glassy conditions if the surf's good. Soon as you lay out a side, the wind comes up. I don't know how it knows."

* What kind of waves do you surf now?

"Small. I don't have the range. An 8- to 10-foot wave is startin' to look pretty big to me these days."

* Peter Cole said he was amazed how many Windansea guys did well in Hawaii. He figured it's such an open-ocean type of wave, it was good preparation.

"It was more of an attitude."

* Peter also said he wanted to catch every wave in sight when he was younger, and that he got his patience in big surf from you.

"Peter's the greatest. He didn't learn anything from me. I never saw anybody enjoy surfing so much. He's my hero."

* The old guys say you made a science of Waimea, that you were the ultimate craftsman and the first to really study the place.

"I don't remember being that serious."

* What kind of memories do you have of the North Shore days?

"It was the right time. People talk about the crude equipment we had. It wasn't that bad. And there were no crowds. I was young then. Best time of my life."

What was it like on that first day at Waimea in 1957?

"We thought it was maybe 12 feet. We got a big surprise when we got out there. I don't think anybody made a wave."

How do you feel about the success you had there?

"I guess I had more luck at Waimea than the other places. Actually, I had no idea what I was getting into. I'm such a shitty athlete, I had problems in small waves."

You left there in your early 30s, your physical prime.

"Well, it was gettin' crowded, and I was getting ready to do something else. I'd done everything I wanted to do there."

What did you think about Noll hanging it up after riding that 30-foot wave at Makaha?

"Well, he was taking some big chances. I think that wave made him sit down and think."

Did you ever have that feeling?

"I never did. We were diving a lot, which prepares you for times like that. We were in such good shape, you'd have to tell yourself to come up. Jose Angel used to go for big turtles, 280 to 300 pounds, maybe 65 feet down, and I saw him stay down a long time. Claimed he just wasn't hungry for air. One time we were off Laniakea and he didn't come up. He was almost to the top, maybe 8 feet under, then I saw his eyes roll back and he started sinking. Neal Tobin and I were right there to bring him up. When he comes to, he says, 'Let's go get some lungs and get those sons of bitches.' Those were his first words when he came back to life. He was purple. I said, 'Go home, Jose.'"

How much of Tom's career can you follow from this distance?

"Not much. It's OK. There's still a big difference in our ages. Maybe later. The ages gotta converge a little more. Right now, he don't buy my act."

Do you see any of yourself in Tom?

"I can't see myself. I don't know how I could see myself in him."

You haven't been to many of those old-timers' reunions. Are they not worth the trip?

"Well, you see this sign, 'Welcome Surf Pioneers,' you get a couple of drinks, start moving down the line, seeing some of the guys, then they kick you out at 9:30."

Is there enough carpentry work out here to keep you going?

"There's not a whole lot of work, but hell, I'll be drawin' Social Security pretty soon. What do I care?"

Mind if I ask your age?

"I'm 62 . . . in fact, I turned 62 today."

It was Pat Curren's birthday. I got the feeling if Jim Hart and I hadn't shown up, nobody would have noticed.

And then, in a context I can't recall, I made mention of Jeanine.

"Let's don't talk about Jeanine," he said.

She answers the door in a smart, black-and-white outfit with a bow tie. Jeanine Curren lives about 10 miles north of Rincon, and she's working as a waitress in a local hotel. Now in her early 50s, she looks fit and tanned, the picture of health. She remarried in August, to a pastor named Jerry Bloom, so the Curren name is absent, like the man himself.

Friends said they never quite understood them as a couple. Pat was so damned quiet, and Jeanine never stopped talking. But they had their moments. Recoiling from the crowds, Pat moved the family from Newport to Dana Point and finally to Santa Barbara, where they ran a successful bathing-suit business out of their house and eventually opened their own shop. Pat also had a variety of talents with his shaping, diving and expert touch as a finish carpenter. In the 10-year period from 1964 to 1974, the Curren family was in its glory.

The final chapters were not pleasant. There were some poor financial decisions, a shortage of funds. The young Tom Curren got wild—delinquent wild. Pat became even more sullen than usual, and according to Jeanine, he made a slow retreat from the family. In 1975, Jeanine became a born-again Christian and pursued her new life with a passion. She prayed that Pat would also be saved, but he wasn't buying it. The separation of personalities became greater and more painful, until Pat finally left in 1980, triggering their divorce. Told that Costa Rica was the new frontier, he settled there until 1986. And then he moved to Baja, where he's been ever since.

On a gorgeous summer morning this August, Jeanine was quite willing to discuss both the good and bad times:

"I was 16 when I met Pat at a surfing movie—I believe it was the original *Big Wednesday*—and he made quite an impression. I pretty much started following him around after that. I was from Coronado, but I started going to Windansea because I knew he'd be there. One day he asked if I'd go tandem surfing with him, and this was a big day, maybe 8 feet. I was pretty coordinated and a good athlete, but that was the biggest surf I'd ever been in. I remember we got on a set wave and he said, 'Here we go—don't look down.' That was really exciting, the beginning of our romance. I think it really impressed him that I went out there. Two years later, in 1961, we were married.

"Pat's definitely an Irishman, both sides of the family. Raised Catholic. His mother was very strong and intelligent, one of the first women licensed surveyors in California. His parents were in the surveying business together, and Pat was a draftsman before he put his energy into surfing. It was so easy to see where Pat got his humor. When his family got together they had their own language, their own dry wit, and unless you knew them, you didn't understand a thing they were saying. They'd get to talking and drinking and playing Scrabble, and they really enjoyed each other's company. Yeah, Pat's humor was definitely inherited. It was good; probably kept him sane in some situations.

"They lived in Mission Beach and they had a great life until around 1964, right before Tommy was born. Pat's mom smoked a lot, and she accidentally caused a fire in the home one night. The smoke went upstairs and asphyxiated her husband. Things were never the same in the family after Pat's father died.

"Pat had an amazing way of connecting with people. A lot of California guys sort of brawled their way into acceptance in Hawaii, but Pat never had to do that. He had younger friends that looked up to him, but he was close to older guys like Rabbit Kekai and George Downing, too. Pat's friends on the North Shore didn't really get along with his friends in town, so the day we got married the country guys came later, very politely, so there wouldn't be trouble. It was amazing. Pat had friends who were locals, not even known for their surfing, people who would come over, bring the whole family, make dinner, clean up, then leave and just say thanks. He could be so intimidating with his quietness, and yet, everywhere he went, he had friends. And in all the years I knew him, I never saw him get into a fight.

"Living with Pat on the North Shore was, well, a test of your flexibility. You'd have guys coming over wanting to drink six cases of beer. The 'kitchen' was really just a place to shape and patch surfboards, and the butter tasted like resin. People were always looking for a deal or a place to stay, and Pat was always, 'Come on in.' After that last winter, 1961–62, I think Pat was ready for a change. A new era was coming in, with a lot of hype, and once Hawaii started to change, it was no longer his first love.

"Pat and I were so opposite. A lot of people felt that was good for Pat, but I know there was some resentment. We had some unhappiness at the beginning of our marriage, and it was never really resolved. Although Pat was a good man, a likable man, he was self-centered in a lot of ways, not real communicative to me.

"And Tom was running away. When he was 10 years old, he was smoking pot first thing in the morning, every day, and I'd be chasing him all over town. Pat was concerned, he just didn't know how to deal with it. He wasn't communicating with me or giving me any support. I finally came to a place where I just surrendered. God became my answer. It gave me a life where there was hope and peace.

"I bought into it 100 percent. I was not lukewarm. I was on fire. And that was hard for my husband, for he did not accept God's grace and liberation. He hardened his heart. He saw our life as an impossible situation. I could sense a real sadness come over him. He made a toolbox, put his tools in it and said goodbye."

In surfing circles, it is said that Pat Curren left without warning, that he told Jeanine he was going out for a pack of cigarettes and never came back. "No," said Jeanine firmly. "He's not an evil or cruel man. He was discouraged, and he didn't know what else to do, so he went out in the wilderness. People say, 'He's a survivalist. He's a real man's man.' That's a bunch of BS. He's humorous, he loves people, he's just filled with that kind of stuff. But he's going to die a lonely old man, and because of what? It's a lie. The whole thing is a lie from hell.

"I know he probably feels a lot of guilt for what he did, but his pride—that's what keeps him there. I've tried everything to bring my husband to the Lord, but he just doesn't see it. I don't hold it against him. I've forgiven him totally for everything. I wish him only the best."

There was a steady wail of sirens on the North Shore when I interviewed Tom Curren. It was January 31, the best big day of the winter, a solid 18 to 20 feet with a gorgeous blue sky and offshore winds. It was also a horrible day, the day Jim Broach disappeared at Phantoms.

Tom was oblivious to the sirens. He was watching Rockpiles, the spot directly outside. It was more terrifying than beautiful, just a howling, uncontrollable thing, but he was eyeing it all the same. We sat down over a six-pack to discuss his father, Pat Curren, the man he hadn't seen since the mid-1980s.

"I have a lot of admiration for what my father did," said Tom. "The only recognition he got was from his contemporaries, and that's all that really matters. He was getting big waves on modern equipment that he shaped himself, and he didn't really need to talk about it. He just did it. That sort of says it all."

It seemed to blow Tom's mind that Pat didn't start surfing until he was 18. "But from all the diving he did, he had a way to control his breathing, and his mind, so when he wiped out he didn't use up all his air. And for him, hotdog riding was a less realistic way to improve than just getting out there in the big stuff, when most guys were pulling back. I think the way he looked at it, when you've seen a 50-foot wave, a 30-foot wave doesn't seem as bad."

Tom's surfing education began . . . well, how far back can you go? "There's a photo of me and my dad at Honolua Bay. I'm six months old and I'm on the front of his board. I don't know if that counts. When I was 6, he took us to the south shore of Oahu, and that's when I picked it up. Later on, we stayed at Jose Angel's place and other spots on the North Shore. My dad didn't really push me into waves or anything. He bought me a board for 10 bucks in Haleiwa, and that's all it took. I started out as a goofyfooter, actually.

"My dad really went out of his way for us to see different parts of the world. Hiking, horsebacking, we did all this stuff. He definitely enriched our lives—my brother Joe and my sister Anna, and especially me because I was the oldest. That influenced me, at least with my own kids, to show them things that might jar them in a pleasant way.

"He got me started surfing Hammonds, which became my spot, and we had some great surfs at the Sunset Cliffs area. Sometimes just the two of us. Big set would come, he'd paddle out, and I'd just paddle right along with him. We only went out when it was pretty good size, and even then, I knew it was like puddles in a pond for him. I saw him take some great wipeouts, though (laughs). One time, maybe around 1974, we got caught inside and we lost our boards. Took us about 20 minutes to get in, and when we went up on the cliff and looked out, we thought we saw 'em way out to sea. But they were so far out, we just left 'em. Couple years ago, I heard somebody found that board, all rotted out, the 6'4" my dad shaped for me. Great board."

Tom claimed the family breakup wasn't devastating—at least to him. "We could see it coming," he said. "I was surfing all over California at that time and didn't see him that much, and I handled it fine. When you're 17 years old, it isn't a major trauma. It was hard on him. Hardest thing he'd ever been through."

They are probably the greatest father-son surfing combination of all time, up there with the Keaulanas, Downings and Hamiltons. The difference is that the Currens barely know each other. Tom's younger brother Joe, now 20 and a fast-rising surfer, has made several trips to see Pat in Mexico and said, "I've never held anything against him. Not at all. Things get to my dad pretty easily, and he's kind of where he should be, I think. We've had some good times together. With Tommy, I don't know . . . he's never been down there. But he's talked about it. I think it will happen. We've talked about having a whole reunion down there."

The way Tom sees it, "I don't think it's going to be any big deal when I finally catch up to him. It's just a matter of time and effort. I have no problem with what he's doing. I think this is absolutely what he was destined to do. I figure he'll always be somewhere in Latin America, because that's where it's all happening. I don't see him coming back. I wouldn't recommend it (laughter). I wouldn't go any farther north than where he is."

Peter Cole, who has had the pleasure of knowing both generations, can't get over the similarities. "Tommy's so much like his dad. He'll start to say something, kind of look out to sea, and there's this wave out there, and then his mind wanders, and he forgets what he was talking about (laughs). When my wife and I were in France, Tommy and Marie had us over for dinner. It's funny, in my house, I have pictures of myself surfing big waves. Same thing at Ricky Grigg's place. We like to show it off. You go into Tommy's house, and there's absolutely nothing. You don't see a trophy, a medal, a picture. You wouldn't even know he's a surfer. Then way in the back, where he has his boards, all the stuff's sort of piled up in a corner. Pat was exactly the same way."

Some might draw an unsettling parallel as Tom, divorced from Marie, has taken on something of a nomadic lifestyle—though Tom, unlike his dad, has already remarried. When I ran that past him, he took an unusually long pause and finally said, "Yeah, there's a little of that in me, too. I don't know. There are some things I can't really talk about. I've thought about it, too. I don't know . . . I can't really . . . " And he let it rest that way.

It was a breakthrough winter for Tom, who had never stayed past December on the North Shore. Now he was settling in for January and February and savoring the rewards. "It makes me feel good to know what my dad did over here," he said. "Makes me feel like, somewhere inside, I've got it. I've made my career winning contests in small surf, but I'm not interested in that anymore. I want to surf big waves now, good waves. I'm just gonna surf Sunset if it's breaking, Waimea if it's breaking, outer islands, anywhere it's good. When the next Eddie Aikau contest comes along, I want to know I'm ready, that I'll have a board I like, and I'll know what the hell I'm doing when I'm facing a 25-foot wave that's top to bottom."

He paused and looked out at the grinding, impossibly large Rockpiles. "Some nice waves out there," he said. "I might go out and get one."

There was one other surfer out, getting worked big-time as Tommy paddled out. Only a few people on the beach were even in position to notice Curren in this heroic act; we felt lucky to be part of it. Suddenly there he was, dropping into a right that was 15 feet Hawaiian-style, easy. He glided down the face and into a huge bottom turn, then zipped out the back as an ominous section began to close. Sets were beginning to feather a half-mile out and Curren kicked for the horizon, well past his original takeoff spot. The other surfer was nowhere in sight. Now Tom was stroking into a left, and we all yelled in amazement as he did a huge fade, for seconds on end, then descended into the pit, did some fast-track ripping and gracefully pulled out before the slaughter.

The rest of the set simply buried him. He was a speck in an avalanche. Fearing the worst kind of pounding, he released his cord. It looked for a moment he was headed for the inside rocks, but of course, he made it safely to the beach. I had seen Curren rip unspeakable Pipeline backside on a day so dangerous they called off the Masters contest. I had seen him pull small-wave maneuvers at Maverick's the first time he ever surfed the place. But this performance, I reckoned, was in a class by itself.

With the sweet days of fall and winter opproaching, Pat Curren fills his life in simple ways. A little surfing, a little shaping, a little carpentry work from the surfers and opportunists building dream houses near the tip of Baja. Give him this, a cold beer and his beloved little dog, and he couldn't be better.

Selling out? Missing the boat? Not in Pat Curren's mind, nor in those of his old friends. "You know what's so bitchen," said Greg Noll, "is that he's doing the same shit that he found enjoyable back then. He's away from the takers, the people who want to grab onto your surfing shirttails and make a fast buck. He has kept his life simple, focusing on the things that count. If people think that's not being successful in life, I have to disagree."

Ricky Grigg: "Part of his pure quality was his inability to compromise with society, which was why he came to Hawaii in the first place. The fact that he's in Mexico, in that setting, is completely consistent with that attitude."

Van Dyke: "I always saw him as sort of a Hemingway character, living on strictly his own terms. He'll never wear shoes, so to speak, and I envy that sort of freedom. I taught school for 34 years, and over that time I probably surfed less than Pat in the five or six years he spent in Hawaii. He just said the hell with everything eise. And that's a big reason why he was so great."

Here's how Pat Curren puts it: "We keep getting pushed into these little corners," he said. "The last time I surfed Malibu had to be 1952. Couldn't believe how crowded it was. Never went back. La Jolla got all f—ed up, then Hawaii, then Costa Rica. I'm runnin' out of places. Then again, I'm runnin' out of time."

How long does he figure he'll stay put?

"Well, this road hasn't kept out the riff-raff (laughs). There's a lot of room up the coast. Doesn't take you long to get out of town."

The last time I saw Pat Curren, he was surfing a well-known point-break not far from his trailer. The waves were about 6 feet, with an occasional bomber set, and I had just paddled out into an intense, super-talented group of surfers when I noticed a gray-haired man sitting way outside of us, all alone.

He probably sat there for half an hour, with his back to us. But then came the set he wanted, sure as the rising sun. He picked the right wave, the perfect wave, the wave of the day, and he glided past me with a little smile on his face. He rode that thing all the way to the beach, stepped off, then disappeared into the land of burros and cows. ◪

Tragic Kingdom:
Looking for Magic in the North Shore Amusement Park

By Todd Chesser · SURFER Vol. 38 No. 4 · April 1997

Oahu's North Shore changed rapidly in the boom period of the mid-1990s. Roosters and livestock gave way to highway bypasses and sprawling business parks, and old plantation homes were replaced by the gaudy estates of "coast haoles." The annual winter crowds swelled into gridlock as surfers and tourists alike invaded the "tragic kingdom." For lifelong residents like Todd Chesser, all the waiting in line for a ride spoiled much of the fun, but there were ways that locals could cope with the onslaught and recapture some of the lost magic.

When I was a grommet growing up on the South Shore of Oahu, I was deprived of the one thing that virtually all Mainland kids have the privilege of knowing and loving: Disneyland. Theme parks are non-existent in Hawaii, and the only way I found thrills similar to the rides I'd heard about at Mickeyville was on a beat-up Aipa sting my mom gave me. Mickey was just some oversized mouse that I watched on TV.

Due to a lack of options, my Magic Kingdom became the North Shore, and the characters that I looked up to were big-wave riders that my mom told me about: guys like Jose Angel, Barry Kanaiaupuni and Eddie Aikau. If Goofy and Jose Angel were standing side by side, I would've run and hugged Jose, and ignored the weirdo with the stupid laugh and oversized nose. Before I ever even made the 45-minute trek to the other side of the island, I thought of the North Shore as Fantasy Land, a place where dreams come true.

These days, after what seems like 90,000 seasons on the North Shore, I've found that my childhood dreams were a warped distortion of reality. There is no Santa Claus, Goofy's a kook and Mickey will do anything for the cameras.

Just recently I found myself out at Off the Wall. It was the day after Halloween, and a lack of sun, photogs and hangover remedies left me alone at "Kodak Reef" for a few hours of bliss. It was shifty and far from perfect, but it was fun and it was all mine. The next day, it was same place, different story. Photographers, reveling in the sunlight, jockeyed each other for the best angles as a herd of surfers and bodyboarders did the same. Ross Williams, Kahea Hart and I bobbed in the lumpy lineup while all 'round us the illegitimate offspring of Tom Morey kicked and squirmed their way into well-lit closeouts. One prone disciple went so far as to wear a Dallas Cowboys football helmet, face mask and all, complete with his sponsors' logos on it. This guy was out to get the shot, no matter what silly antics were required. "Jesus," Ross muttered in disbelief, "isn't it a little early for this kind of thing?!"

Just like its Orange County counterpart, the North Shore seems to be a crazy mix of foreign tourists, naïve young couples, cartoonish characters we all recognize and more cameras than a White House press conference. Even though the tourists know only verbal directions to the spots ("That man told me the Banzai Pipeline is over here, honey!"), prime time at the 7-mile miracle is more chaotic than Labor Day at Space Mountain. There's only a couple of rules at this park: be psycho (or at least make everyone think you're psycho) and devour all those who are lower than you on the food chain.

And the rides! With lifeguards at only the best-known spots, there's not much holding back the most inexperienced clods from entering the jaws of death. The North Shore really needs Disneyesque warning signs. Pipeline, for instance, should have a sign with a caricature of somebody like Mark Cunningham on it that reads, "Caution: This is a dangerous ride. If you are recently transplanted from the Mainland and are paddling out to impress your bros, please refrain from going beyond this point." And if you're the passenger in the truck of Shawn Briley, Hawaii's own Mr. Toad, you'd better handcuff yourself to the floorboard, because this boy gets wild. If you're still alive and in need of more thrills, then rev up that ego and prepare your lungs for some exhaust as you "get strapped" with Big Wave Hero Alec Cooke and tow into "the big ones" on the outer reefs. The ride was temporarily out of service after the self-proclaimed Ace Cool got slaughtered earlier this year on an 18-foot day and lost his ski. Word is he's fully recovered and ready to rock, regardless of how many paddle-in surfers are in the lineup.

Getting hungry? Thought a hot dog and a Coke at the stand by the Matterhorn was pricey? Stop into Foodland Supermarket and get taken for a real ride. Grab a cart, put on that "I was just ripping!" face and trade the day's surf stories as you dig deep into your pockets and exchange your life savings for a box of cereal and milk. No tales to tell? Just make one up; you don't want to feel left out.

I know it's a small world and all, but the flags that've been flying in my backyard are starting to get a little ridiculous. Early this November, the equivalent of the Jamaican bobsled team set aside their politically neutral and watch-making reputations for a new national pastime. Switzerland is now the proud owner of a surf team. With their country's colors prominently displayed on their rash guards and Swiss army knives airbrushed on their boards, the five of them hit the Sunset lineup with an uncharacteristically aggressive abandon. "I was almost decapitated by Hans or Franz—I couldn't tell who was who because they all looked the same," uttered Sunset Beach resident Porter Turnbull. "Just think, next year they'll be doing tow-ins with the Italians and French!"

Of course not all the magic that I once knew has been diluted and distorted by the park's renovations over the years. Michael Ho, another one of those eternal legends I would've run up to and hugged as a kid, won the XCel Pro this year in some meaty waves. On the other end of the scale, I watched the 20th annual Haleiwa Menehune surf meet in late October at Ali'i beach. Watching hard-core surf-stoked kids like Daniel Jones and Sean Moody rip the 1- to 2-foot surf to pieces assured me that there are still local kids out there who see the North Shore the same way I did when I was a keiki. Unfortunately, special little moments like these have become an exception to the rule.

And yet miracles still happen. It was after four days and four nights of solid rain, and the North Shore was being cleansed of the filth that had accumulated since the last big soaking about five years ago. I woke up early, called the buoys, and nearly jumped out of my skin: 25 feet at 17 seconds. I grabbed Chris Malloy and we jumped in my ark and floated down the Kam Highway to Waimea. Despite the rumbling surf, there was a strange quiet in the air: the vermin were nowhere to be seen. There wasn't one surf car in the parking lot, and besides the few tourists who seemed to be impatiently waiting for the first victims, we were alone. We looked out into the muddy brown lineup and saw a 25-foot wave feather across the bay. One of the heaviest waves in the world was operating full-tilt and there was no one else in line. It was like showing up at Disneyland on a day when every tourist in California thought the place was closed. After surfing with Chris, Ross Clarke-Jones and Elijah Young for more than three hours in perfect 20- to 25-foot surf, I was struck with a revelation. All the stories my mom used to tell me about, all the legends that make this strip of sand so special, became as clear as they were when I was a pint-size punk stuck in town. Although it's a little harder to find these days, there's still a little magic left in the Tragic Kingdom. 🏄

Heavy Duty:
The Rise, Fall, Rise, Fall and Rise of Mark Occhilupo
By Matt Warshaw · SURFER Vol. 38 No. 7 · July 1997

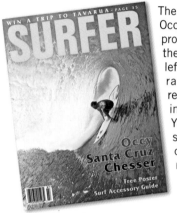

The rivalry between Australian wunderkind Mark Occhilupo and American champion Tom Curren provided for some of the most exciting clashes in the first decade of the ASP tour. But after Curren left the tour on hiatus, Occy seemed to lose his raison d'être. He followed Curren into semi-retirement, but in the ensuing decade spiraled into a vortex of drugs, depression and obesity. Yet, his fan base and sponsor support remained stubbornly intact, and, in 1996 his sponsors convinced him to attempt a comeback. Occy's return and eventual redemption went on to become one of the most remarkable stories in surfing history, as well as the vital antidote to the blandness that had plagued pro surfing since the disappearance of the Curren/Occy Show. Catching Occy at the apogee of his emotional comeback, former editor Matt Warshaw gave *SURFER* readers an undaunted look at Occy's wild 15-year roller coaster.

Mark Occhilupo will likely get fat again. In five years, his weight ricocheted from 165 to 200 to 165 to 245 to 170, and with middle-age spread still to come—well, a pattern suggests itself. Occhilupo's wife Beatrice witnessed the last gain/loss cycle, and won't bet on his future physique, saying, "anything is possible." She also admits that "he was actually pretty happy when he was big."

This is a comforting thought. It supports my own idea that if Occhilupo does take his place in the small but distinguished family of corpulent surf legends, he'll stand with the cheerful and gregarious Chubby Mitchell instead of the withdrawn and tortured Michael Peterson.

But knowing that Occhilupo's career so far can be told as a series of faulty predictions by people like me, why not substitute Gerry Lopez for Chubby and imagine Occhilupo as a man of perpetual fitness, bending Pipeline, Kirra and Jeffreys to his will for the next 25 years? "He's thrilled us like no other surfer—maybe ever."

It was certainly a thrill to watch Occhilupo lose 75 pounds in 1994 and 1995 and return to the top of his profession—13 years after his rookie season. He was a world-title contender in 1984, and some believe he will be so again in 1997. What athlete has done that in any sport?

Furthermore, he returns to the ASP World Championship Tour this year as one of the last practitioners of a dying art: full-time power surfing. Occhilupo today rises up like Mr. Clean before all surface-skimming, pencil-limbed New Schoolers and Pre-Schoolers, strongly muscled and smiling down with a touch of contempt.

There is, too, a perverse thrill in recounting Occhilupo's bouts in the not-so-distant past with insomnia, drinking, depression, mania, profligacy and chronic anxiety. He's stretched himself psychologically to a degree far greater than anything he's ever done with his surfing—or his waistline, for that matter. Which means that Occhilupo's current state of well-being can seem a little suspect. Not that I expected him to greet me with rolling eyes and a gang of invisible friends when I knocked on his patio gate in Hawaii last December, but there was a slight disconnect in trying to match what I knew of his mental history against the smiling, confident 30-year-old now walking toward me, hand extended. I still wonder: how does today's evident stability grow from yesterday's disorder? Or a more specific question: how does a 245-pounder, unable to paddle more than a few yards without gasping for breath, change himself, in just 18 months, back into one of the world's great surfers?

In part because he never entirely lost his sense of pride and position. A quick example: Billabong, Occhilupo's longtime sponsor, was ready to stand by him with clothes and a monthly paycheck, even through the rough years. Occhilupo, however, was uneasy with the relationship as he gained weight. When his waist size hit 36, he still took delivery on his free walk shorts and trunks. At size 38, then 40, he instead drove to a remote surf shop, picked the needed Billabong items off the rack, ducked his head at the counter, and paid retail. Keeping faith with his sponsor, in other words, while trying to keep faith with his reputation.

"In the quarterfinals against Gary Elkerton, I told myself to lose the heat no matter what. I'd sort of tried to throw heats the day before, and it hadn't worked. And against Gary, I swear I wanted to lose straightaway, but I just had a rip attack. Full on. Every good wave came right to me, and I was ripping. I couldn't help myself." Occhilupo at this point slumps in his chair, lifts his eyebrows in sad resignation and sighs. He's making fun of himself—and tipping his hat to his own talent. It's a tossed-off remark, but delivered with style, and I feel a little rush of gratitude, safe for the moment against the creeping blandness of today's famous surfers.

Occhilupo, shirtless, is sitting across from me at a small table on the balcony of a rented house near Rocky Point. Freshly shaven and with a new haircut, he looks much as he did at age 17. Same marble-cut torso. Same smooth, bulging lower jaw and full-lipped mouth. Because he's not well educated and has little inclination to read, and because he's a famous mangler of words and phrases ("I really wanted to win a contest last year," he told me, "but it deluded me"), Occhilupo has been called dim. This is wrong. He's perceptive and aware, and has a natural feel for irony. His sense of humor is more sly than direct. He's a good listener. Several times I watched him defer an answer to a question as he built a footing of background and anecdotal information. Once done, he would invariably say, "So, getting back to your question . . . " then answer concisely.

He continues with the story of his heat against Elkerton in the 1988 Op Pro: "Finally I went, 'Look, that's enough. It's time to lose.' So I did this blatant paddling interference, got called, and that night I flew back to Australia. I was completely sick and tired of pro surfing. I wanted to see my mom and dad. I wanted to go back home to Cronulla, so I did."

When Australian surf journalist John Witzig wrote in 1983 about the "quite remarkable beauty" of the Sydney beach cities, he made an exception for the working-class town of Cronulla, describing it as "city surfing at its ugliest." Little has changed in 14 years. Rows of tedious red-brick apartments march back from the beachfront, and local industrial sites include the Continental Carbon factory, the Kurnell Oil refinery and a sewage outfall. Generations of local surfers have molded themselves to a Cronulla standard: funny, loyal, reckless and slightly morbid. The town's original favorite surfing son, Bobby Brown, New South Wales champion in 1964, was killed in a Cronulla bar fight. Heroin moved through the native surf population like the plague in the '70s. In 1994, Robert "Bear" Jackson, machine operator, goofyfoot, neighborhood legend and diagnosed manic-depressive, killed himself.

But lack of ambition might be the Cronulla surfer's single most distinguishing trait. As local and international surf guru Jim Banks phrased it, "Nothing really happens to anyone from Cronulla." Gary Green was rated sixth in the world in 1987 when he quit the circuit and flew back to his Cronulla apartment, saying, "I'd just rather be at home, surfing with my mates."

Occhilupo returned one year after Green. He surfed and occasionally socialized in Cronulla, but for the most part went to ground at the home of his parents, Pam and Luciano, in the adjacent town of Kurnell.

The perpetually occupied Luciano Occhilupo had little to say about Mark's return. An Italian-born, university-educated engineer, Luciano had immigrated to Australia by boat in 1953 at age 25. He married Pam Raphael, a New Zealander, then moved to Kurnell, where, to his slight consternation, he fathered three daughters. The couple's fourth and final child, Marco Luciano Jay, was born June 16, 1966. Hugs and encouragement rained down on Mark from the females in the house, while Luciano pinched his son's cheek and told him again and again to grow up strong.

Mark, instead, grew up lazy. After his first afternoon on a construction site, at age 15, he came home and said he'd never work another day in his life—a slap to Luciano, who not only worked continually, but attended Sydney University part-time for 16 years. Mark then announced that he wanted to become a professional surfer. He and Luciano fought about it, then Mark left home and shared an apartment with some friends in Cronulla while he finished the 10th grade. In July 1983, Occhilupo signed on as an ASP trials competitor. Fourteen months later he was leading the world ratings, and American surf journalist Bill Sharp spoke for pretty much the entire surfing community when he wrote, "Where did he come from? Where is he going? Will he last? And of course, just who the hell is Mark Occhilupo?"

The surprise was due in part to the fact that Occhilupo was fourth in a series of world-class teenage sensations, following Tom Carroll, Tom Curren and Martin Potter. "But it was different with Tom Carroll," Wayne Bartholomew recalls. "People in Australia had been talking about him for ages, 'Watch out, here comes Tommy Gun.' Same with Tom Curren in California—years of advance notice on that one. Occy just appeared. Just a bolt from the blue. Potter did the same thing a couple of seasons before."

Occhilupo's most conspicuous talent was power. At age 17, without a single day's work in the gym, he had the body of an Olympic speed skater: well-muscled (but not grossly so) trunk and arms, a wide, low ass, and a pair of enormous thighs. His broad feet moved automatically into a spacious utility stance, and his back would twist and straighten like a torsion bar—only Curren and Kelly Slater would be better planted on a deck of a board. Occhilupo's hands, meanwhile, were soft and open, and seemed to guide him through the fallout of his own gouging turns.

Curren was the ultimate foil to Occhilupo. Both drew faultless lines, but Curren's accents were elegant, while Occhilupo's were slightly ravenous—even feral. Curren was probably the closest thing we'll ever see to a perfect surfer. But the warmth, joy and emotion of the act came across more clearly with Occhilupo, which at times made him the more attractive surfer.

Despite the rocket start, Occhilupo didn't hold on to win the 1984 world title. He finished third that year, fourth in 1985, and third again in 1986, by which time he'd won eight world tour events, plus the non-rated 1985 Pipeline Masters, and was earning about $125,000 a year from his sponsors.

Progress at home, meanwhile, was uneven. A high point came at the 1984 Beaurepaires Open, held at Cronulla. Up to then Occhilupo's father had yet to see him surf. "Luciano," recalls Mark's mother, "said he'd go watch Mark if he did well in the competition." Occhilupo won the contest and was interviewed live for Australia's Wide World of Sports. If the Beaurepaires contest didn't exactly produce a father-son breakthrough, it was nonetheless a proud moment for both.

Luciano returned to the beach three years later, for the 1987 Coke contest. Mark lost in the semifinals to Tom Carroll, and the next day he asked Luciano what he thought about the match. "Pretty good, pretty good," Luciano replied. "But how come you fall off with Carroll so many times? You deserve to lose twice for that."

Sixteen months later, Mark answered Luciano with a passive-aggressive masterstroke. He quit the tour and moved back home.

Derek Hynd wrote that Occhilupo, beginning in 1987, had gone into a "downward spiral" leading to "radically dangerous territory," and that some of Occhilupo's friends thought he "faced certain death."

Occhilupo looks irritated as I read these quotes back to him in Hawaii. "Well," he says after a pause, "part of the reason I quit the tour was because of guys like Derek Hynd."

Which isn't fair to Hynd. Occhilupo did have a breakdown of sorts in 1987 and 1988, and if it wasn't, as he puts it, "half as bad" as a subsequent breakdown in 1992–93, friends and family were justifiably alarmed by his erratic behavior. He bought a Cronulla penthouse and sold it a few months later. He was a no-show at the first ASP contest of 1988, in January, announcing that he'd just bought a hillside lot overlooking Sunset Beach and was moving to the North Shore. Pam and Luciano flew to Hawaii intending to bring their son home—and failed. Weeks later, however, he was back in Cronulla of his own accord, and his Hawaiian property was up for sale. He gave up yoga, fruit juice and lentil soup for cigarettes, meat pies and drunken nights on the town. During Easter week he surfed in the Bells contest and placed third. He was back on the tour.

In California he threw his heat against Elkerton in the Op Pro and came back to Cronulla. He was back off the tour. This time, he announced that he was ready to begin a new career as a blue-collar worker. "Laboring's where it's at," Occhilupo said, forgetting the horror of his construction site experience as a 15-year-old. "Anything else wouldn't be a reality after being a surfer for so long."

Evidence aside, Occhilupo tells me he wasn't manic at that point. He says, first of all, that he was tired—which I believe. The ASP's yearly schedule in the mid-'80s had double the contests it has today, and by the end of 1987 Occhilupo had competed in more than 100 international events without any real break. Drugs may have taken a toll. I ask Occhilupo about what was said to be an impressive mid-'80s cocaine habit. He first answers that it was something he'd "tried," then says it was something he'd "abused," then attempts to steer somewhere in-between. "People said I was going through a ton of coke, but that was really an exaggeration."

I bring up the idea that he simply may have been destined for a collapse in 1987. He might have given up and moved home, I suggest, if he'd been an engineering student at Sydney University. "Yeah, I've thought about that," he replies. "I don't know how much of anything you can blame on other people, or whatever's happening around you. Things seem to happen on their own sometimes. That's a hard one."

We're still sitting at the balcony table, and Occhilupo at this point clasps his hands together, leans forward slightly, and gives me a quiet look. We've been digging through the difficult part of his story for most of the afternoon. He has, in fact, taken me all the way from childhood to 1994, and I'd circled back to the late '80s to gather details. Occhilupo so far has been nothing but open, thoughtful and gracious, but I know that his mood can turn, and turn quickly, and I wonder for a moment what kind of margin I'm working on. Occhilupo brings the conversation to an end, summing up his 1988 withdrawal from pro surfing: "It wasn't like I was sitting at home going, 'Oh, man, I've really blown it here.' Not at all. I didn't miss the attention, the competition, the image, the media, anything like that. It was more like, 'Unreal. Glad to be done with it.'" This last point is said in a slightly defensive tone. Now his voice goes back to normal. "But I wasn't really on top of my surfing the way I had been. And that part I missed—a lot."

The following morning, sitting on the beach, I watch Braden Dias paddle for a shoulder-high wave during a first-round heat of the 1996 Pipe Masters. The swell is small and from the north, and the contest is more or less an insult to Masters events of the past, but every few minutes a little right will peel neatly across the forecourt. Dias is probably the best young surfer in the trials. On this particular wave he banks off the top once, then twice, then races down the line before floating the last section in the shallow water near Off the Wall.

Mark Occhilupo had ridden a similar wave three heats earlier. Like Dias, he did two hooking moves on the face, then finished with a reentry. But Occhilupo was plainly surfing to a different standard; not just from Dias, but from every other young surfer in the event. His body was steady over his board, his board was steady through the water, and the gears were engaged, one to the next, up or down, with such a smooth hand that changes in speed almost didn't register. Each turn was full and rounded off. Dias, in comparison, attacked like a Supercross racer. The nose of his board chattered between maneuvers, while the tail moved forward, held, slipped, inched backward, then again moved forward. Dias can accelerate and decelerate in an instant—quicker than Occhilupo. He's more nimble. He can place his board at angles on a wave that Occhilupo can't. Occhilupo, of course, understands all of this perfectly. Earlier this year he spent time working on aerials and reverses, then quit, and now says the neutral-rail technique is "kind of irrelevant to the way I surf."

Dias and Occhilupo both win their heats, but Occhilupo is the standout surfer of the morning, and I remember something Tom Curren said to me recently: "If Occy surfs next year the way he did 10 or 12 years ago, he could win pretty much any contest he enters."

Curren's right. And, really, it's an amazing thought. Occhilupo has done little more than spit-shine his 1985 act, yet he's again in company with the world's best surfers. I don't know if Occhilupo's return is as much a testimony to his great natural talent as it is a condemnation of the New School. I *do* know that Slater, alone among his generation, has moved ahead of Occhilupo. The rest have simply moved sideways—literally and figuratively.

And because sideways surfing likely won't win the big WCT prizes this year at Jeffreys, Grajagan, Reunion, Sunset or Pipeline, it's not impossible to say, as Hynd did recently, that "a world championship is dead ahead" for Occhilupo. But I don't think so. He wasn't a particularly nimble competitor in the mid-'80s, and—despite a World Qualifying Series victory in Australia in early February and a third at the WCT season opener at Narrabeen in March—I don't expect he'll be one in 1997. It's been 11 years since he last won a major event. "He's not a competitive person," his sister, Fleur, said in 1990. "He's not ruthless that way." (Occhilupo sighed when I mentioned Fleur's remark. "That's true, you know. I really have no interest in hassling. I mean, I wouldn't paddle over someone's back to win a heat.")

But forget the rankings. I'd drive from San Francisco to San Diego in pouring rain and hand-deliver my $24.95 to get a highlight video of Occhilupo surfing next year's circuit. I'd probably do it for Slater, too. But nobody else on the WCT. Competition is just one reference point, in other words. The surfing world is simply a better and more interesting place with Occhilupo back on stage. It's certainly a great relief for Occhilupo himself—partly due, of course, to his new $200,000-a-year sponsorship contracts, but more because he's again met his own promise. "Years ago," he says, "when I told everyone I was quitting the tour to be a laborer—well, I was kidding myself on that one. It wasn't going to happen. I'm such a softy; I always have been. It's a really, really good thing I can surf."

Laboring didn't work in 1988, nor did a world tour comeback the following year. In 1990, Occhilupo again moved back to his parents' house, where he stayed indoors, didn't answer the phone, went days between showers, drank beer, and gained nearly 50 pounds. He still surfed on occasion. "I'd drive to this place where I'd run through a golf course, dodge around this electric fence, then climb down to where I knew nobody was going to see me. I'd have my little surf session down there. I'd get my little fix."

Then two of Occhilupo's friends died in relatively quick succession: Ronnie Burns in 1990 and Mark Sainsbury in 1992. On June 15, 1990, Occhilupo's father died of a brain tumor. "That was a hard one," says Wayne Bartholomew. "They went through rough times, but Mark really did love Luciano, and when he was gone Mark was just devastated."

In 1992 Occhilupo trimmed down and again joined the world tour, climbing as high as 20th in the ratings before having a long and semi-public breakdown during the European leg of the circuit. At Lacanau,

Occhilupo paddled in halfway through a heat, tossed his contest jersey in the air and walked away. In Biarritz one afternoon he buried his surfboards in the sand, and returned the next morning to find them smashed by a tractor. He slept just three or four hours a night. He spent breathtaking amounts on dinner and bar tabs. He challenged soon-to-be world champion Kelly Slater to a fistfight. "I was going so fast," he says today, thinking back. "I was running around, just non-stop, and not making sense at all to other people."

Occhilupo left France in September and took an apartment in Queensland. He could still be lucid and funny. But the insomnia continued, as did the drinking, and he generally felt both anxious and lethargic. He wasn't using cocaine. "If I had been on hard drugs at that point," he says, "I probably would've blown my head off."

Bereavement for Luciano had so far been the all-purpose explanation for Occhilupo's conduct. But in Australia, "I finally began to figure out something else was wrong with me," he recalls. "I just wasn't ready yet to find out what it was."

Four important things happened between Occhilupo's return to Australia in September of 1992, and the first realization, sometime in late 1994, that he might work his way back to top surfing form.

First, with the help of Wayne Bartholomew and Billabong owner Gordon Merchant, he spent his inheritance money on a beautiful piece of property at Bilambil Heights, in the hills behind Kirra.

Second, he met and married Beatrice Ballardie.

Third and fourth (simultaneously), he spent a year in therapy and put on 80 pounds.

Ballardie was introduced to Occhilupo not long after his return from France. She was a 35-year-old single mother raising a 10-year-old son, Raynor, and studying to be a drug and alcohol rehabilitation counselor. "I didn't think at first that I'd want to get involved with Mark," she recalls. "He really did seem a bit crazy." But Occhilupo's better qualities hadn't been totally obscured, and she took him on as a kind of project. Others had done the same over the years. Radiant charm and vulnerability have always made Occhilupo the great lost puppy of professional surfing, and with wildly mixed results, he's moved from one caregiver to the next: Hynd, Cheyne Horan, Bartholomew, Paul Sergeant, Brian Surratt, Merchant, Jack McCoy and now Beatrice.

"I told Mark he had to straighten out to stay with me," Beatrice continues, "and he agreed right away. Not because he was *that* madly in love; he just wanted to. He was sick of the way he'd been acting, and he needed someone strong to help. I was kind of the right person at the right time."

"Right after I met my wife," Occhilupo adds, "I started to sleep at night." They were married on February 12, 1993, four months after being introduced. Later that year, Mark, Beatrice and Raynor moved into a newly built two-story house on Mark's property.

Beatrice assumed the mantle of head of the family. She did the banking and check-writing. She insisted that Mark improve his language and table manners, to set a better example for his stepson. Occhilupo was still going through periods where everything felt speeded up. It was Beatrice who suggested he might be manic-depressive, and she made an appointment for him to see a psychiatrist. "By that time," he recalls, "I really wanted some kind of evaluation. I had a couple of friends who were manic-depressive, and they got on the lithium, and had it under control. So I thought maybe that was what I needed to do."

Occhilupo saw four psychiatrists in one year, and was diagnosed as having manic periods. But the prescription was for continued therapy, not lithium—a relief to Occhilupo, as he'd been warned of the drug's emotion-numbing side effects.

Once he'd brought the problem to light, Occhilupo began working on underlying causes. How that transferred into a one-year stay on the living-room couch, fattening up to 245 pounds on a circular diet of beer, potato chips and daytime television, is something he can't really explain. It wasn't really depression, he says. "More like hibernation." He didn't surf. Beyond a certain point he was so embarrassed about his size that he felt he had to stay indoors.

Then, as had long been expected, Merchant told Occhilupo his salary would soon be contingent on a real effort toward getting back in shape. Occhilupo cried when he left Beatrice and Raynor and flew off to Western Australia, where for three months he ran, surfed and dieted under the supervision of filmmaker Jack McCoy. He returned home nearly 50 pounds lighter. He again wanted to surf—all the time. The sandbar waves at nearby Duranbah became a training ground, where Occhilupo's strength, timing and positioning all came back without any real resistance. He was still big around the midsection. "But," he says, "I think I actually turned *harder* when I was chubby."

In the fall of 1995, he competed in the inaugural Billabong Challenge, held in beautiful 6- to 8-foot surf in Western Australia, and suddenly found himself on pace with two world-title contenders, Kelly Slater and Rob Machado. All the extra weight was gone by this time. He felt welcome and involved. Before the event finished, he'd decided to give the ASP another shot.

The afternoon trade winds gust through the yard and across the patio, and it's obvious, as Occhilupo recalls his experience in Western Australia, that the Billabong Challenge is where he marks the end of his rehabilitation and the beginning of an ongoing phase in his life and career.

He steps inside to find a sweatshirt. I do some quick additions, and when he returns I point out an obvious difference between his two rehabilitations. In 1992, he was able to get back in shape in just a few weeks. This time around it took about 18 months. He nods. "Yeah, that was on purpose. The first time, it was only a weight thing, which is really easy for me. I can put weight on and take if off like *that*. This time I got my head right first and did the weight after, and the whole thing took a lot longer. Slowly but surely—that was the way. My wife said it, the doctors said it, and that's really been the difference."

So, the last question is: Is Occhilupo in the clear? Bartholomew and Merchant tell me, without hesitation, that the hard times are over and done, and that he's home free. People who don't know Occhilupo, but know about mental health, as either patients or doctors, tell me Bartholomew and Merchant are kidding themselves.

Occhilupo looks evenly into my face when I ask the question, then offers a genuine demonstration of self-knowledge: "I can't say I'm completely in the clear. Nobody could do what I've done and say that. I still get nervous sometimes thinking about all the things that can happen. Accidents, or people dying, or just anything. Who knows? Pretty much whatever you have, you can lose. But I found out what was wrong with me. It used to be I didn't even want to know; I just sort of went along hoping things would take care of themselves. Then after I found out what was wrong, I wanted to get better, but I also wanted to know how it was going to happen. That means if I start going too fast again, I'll hopefully know what to do. Same if I get back in front of the TV for too long. Knowing all that—well, it's good. It's the best thing."

Three weeks later I was back home, watching Jack McCoy's gorgeous documentary of the 1995 Billabong Challenge. A bleary-eyed Occhilupo is shown walking along an oceanfront bluff on the morning of the contest. "I just got the flu yesterday," he says. "I feel like a ton of bricks." He struggles to lift an enormous board bag up onto the roof of his car, and remarks that everybody at the contest had dropped by with a flu remedy, and he'd tried them all. With forced good humor he looks ahead to his first heat and says, "We'll see how it goes." He then gives a laugh, followed by a cough, and there, visible for a moment, is the fault line between his strength and fragility.

But strength carries the day in Western Australia. Occhilupo paddles out, air-drops into his first wave, leans into a turn and settles into the tube. He looks powerful and relaxed.

Two years later, he still does.

A Beautiful Fight:
Hawaii Says Goodbye to Rell Sunn
By Bruce Jenkins · SURFER Vol. 39 No. 5 · May 1998

Rell Sunn's profound impact on the Hawaiian surfing community stemmed from the tiny things that make up the Aloha spirit. Her front door was always open, her towel was your towel, and if the ice cream truck rolled up and you were a penniless *keiki*, the loose change in her ashtray was fair game. But her warmth and guiding hand veiled the courageous warrior inside: she was also the woman who dove amid sharks, became Hawaii's first female lifeguard, stood up to belligerent bullies, and fought off cancer for fifteen years. In the end, it was the time she spent with you that was Rell's greatest gift, and she gave it freely to thousands of locals and visitors alike in her 48 years on earth. When she passed away in 1998, she was honored with a Hawaiian ceremony reserved for royalty, the kind that brings the gods and giants of Hawaii to tears. Bruce Jenkins captured the mood and magic of Hawaii's final tribute to Rell Kapoliokaehukai Sunn . . . a fitting send off for The Queen of Makaha.

A gentle rain fell on the Makaha Valley as they laid Rell Sunn to rest. It's OK to cry, they said; the heavens are crying. It was a gray, gloomy, perfect Saturday on Oahu's West Side, a day for tears, memories and the celebration of life.

To hear the locals tell it, Rell's guiding hand was everywhere. From the rains came blessing. From the depths of the ocean came a sign. The instant her ashes were spread, the surf got better. In their prayers, many had asked Rell to send more angels this way, more spirits just like hers. For this day, there was no need. The Queen of Makaha was presiding—smiling, vibrant and youthful.

When she died at 47 on the second day of 1998, nearly 15 years after being diagnosed with breast cancer, everyone was prepared. And everyone was shocked. As inevitable as her passing might have seemed, it was incomprehensible. Not since the great Duke Kahanamoku had a Hawaiian surfer touched so many lives. It was hard to recall anyone, in any walk of life, with such a well-rounded list of accomplishments.

But for those who saw Rell at the very end—withered, drawn, unable to speak—there was a proper sense of closure. "It was good that I got to see her then," said one of her best friends, Jeannie Chesser, who lost her son Todd to the 25-foot surf of Oahu's outer reefs last winter. "I saw her several times, and each time it was worse. It got to the point where I couldn't bear to watch."

By the time they cleared the water for Rell's ceremony at Makaha, a sense of perspective was gained. It was a wonderful time for the imagination, gazing out into the empty waves, remembering Rell at her best. "The only person allowed in the water will be Rell," said Brian Keaulana during the week's preparation. "We'll see her riding, we'll see her surfing style and her smile. We'll see the true beauty of Makaha and why she called that place home."

Keaulana was responsible for coordinating the event—he felt as if "my whole life was going to school for this"—and he was one of many vital figures on the beach that day. There were Rell's parents, her daughter Jan, brother Eric, and sisters Anella, Kula and Val. There was her husband, the incomparable Dave Parmenter, steeled for the occasion through sad, reddened eyes.

It was Parmenter, in conjunction with Drs. Mark Renneker and Keith Block, who led Rell down the most civil path through cancer. They were all in San Francisco last August when Rell's condition hit a new low—and her spirit stunned a community.

"The tumors had spread from her chest to her brain, and her Hawaiian doctors were fairly grim about it," said Renneker, who specializes in alternative care for patients with life-threatening illnesses. "When cancer doctors start talking that way, they're expecting you to die. She'd been having severe headaches, vomiting, and she was on a very high dose of steroids, which make you swell up like a pumpkin and, worse yet, cause your muscles to atrophy. So she was losing her ability to surf, or even paddle."

Always open to every type of therapy, Rell and Dave came to the University of California at San Francisco for what is known as gamma knife treatment—"a cutting-edge, experimental type of therapy, a kind of bloodless surgery that applies specific radiation," said Renneker. "The night before the surgery, they were at my house and I heard these plunk-plunk sounds and a lot of laughing. I peered through the door to the next room, and I see Rell and Dave just rolling around the bed in laughter. Dave had a ukulele, they were fooling around with some silly Hawaiian kids' song, and they were just in hysterics. It was like that the whole time.

"When Rell signed her consent form for the procedure, she put a big smiling face on it. Just imagine that. It wasn't some pathetic *Terms of Endearment* thing; she really meant it. She really wanted to thank these people for doing something for her. The whole department became different because of that single, simple action."

The surgery brought Rell's brain tumors under control, she was able to taper down her medication, and she began surfing again. But still there were problems; they never stopped. Back home at Makaha, Rell had been devastated by the sudden death (also of breast cancer) of her dear friend Pua Mokuau, herself a great surfer and lifeguard. Rell had been unable to attend the annual Biarritz surf festival honoring the living legends of Hawaii, or even her own menehune contest—celebrating its 23rd year—at Makaha. When Rell surfed her home break about two weeks before Thanksgiving, helped into the surf by Dave and Luana Froiseth, it would be the last session of her life.

In the final hours of 1997, Dave summoned Rell's closest friends to her bedside with a sense of urgency. It was apparent that her time had come. "They set it up so beautifully," said photographer Linny Morris Cunningham. "It was all color and light, tapes of the world island music, picture-window view of the Waianae mountain range, and Rell was on a bed of brightly colored sheets and aloha print quilts. There wasn't that dark, grim feeling of the hospital. The difficult part was seeing how terribly weak she was. She couldn't even squeeze our hands. But she could smile. That was one of the last things she gave up, her smile."

On New Year's Day, Dave and some friends carried Rell on a stretcher to the Makaha shoreline, where her family had placed a bed. "It was her last wish," said Parmenter, "to taste the sea on her lips once again."

To the absolute end, she was Rell as the surfing world had always known her. "If you can imagine the kind of courage it takes to get up every morning and face that—every single morning—and never have a moment's respite from that fear," Parmenter said in an interview with the *Honolulu Advertiser*. "And every time you go to the doctor, the news is a little worse. She never wept or felt pity. She was unvanquished."

Parmenter's loving touch had made an indelible impression on the Waianae community, and now he rose higher in their estimation. "With Dave, once you're married to Rell, he married all of us guys," said Keaulana. "His heart is Rell's heart. He has Rell's blood in his veins. Rell did not marry him for just any reason. He became Rell. We have never seen anybody so totally dedicated to a person."

It was Brian's mother, Momi, who captured the essence of Rell's passing. "I asked Rella to do me a favor," she said. "I told her, 'You fought such a beautiful fight for so many years, but when you are through, just close your eyes and go to sleep.' And that is what she did."

Rell Sunn was a person who took surfboards to bed with her as a child, caressing them as she drifted off to sleep. She had a canoe in her front yard and paddled it with expertise. She was one of the world's great free divers, catching fish out of fairness and sport with nothing but a three-pronged spear and the air in her lungs. She was flat-out the best female longboarder of all time. She surfed with style, feminity and vintage Hawaiian good humor: on a lawn chair, with her dog or with the ingenious maneuvers required in the annual Buffalo Big Board contest: Scooter Boy, Allen Wrench, Dying Cockroach. These were the wonderful memories shared in the day following her death. But someone had to prepare Makaha for the arrival of 3,000 people on that special Saturday. It was Brian's dad, the great Buffalo Keaulana, who took charge.

The parking at Makaha is pretty much where you find it, on thin stretches bordering the Farrington Highway. The locals' only hope was to clear away a hillside covered with thorns, weeds and kiawe bushes. "But nothing was happening," said Brian. "Finally my dad comes out with a machete, jumps into the bushes and starts hacking away. Across the road the surf's going off. All the beach boys going, Buff, what are you doing?" He goes, 'I don't care if anybody's gonna help me. I'll clean this place by myself.'

"Next thing you know there's like a hundred guys over there with shovels, rakes, pitchforks and chainsaws, just attacking this field of thorns. Finally one guy brought a dozer and cleared the whole four acres. Everybody's all stoked."

What about permission?

"Didn't get it," said Brian. "No environmental impact, no red tape, no nothing. Just the Hawaiian law."

The Friday night before the ceremony was left to more unsung heroes. The great watermen of Oahu are people like Keaulana, Terry Ahue, Mel Pu'u and Dennis Gouveia: lifeguards, Jet Ski operators, big-wave riders, purveyors of heroism and safety. On the Mainland, dignitaries hire a work crew to do the dirty work. At Makaha that night, they were the hard laborers: cleaning, clearing and building structures instead of drinking beers and talking story. Their moment's respite came after the preparation was complete, throwing small beach parties the Hawaiian way: tents, barbecues, flatbed trucks. Around midnight, one could hear songs of the sea ("Everybody go surf/Ala Moana and Makaha, too") and the soothing sound of Pu'u's guitar. They handled Saturday's tear-down with equal efficiency and dedication; in essence, they did everything.

On Saturday morning, as if on cue, the surf came up. A week of perfect weather vanished into sheets of rain, flowing easterly across the landscape. Keoni Watson and Mark Cunningham greeted the first signs of light with a roaring bodysurf in some heaving 4- to 6-footers along the Yokahama stretch. The Makaha lineup filled quickly, and the beach became a once-in-a-lifetime history of Hawaiian surfing: George Downing, Wally Froiseth and John Kelly, leading to Fred Hemmings, Ricky Grigg, Peter Cole and Fred Van Dyke, followed by Barry Kanaiaupuni and Clyde Aikau through Laird Hamilton, Darrick Doerner, Dave Kalama, Sunny Garcia, Johnny-Boy Gomes and Derek Ho. And countless more. West Side mainstays were everywhere, people known by nicknames given long ago: Bunky, Boxer, Boogie, Flash, Tinky, Bird, Buffalo.

Visitors filed through a magnificent gallery of photographs, showing all sides of Rell from her childhood to her early-40s prime. Lifeguard, schoolteacher, radio personality, co-founder of the women's pro tour, hula instructor, writer, Hokule'a crew member, advisor to countless Hawaiians on cancer awareness, world traveler—gracious, what a life she had. The *ho'okupu* (offering), as Brian explained it, was "surf, sand and sound. Bring sand from your beaches, water from your surf and a conch shell, for the sound of a thousand blowing at once. That's how it was centuries ago when Queen Emma was put to rest. It's a sound no one has heard for ages."

As the morning progressed, the ocean water filled a large wooden bowl. The sand from many beaches formed a handsome pile. Pure, essential music flowed from the likes of Brother Noland, Jerry Santos and the Cazimero brothers. People arrived from the North Shore by way of the Kolekole Highway—magically opened by the military for this one day. The eulogy, beautifully written by Parmenter, was read by Ron Mizutani, a local television broadcaster, and the task overwhelmed him. He twice backed away from the podium, crying, but when Jan and Momi came to his side, touching his shoulders, waves of encouragement and applause washed his way. Waves were literally part of the ceremony as they slammed into the backwash, rushed up the bluff and doused the ankles of onlookers on the outer edge.

Rell's ashes were safely inside a glass ball—so appropriate for the woman who once wrote, "I often think of myself as a gypsy glass ball floating from one shore to another in perfect surf, fragile, yet arriving and departing in one piece." Now she was in Dave's hands, and he held the ball as he boarded a four-man canoe with Brian, Jan and Eric. It was Rell's canoe, her middle name hand-painted in pink: Kapolioka'ehukai ("Heart of the Sea"). Right about then, the fine mist lifted. The canoe was about to embark into the empty Makaha lineup. And the conch shells blew, a haunting, mournful sound that requires no technology or electrical power, only knowledge.

It was Rell's request to have her ashes dropped at the Blowhole, her favorite lineup spot on fun-size days. Brian knew that some formidable surf was coming, "and whatever happens is destined," he said. "We might make a clean getaway, or it might be one of those things. We might get whacked by waves, which to me will be Rell saying, 'Heads-up guys,' in a fun way."

Brian knows Makaha like a mother knows her child, but as he steered the canoe into the lineup, he became slightly uncertain. "I think Rell was playing hide-and-seek with us," he said. "The Blowhole is not just anywhere, it is exactly one place. Lots of water moving around, not much time . . . for a moment there, we couldn't find it.

"And then Rell's arms just reached out and guided us," said Brian. "There was a bubbling, a boiling in the water. She just blew it up for us."

The utter jubilation was something only those four people could truly know. Dave released the ashes and within seconds, a large two-wave set headed their way. Snapping out of funereal mode, they furiously escaped the first. With Brian in charge and Dave up front, there would be no mistakes. They glided expertly into the second wave and rode it all the way to the sand, Dave still clutching the beautiful glass ball. On the beach, there were tears, joyous shouts and "chicken skin." This happens only in Hawaii. Nowhere else.

As it turned out, Rell had one more wonderful surprise. A solid 200 surfers were now unleashed on the waves, and the ocean was completely different. Trade winds suddenly returned after more than a week's absence in the islands. They didn't last long, maybe a half-hour, but as the ceremony gave way to surfing, the wind turned offshore. And what a spectacle: everyone riding a wave for Rell. Two men clasped hands on separate boards; two others climbed on a board together. There were eight people on one wave, all of them tossing leis into the air. Except for a few kids, gorging out of pure stoke, a single wave was enough. The big people rode one for Rell and happily returned to the beach.

"This whole day was so wonderful," said Rell's sister, Anella. "I just can't believe how perfect it was. I'm pretty OK right now, but there's so much emotion. Just when I thought I was done crying, it all starts again. Did you hear what Brian said? He said Rell was playing with them."

Rest easy, Rell Sunn. Come see us often. 🦎

Most Influential Surfers of the Century: Kelly Slater

By Jason Borte · SURFER Vol. 40 No. 10 · Oct. 1999

SURFER marked the end of the millennium with a list of the Top 25 most influential surfers of the 20th century. The net was cast wide, and hauled in statesmen, surfboard designers, inventors and performers. Though a full two years into his early retirement, the then six-time world champion Kelly Slater still carried the torch for the high-performance vanguard. Such overwhelming dominance may have surprised some, but not fellow East Coaster Jason Borte, who saw the kid coming light-years away.

20. Kelly Slater

In 1985, I saw the future, and it made me want to quit. Reaching the boys' division man-on-man semi-finals of the Eastern Surfing Association Championships was already a stretch. I was a dreamer, but my next foe was Slater, a harmless looking, puka-shelled 13-year-old, and already a legend. For me, avoiding embarrassment took precedence over winning. But what if? No time to think—he opened the heat with an average looking left, whack, whack . . . what the hell?! The elfin terror in Sundek rainbows exploded through the lip, flipped a barrel roll and continued down the line.

God help me.

Child prodigy, demigod, superfreak. Kelly Slater makes anyone else riding a surfboard look stupid. He is too far removed to be considered a role model. Watching his act doesn't inspire us to surf, because not even our mind surfing can touch him. The six-time world champ nonpareil remains the most electric surfer in the galaxy, and his equal is likely still unborn.

What of the road from Cocoa Beach to Oz, one that Kelly drove in his sleep? First and foremost, his natural ability is staggering, with quintessential build and rubberman flexibility. Watch him switchfoot at maxing Pipe, and it becomes clear that with some practice, he could restart his career as a goofyfoot. Second, desperation breeds desire. A childhood spent in soggy Cocoa dribblers begat an unwavering hunger. Bloom at a perfect pointbreak, and beachbreak boredom is a killer. Finally, imagination. Riding anemic vessels that are mere extensions of his feet, he sees virgin lines and creates a visual symphony. In layman's terms, he's a visionary.

Just how bright is Kelly's star? Forget his attempted crossovers into TV and rock-stardom. If anything, they diluted his image and boosted our egos by exposing his mortality. His god status is purely based on his performances in the water, and, in that arena, he's a man among boys. On tour, the best surfers in the world watch him with awe, lining the beach for his heats like giddy grommets. He alone sparked the New School revolution, a shameful feat to the over-30 crowd, perhaps, but immortalizing him to the next generation. The kids. That's where Kelly's influence is immeasurable. They drive the market, and Kelly drives them. No one, least of all Quiksilver, would question his seven-figure salary. From Sebastian to San Clemente and Sao Paulo to Sydney, his popularity is unprecedented. Generation Next thanks him, not realizing the Jordanesque shoes he will leave them. For better or worse, kids believe in fairy tales. Pumping down the line, they come to a section and think, "What would Kelly do?" The truth is, they'll never know.

Simple Procedure

By Rob Gilley · SURFER Vol. 41 No. 10 · October 2000

Every surfer's life centers on an endless pursuit of an elusive and evanescent quarry. A vision haunts us: that at the end of some faraway deserted road, the perfect wave is unspooling onto a tropical reef. The urge to see what is around the next headland is so strong, it seeps into every part of the surfer's life. A Friday night at the movies, for example, finds our fellow theatergoers engrossed in a make-out scene on the beach, while the surfers in the crowd zero in on the wave peeling in the background and wondering if the love scene was shot at low or high tide. We see potential surf everywhere; no car commercial or magazine or even, in Rob Gilley's case, dentist appointment, passes without assiduous sifting of some potential clue to the whereabouts of an untapped vein of surf. And sometimes, as Gilley points out, our vigilance pays off.

I've never really been able to figure out why dentists seem so intent on conversation while they work on you. One would think that with all the education required to be a full-fledged oral practitioner, they'd have learned that it's a little difficult to speak without the use of lips and a tongue. Nevertheless, I recently found myself lying there, mouth agape and full of dental paraphernalia, desperate to pry some conversation out of my dentist while gargling, rinsing and trying to get the good doctor to talk about a secret island with perfect surf.

Maybe I should back up. I had recently discovered that my new dentist, Dr. Bridges, was an avid scuba diver, and that every few months he'd close up shop for a two-week vacation. Apparently he has done this without fail for the past 20 years. Three trips a year for two decades, 60 trips in all.

Bonus frequent flyer miles for every root canal? What a friggin' scam.

On one of my first visits, I noticed a few photographs on the walls of his office. "Isn't that Fiji?" I asked, pointing to an aerial shot of a fairly nondescript lagoon.

"Yes, how did you know that?" the doctor responded, sounding a little surprised.

"I happen to have been there a couple times on surf trips," I answered.

"Oh, yes, you must have gone to Tavarua. We went by the outside reef there a couple of times on our way to do some ledge diving. It looked like there were a few fellows riding some really nice breakers there."

"Ever been to Moorea?" I asked, ready to impress him with my worldliness.

"Yes, twice actually. Once in '88 and again in '96. We did some night shark dives last time I was there."

"How about the Cook Islands?"

"Sure, we did an outer island trip to Aitutaki this last time. A beautiful, beautiful place."

"Mauritius?"

"Yes."

"Bali?"

"Yes."

Now I was getting desperate. "Australia?"

"Yes, of course, the Great Barrier Reef."

"What about the Bahamas?"

"Yes. That's actually where I got certified."

I could tell I was starting to bore him. Since I'd almost run out of islands that I'd traveled to myself, I decided to probe the depths a little more. "What about Papua New Guinea?" I wagered, with a gleam in my eye.

"Last year. Extraordinary place."

"The Solomons?"

"Great wreck dives."

"The Virgin Islands?"

The old guy actually chuckled. "Yes."

"The Seychelles?"

"The most beautiful islands in the world."

Well, I had to admit he had me. And like that, my attitude went from competitive zeal to complete respect. This guy was gnarly.

But it didn't hit me until a few days later, when I experienced a rare moment of clarity. If this guy has been everywhere under the Seven Seas, then he's probably passed by plenty of perfect surf and not even known it. Scuba divers like to frequent the outside reef passes, so if properly debriefed maybe this guy could point me to some other places where he's seen some "nice breakers."

Dental pain to the rescue. A few days prior, I'd been pleased to discover that a temporary filling was starting to cause me a significant amount of discomfort, and in a bizarre twist of fate, I was actually looking forward to my dentist appointment. I even spent some time rehearsing a line of questioning so that when I walked into Dr. Bridges's office, I could take the shortest route to determining whether he could lead me to unmolested surf. When he finally greeted me, he explained that he was running behind schedule, so we'd have to talk while he was removing the temporary filling and replacing it with a permanent one.

He could have pulled out a tooth with rusty vise grips for all I cared, so long as I had enough time to get the goods out of him.

While the doctor numbed the area and prepared the drill bit, I gave him the short course on what surfers look for or, rather, don't look for in good waves (closeouts, exposed reef, large man-eating sharks, etc.), and then mentioned a group of islands that were rumored to have good surf somewhere in the broad expanse of the Equatorial Pacific.

This next part is where my memory takes on a crystal-clear, slow-motion quality. I can still see the metallic curvature of the saliva extractor and the side-lit outline of the hygienist's face in my periphery as I watched the following words tumble from Bridges's lips:

"Yes, those islands are actually a very popular destination for divers, some of the best underwater visibility in the world. And come to think of it, on one of the islands, I think it was called . . . yes, that's it, we dove outside a reef that had the exact same type of breakers you're talking about. In fact, I distinctly remember remarking to my dive buddy that those waves looked a lot like the ones we'd seen in Fiji, except that they were breaking in the opposite direction, if that makes any sense."

Because of the novocaine all I could do was grunt, but it was possibly the most joyfully expressive grunt in the history of dentistry.

After my appointment, I immediately drove to Barnes & Noble. Out of the thousands of travel books on the shelves, I could only locate one on the area, but it was well worth the trip. It was too good to be true. Not only were these islands served by a reputable air carrier, but there was comfortable lodging, rental cars, no significant epidemics, English was the national language, and best of all, there were several independent boat-charter businesses that already specialized in trips to the outer reefs. It looked so promising, in fact, that for a while I thought this whole thing might be a cruel, elaborate hoax being played on me by Ted Brambeau.

And so with fresh recruits Dan Malloy and Mike Todd, I flew across the Pacific to encounter the almost unknown, only to find myself, less than four days later, hip-deep in perfect, empty surf. It was all so simple. Land on the island, find a modest, clean hotel to stay in, charter a boat for a run to the fringing outer reef toward where my dentist indicated he'd seen waves and . . . well, when we pulled up to the inside of the reef pass, all our jaws dropped simultaneously. In front of us stacked a series of double-overhead, tapering rights that wrapped around the reef at the optimal angle to catch the sideshore trades straight up into their face—and best of all, there wasn't another soul around for miles.

Surf trips aren't supposed to be like this.

What ensued can only be described as surfer heaven. Dan and Mike scrambled out of the boat and proceeded to get tubed out of their minds, then carving themselves silly in the perfect cutback position. Both referred to the session as "the quickest 2 hours of our lives," and said that the wave was as good or better than Lance's Rights in Sumatra—only here there wasn't a chance that a boatload of Brazilians was going to show up before dark.

On land, this innocuous little island proved itself to be almost exactly as the guidebook had labeled it: an unpretentious Pacific backwater with a very friendly attitude toward outsiders.

In fact, the only thing close to a disappointing experience we had was when we decided to hike up to a waterfall in a remote part of the island. At the beginning of our trek, some local kids saw what we were up to and tagged along with us all the way to the top. When we reached the summit, water poured over the edge of a deep cave that offered a breath-taking view of the lush, palm-studded slope and the reefs beyond. It was a nice, quiet change from the din of Southern California rush hour that we'd been immersed in just a few days prior. One of the local kids even began to serenade us with a melodious chant.

Just as we thought we were having this culturally pristine experience, however, Mike recognized the "chant" as a song from the Backstreet Boys' *Millennium* CD. Then the oldest kid tapped me on the shoulder, and in all seriousness said, "That will be nine dollars, please,"

But this was an insignificant event compared to what happened during our next session out at the reef the following morning. A few minutes after the boys hit the lineup, we could see another boat approaching, and as it got closer, we could clearly make out white men and surfboards.

"Oh shit," I thought. "Here it comes." We'd stumbled across a couple of surfers' secret garden, and they probably thought we were trampling all over it. I half expected loud yells and maybe a few threats thrown in, but when they anchored and paddled to the lineup, there was nothing of the sort. Dan later paddled back to the boat and said, "Those guys are super-cool."

It turned out that our new friends were both Americans and stood in stark contrast to the bitter expat stereotype. In fact, Mike, an attorney, showed us nothing but hospitality and was almost exploding with the desire to talk to other surfers about how good the waves were here. He could barely believe his luck: here he was with a good job (he worked as a legal counsel for the government), a free house and was sitting on one of the best uncrowded waves in the world. Of course, he recognized that our presence represented a potential threat to his little heaven, but when we said that we wouldn't name the specific island or island group in the event of a potential article, he seemed visibly relieved.

During a 36-hour spell of pounding rain, we used the downtime to get to know Mike a little better, and when the next swell arrived, he gave us a ride out to the reef. En route, he explained that he'd been living on this island for a couple years, and before him, a surfer from Kauai had lived here for about 10 years. It boggled the mind to think how many barrels that guy must have logged in a decade.

When we reached the pass, another super-clean, slightly overhead set of waves barreled across the reef, each alternatively spitting light clouds of mist from their chambers, each lightly groomed by the offshore winds. This was one of those moments when I was half-torn between shooting photos and tossing my equipment into the drink and just going surfing—a glorious dilemma.

During the last few days on the island, we were able to reflect on the whole scenario a little bit, and we wondered how such a perfect—and perfectly accessible—wave could exist in the year 2000. With merely the slightest deviation from the Indo/Fiji/Tahiti flight plan, we had run across an island with all the comforts of home, yet it was untouched by the masses. Still, the procedure of getting here was so elementary it almost didn't seem fair. Or, were we just the luckiest surfers in the world?

Consider what happened on the way home, when we stopped on a neighboring island reported to have good waves. There we met yet another expatriate American surfer, Ken, who was also extremely friendly and shared his surf spot with us. Rather than running away form the California apocalypse with a bad attitude toward his fellow humans, Ken had simply got sick of the rat race at home and was now living on this beautiful tropical island, working a job he enjoyed and that the local people appreciated, surfing empty waves by himself as much as possible.

One rainy day, Ken told us about another perfect wave that was "as good or better than G-Land," and as accessible as the wave we'd been surfing the week before. At first I had my doubts, until I discovered Ken's line of work.

The man was a dentist. 🐉

Water from the Moon
Sailing Back through Time in Indonesia's Fabled Spice Islands

By Steve Barilotti · SURFER Vol. 42 No. 9 · Sept. 2001

While scientists adamantly deny the possibility of time travel, surfers argue that they have already made the fantasy a reality. You just have to know, they point out, where lie the doors to the past. *SURFER*'s itinerant scribe Steve Barilotti uncovered one such wormhole to another time somewhere off the coast of Irian Jaya, when he and his intrepid crew set off to explore disputed territory in the chain once known as the Spice Islands. On their voyage they were visited by the ghosts of wars past and present, and stumbled into the crossfire of a century's old struggle. The lesson? That the past is just as likely to be a quagmire of grimy quicksand as it is a utopian high meadow.

Corporal Keishichi Kishi sat on the beach, looked hard and long towards Japan, and cursed under his breath. The ragged 35-year-old foot soldier, bearded as his ancient grandfather and nearly naked except for a crudely woven hemp loincloth, sat atop a large driftwood log. Narrowing his eyes to gun slits, he peered hard over the crest of a large East Indies swell humping up on the outside reef.

He briefly considered his rifle, propped next him like a favored walking stick. It was a vintage, bolt-action 7.7 Meiji type-99 with right-hand twist and an imperfect sight that required a certain degree of Zen to hit its mark. A relic from his mummified soldier's life.

Corporal Kishi desired many things—cooked rice, a hot bath, warm sake, Fred Astaire movies, cigarettes, chocolate, a soft giggling Tokyo girl nestled in the crook of his arm. But what he yearned for above all was to be a corpse rotting away in the jungle along with his comrades who had the good fortune to be killed in honorable combat over a decade ago. The day when a plague of gaijin soldiers streamed into the jungle with mortars and flamethrowers and began picking them off like flushed quail.

But it had all been so confusing in those last days. Kishi, a rear-echelon cipher clerk stationed in the Moluccas, suddenly found himself on the front lines of a last-ditch invasion force sworn to take back the island of Morotai from the Allies in late December 1944. Unprepared for battle after two years of garrison life, the Japanese defenders were methodically slaughtered by the ferocious, battle-honed Allies.

In the chaotic rout that followed, Kishi and ten others fled deep into the jungle. Cut off from all communication, the lost squad became *zanryusha*, stragglers, although they believed they were still fighting the war. Their last orders, from a sergeant now long dead, had been to stand by. And on this matter, the Bushido code was quite clear. Victory or death.

And there they stayed, long after the guns were silenced, long after the gaijin soldiers had left.

The local militia had been after him and his men for years, but could never catch them. If chased, the police would only get off a few wild shots before the starved, half-naked little soldiers evaporated into the jungle. In time the villagers accepted them as part of the spirit culture that permeates every aspect of these queer lush islands. They became hungry ghosts, stuck in time, stories to threaten bad little children with. Kishi pondered his home beyond the reef and this oppressive vast blue ocean that marked the perimeter of his exiled life. It being November by his calculations, it would be snowing in the mountainous Yamagata prefecture where he grew up. He smiled at the memory of cold.

The swell feathered and pitched forward with a dull boom.

Corporal Keishichi Kishi looked over the waves and saw great cold flakes of snow falling on his mother's roof. He contemplated his rifle and the two remaining bullets in the clip. He could die a soldier after all. He thanked all gods and ancestors for this gracious opportunity to redeem himself.

Clove. It's the first thing you smell on deplaning in Makassar. Clove, and the wet fecund smell of rotting vegetation. Kreteks, clove and tobacco cigarettes, are the logical incense to all the gods of sweat and poorly paid heavy labor. Originally sold as an herbal cure for asthma at the turn of the century, kreteks quickly became the addiction of choice among Indonesia's poor. They found a sweet calming balm and cheap entertainment in the "tek tek tek"—the crackling gecko song of these beautiful tortured islands.

It was the sweet Christmas scent of cloves and nutmeg that first lured the Arab traders, and later the Dutch and the English, to these small fragrant islands strewn along the equator. In the 1600s, in a time before refrigeration, spices masked the taste of rancid meat and were thought to cure syphilis and the plague. A shopping bag of nutmeg corns, which only grew in the remote Banda Islands, could buy one a comfortable estate in England or Amsterdam. Spices were the lucrative drug trade of their time and particularly nasty wars and colonial empires were built on the back of now-common kitchen condiments. The great trading companies are gone now, with only the crumbling remains of coral-stone forts left behind as a dubious legacy.

Somewhere 30,000 feet below, between the drinks' service and the distinctly unhilarious Dutch inflight comedy shorts, we crossed over the Wallace Line. Named for Alfred Russel Wallace, the genial 19th-century English naturalist, the line is a hypothetical boundary halving Indonesia east and west down the Makassar Strait. The line represents a fundamental shift in species distribution—plant, animal and otherwise—from one side to the other. To the east, oriental Asia; the west, aboriginal Australasia. The line provides a convenient analogy for Indonesia in general, a stitched-together country of fractious islands that seems destined to tear itself apart at the seams.

Wallace, self-taught and self-funded, combed the Malay Archipelago from 1854 to 1862, braving disease, shipwreck and headhunters in his singlehanded quest to collect and study exotic new species. His keen observations regarding the evolutionary process were so eloquent and uncannily similar to Darwin's as-yet-unwritten *Origin of the Species* that Darwin was bound by ethics to share credit with Wallace.

Our journey, a planned 1000-mile surf exploration trip, would be roughly tracing Wallace's route in reverse while compressing four years into two weeks.

Our crew, six in total, descended roughly through the clouds into Sulawesi. Below us, through thick patches of mist I saw miles of verdant rainforest broken only by the occasional muddy river snaking to the ocean. As we circled the spine of volcanic mountains that run the length of this exotic octopus-shaped island, there was an abrupt ascent from coastal wetlands to towering ridgelines.

Our surf crew ranged in age from early 30s to 19 and all possessed exceptional but varied surfing skills. Keith Malloy, newly paroled from the WCT, was eager to spark his creative drive before delving into film projects with brothers Chris and Dan. Hans Hagen, Laguna Beach soul man, had a break between high-end New York modeling gigs and elected to throw in for a no-frills surf adventure. The two young Hawaiians, Aamion Goodwin and Mark Healey, were up for anything.

Ted Grambeau, an old Indo hand who had mustered this trip on short notice, would be photographing the expedition. Having traveled with Ted before, I knew there was a good chance of discovering decent, possibly epic, new surf breaks. Ted is an expert mapsman, and can track a new swell like a Bushman dogging down a wounded gemsbok.

"Luck is the intersection of preparation and opportunity," pontificated Ted as our boards came off the baggage carousel.

The skipper, Rob Nilon, met us in the middle of a torrential downpour that stopped traffic with its ferocity. Rob was a tall gregarious Queenslander in his late 40s who made his fortune doing tilt-up construction on the Gold Coast but preferred running surf charters up throughout Indonesia. His vessel was the *Arythmea*, a spacious 42' Tony Granger–designed catamaran built by Rob in his spare time.

Rob brought his 25-year-old mate Elvis who had been working aboard *Arythmea* for the last two years. Elvis, originally from Nias, was a steady hand and fast becoming a skipper in his own right under Rob's tutelage. Elvis in turn had brought along his buddy Anton who was younger and part Japanese—a legacy from the Japanese occupation of Indonesia 50 years ago.

On the two-hour drive over to Bitung Harbor, Rob let have us the bad news up front: his cook of two years, a devout Sumatran Muslim, had deserted him without notice the night before. Elvis said the cook had heard from some refugees back in Bitung that Christians were shooting and beheading Muslims in Halmahera, the area we were destined to sail to.

Rob said not to worry. He made a decent curry and excellent fish cakes.

Rough passage last night. As we motorsailed east, we smacked head on and blind into a rambunctious monsoon low. Being paying supercargo, the surf crew and I retreated to our fetid bunks and held on as best we could. It got fairly nasty as the waves grew to the size of houses. We took bone-shaking hits over the bow that rattled the boat to her keel bolts. But *Arythmea* put her shoulder to the swells and gamely pushed on.

I came on deck a couple of times during the night to see the skipper and crew in full foul-weather gear. They wore that weary, pissed-off expression of fatigue and anxiety that comes from holding a night watch shorthanded. Rob commented in his genial offhand manner that we had just weathered a 40-knot gale. Elvis huddled around a cup of tea after wrestling down a wildly flapping mainsail that had come unlashed.

This morning I'm driving the boat for a spell to give the crew a much-deserved break. It's easy duty. The sea has settled out and once I have my compass heading I simply line up with a distant landmark—in this case the gap between two palm-covered atolls—and steer with my foot.

Everybody is up now, busying themselves around the salon table with books or scrapbook journals. Ted pores over the charts looking for likely reef passes. Our charts, taken from Dutch admiralty surveys, date back to 1926. There is an asterisk that says to refer to our admiralty sailing directions for areas of former Japanese sea-lane mining.

Rob keeps a hand-carved ship's model of a Buginese *pinisi* in the galley. A cross between an Arab dhow and a 19th century windjammer, the graceful pinisi are the traditional sailing craft of the Bugis, a seagoing tribe from Makassar famed as traders, smugglers and at times, blood-thirsty pirates. In the days of the 17th century spice race the mere sight of a stealthy, black-sailed pinisi on the horizon was enough to make a fat Dutchman soil his breeches. The Bugis were so ruthless that they later became the sharp-fanged "Boogiemen" of children's nightmares.

The Bugis still sail these Indonesian seas, although many have traded in their stately topmasts for Chinese diesel engines. They transport some spices, but the bulk of their cargo is more prosaic goods like Coca-Cola and plastic folding chairs. They sail according to the traditional monsoon winds, and though delivery is often at the mercy of the tide and *jam kerat* ("rubber time"), they are the cheapest, and often the only, supply line for many of the more remote islands.

If the Bugis still exist in the 21st century, so do their darker alter ego, pirates. These days, however, pirates are not storybook rogues with parrots on their shoulders, but small seagoing gangs fitted out with high-speed launches and bristling with surplus AK-47s. They prey on small craft and fishing boats, mugging the occupants for valuables, but will occasionally hijack large freighters, kill or set the crew adrift, and sail off with the cargo to be sold on the black market. There were 113 reported piracies in Indonesia in 2000 and the U.S. State Department has issued a blanket warning against all non-essential travel in the waters north of Sulawesi.

Armed with these statistics I spent a number of anxious hours scanning the horizon doing the calculus of pirates—figuring that they would need to be close enough to established sea lanes to have a steady trade, but far enough from law enforcement to avoid retribution. Using this logic we stayed well offshore when not surf exploring, knowing gasoline in these remote regions was a precious commodity not to be squandered on anything but a sure deal.

Occasionally I would I see a silhouette on the horizon of small low vessel brimming with small hard brown men. If they veered towards us I would become acutely aware of how utterly vulnerable we were; a boatload of naïve white tourists that had somehow floated beyond the safety cordons of tourist-friendly Indonesia. We carried no weapons other than kitchen knives and a speargun. There was no 911 here, no police, no friendly neighbors, no common language and a continent of misunderstanding compressed into a few hundred yards between us and them. That they turned out to be merely curious fishermen who wanted to trade fish for cigarettes did nothing to ease my dreams in these torpid alien waters.

On our third day out, we rounded a small island off Halmahera and were lured inside by a likely-looking left that turned out to be a dry-reef hoax. We traced the densely forested coast for the better part of the morning until we came within sight of a small village. The most prominent building was a prim little New England church with a narrow white steeple.

As we cruised by at a stately pace we saw at least 200 villagers crowding the shoreline and a small wooden wharf marked with a freshly painted sign that proclaimed "Pos Marinar" (Marine Post). They stood silent and wary as statues, no one returning our big friendly waves. It was unsettling, attracting this kind of stony scrutiny by the simple act of transit.

I scanned the wharf with binoculars and saw at least three men dressed in jungle mufti and carrying automatic assault rifles.

Suddenly a single gunshot shattered the thick equatorial air. That lonely report, little more than small firecracker, conveyed volumes of urgent conflicting information. The crowd immediately bolted out of their stasis and began running back to their houses. Our crew quickly scurried back to the cockpit and frantically began calculating bullet ranges and speed/distance ratios.

Keith vocalized the thought that was gelling on everybody's lips: "Let's get OUT of here!"

The skipper powered up but as soon as we were well out of range, the villagers began shouting, waving wildly for us to return. This had little to appeal to Keith, and to tell the truth, I was in complete agreement.

But I remembered a piece of advice given to me by Johnny the Chinese shopkeeper back in Bitung. While he didn't advise us leaving Bitung ("Halmahera . . . many bad Muslims, much fighting, no food, people hungry."), if we insisted on going, he said we should make friends with the villagers and the army. It was likely the marines were simply letting us know they were armed. And there was no telling what was around the next point. We would take our chances with the Christian boogiemen.

We swung around.

As we headed back several villagers, including the soldiers, clambered into narrow hand-hewn sailing dugouts and began paddling out to us at a frantic clip. Elvis and Anton were looking decidedly nervous. "I don' wan a dead," stated Elvis. We reached a likely looking shoal and dropped anchor.

The first boat held four Indonesian men, two of them cradling well-used machine guns with folding stocks. We invited them on board with forced smiles and over-hearty *"Selamat Sores."* It was an anxious moment.

Then I waved to the small flotilla of dugout paddlers now 20 yards astern and closing fast. They waved back. I smiled. They beamed. And within minutes the boat was swarming with beaming, laughing Indonesian men who were wondering what the hell a boatload of big white men was doing drifting around these dangerous waters. We showed them a surf magazine and pointed to our boards lashed on the deck. Then we broke out the trade goods, cigarettes and Polaroids, and engaged the time-honored surfer tradition of T-shirt diplomacy.

With Elvis translating, the first soldier introduced himself as Sergeant Hasibuan of the Indonesian marines. His small ragtag squad wore army-issue cargo pants, and rubber flip-flops. They reminded me of photos I'd seen of VC people's militia. The sergeant inspected our papers and attempted to maintain proper military protocol for dealing with unexpected foreign guests.

From what we could gather, the religious violence in Ambon had been spreading to the outer islands as revenge-seeking Muslims—unemployed city youths mostly—boarded rusty old ferries in Jakarta and took the jihad to the hinterlands. A group calling itself the "Lasker Jihad" had been stirring up trouble in the Moluccas, printing up false reports of Christian violence against Muslims and distributing them in the backcountry mosques. They had been whipped into a killing frenzy by Muslim clerics, or, it was rumored, ousted military cronies from the Suharto regime bent on toppling President Wahid's fledgling democracy.

Muslims and Christians had lived peaceably side by side on these islands for generations but tensions had been mounting after Suharto's political demise. Old scores were being settled and there had been recent flareups on the island.

After a spell the sergeant shooed the villagers off the boat and said he would radio ahead to the other villages to let them know we were in the area and to keep an eye out for us. He waved us on with a *Selamat Jalan* and the barest hint of a smile.

Aamion and Mark hooked up well this morning. Wrestling with the boat's dilapidated trolling rigs they deftly landed two fat rainbow runners and 10-pound Spanish mackerel just after breakfast. We went back for another run and hooked up a big mahi mahi. When the reel jammed, Mark reeled it in barehanded. Within a half-hour the fish were gutted, cleaned and grilling fragrantly on the stern barbecue.

Both young Hawaiians are accomplished fishermen and free divers. Aamion has incredible vision. Raptor sharp, he can spot a bait ball at a hundred yards; a surf break from miles at sea. He is quietly skilled in all the island survival skills—diving, fishing, hunting and husking coconuts. Mark is well versed in tidepool foraging and brought a lure-making kit and a full quiver of self-made Hawaiian slings. In the morning I just point them over the side and say, "go kill something" and they happily comply.

A mile off our starboard beam lies Morotai, northernmost island of the Malukus. Underneath us, a fleet of wrecked WWII ships and aircraft, American and Japanese, slowly devolving to their base elements.

On September 15, 1944, a combined invasion force of over 7000 allied troops dubbed the "Tradewinds Taskforce" streamed ashore at the very northern tip we now pass. Morotai was the last piece of scaffolding that General Douglas MacArthur needed to launch his triumphant return to Leyte Gulf in the Philippines, a mere 400 miles to the north.

Following a short but vicious battle to expel the Japanese occupiers, MacArthur waded through the shorebreak at 10:15 a.m. He stood on the beach and gazed northwest across the ocean to the Philippines: "They are waiting for me there," he orated for the correspondents. "It has been a long time." Final tally—US: 46 killed, 104 wounded; Japan: 870 killed,

10 captured. Approximately 40 Japanese soldiers were rumored to have escaped into the jungle.

The beach this afternoon bore no trace of MacArthur or the war. The jungle was thick, impenetrable, mute, having healed over its battle scars using human bones as fertilizer.

After a rocky start our surf luck has held amazingly well. By the fourth day we chanced onto some decent surf breaking off a small islet that didn't even show on the newer charts. Two miles long and shaped like a miniature Oahu, the south side held a generous anchorage and at least a half-dozen quality setups.

We spent the day sampling each break, which ranged in the chest-high to overhead range, and by morning the outer pointbreak had bumped up to a respectable double overhead. We all took turns naming the breaks: "Hoax Reef," "Midnight Mission" (named for a chaotic mosquito-infested misadventure when the Zodiac ran out of fuel and Keith, Aamion and Mark were stranded two miles up the point after dark), "Mach Reef," a speedy left on one side of a $1/8$th scale Tavarua, and "Barlo's Right," its shallow but mushy counterpart wrapping around the other side.

When the swell dropped we hoisted anchor and unexpectedly sailed into an archipelago lost in time. These islands appeared as insignificant coffee grounds on the chart but in real life presented themselves as a formidable primeval diorama. As we motored into their shadow we wondered at sheer limestone cliffs that erupted straight off the sea floor 600 feet into the sky. A clutch of large sea eagles patrolled the palm-spiked cornice, tacking back and forth on an alienated updraft.

We swam ashore to the loneliest place on Earth. On the beach I heard nothing but the sigh of small shorebreak, a rustle of small birds, the pounding of our own hearts. I sat on a teak log, carelessly lost overboard from a Java-bound lumber freighter, and watched Hans longboard a small inside dribbler for coup. Transparent ghost crabs scurried around my feet tidying up their beach like fussy little groundskeepers. Castaway. The only sign of humanity was the ubiquitous plastic ship debris and dozens of cheap Taiwanese rubber slippers entangled with coconut husks and leaf litter. Except for "Hello Kitty," I was seeing the world through Wallace's eyes.

Back on board Keith slipped *Dark Side of the Moon* on the CD player. Subterranean overtones echoed off cliffs that would likely not hear humans admiring them for decades

As we puttered into a surreal crimson sunset, no one dared say a word.

Somewhere east of time and 12 miles north of the equator Hans grappled with rain that could fall from a cloudless sky.

"It's the curvature of the earth," he speculated. "A cloud can be right over our heads but you won't see it because it's just beyond the horizon line."

I pondered this for a moment, then filed it under "maybe." It made about as much sense as the rest of Indonesia these days. Water from the moon. It's a Javanese saying meaning to desire what one cannot have. Transcendent love, religious tolerance, a Dove Bar on the equator. But for this brief holy moment, I desired nothing.

Arythmea swung gently on her bridle and strained for the open ocean beyond the pass. The stellar left we discovered yesterday would be coming on in about half an hour as the tide filled in.

On the approach to the atoll we encountered a lone dugout fisherman who scurried to shore at the sight of us. On shore we could make out dilapidated shacks built of metal and palm fronds. Our attention was quickly distracted, however, by the sight of a pristine if somewhat pinched barrel pushing towards us at a respectable clip.

"Boys, there's a fucking perfect wave out there!" exclaimed Hans as we pulled into the wide hospitable anchorage that hid behind the swell-lashed outer reef.

Hans paddled out first to flight-test the new wave. Long-period Pacific swells, spawned in Aleutian seas over a week ago, would suddenly jump out of a deep offshore trench and trip over the shallow coral-spiked reef. After sorting itself out along a dry-reef section the wave reeled quickly in a reassuring fashion for the channel. Getting tubed was simply a matter of calculating the depth versus shack equation, and what you were willing to put on the table.

This wave has turned out to be the prize although it suffers from a tantalizingly short tide window. Yesterday, we only got about an hour of consistent waves before it shut off like a faucet. Still, no one felt slighted on their wave count.

On shore, the fishermen hunkered down under a tree on the beach watching us intently. Whenever one of the guys would get a barrel or a long ride, they went wild, hooting and jumping gleefully on the beach.

We've been getting this sort of attention wherever we pull up. The day before, at a fun reef-pass peak fronting a bucolic little village a day's sail from the atoll, a fascinated gray-haired villager sat in the channel a stone's throw from the peak to get a better view of the guys dropping into the slot. No doubt he's been watching these waves for a lifetime, never realizing what they were capable of. Hans left a broken board with kids with instructions on how to glass the nose back on should they ever come across some resin. We could come back in 10 years time and find a thriving surf cargo cult pulling into barrels on handcarved 6'2" breadfruit squashtails.

Yesterday we tracked the swell into a deceptive approach that from a mile out looked like one continuous reef. But Aamion's eyes saw a keyhole entry that we slid through easily given our shallow draft. We entered a wide verdant bay that echoed with caws and shrill whistles. Some small huts were built on stilts over the shallows.

Soon, a small deputation of villagers paddled out. They were Melanesians, extremely dark with wide Aboriginal features, and showed none of the skittishness we'd encountered back in Halmahera. For all intents and purposes we had left Indonesia.

The headman, who identified himself in soft serviceable English as Louis, said the village of approximately 400 West Papua islanders was Christian but had seen no trouble with religious fanatics.

Louis had been an oil rig roustabout in New Guinea where he had learned English and made a decent wage but he grew homesick after a few years and came home. These days he tended his gardens raising pineapple, bananas and papayas, which he traded to us for cigarettes and rupiah. He also showed Rob some good anchorages nearby with possible surf. When we told Louis we were looking for waves he spoke of a good wave down the point that had been surfed by an Australian he called "Mr. Mark." Mr. Mark had sailed up about a year ago and stayed for months surfing and hanging out with the villagers. They spoke of him in almost reverential tones.

We had a busy day yesterday. Three sessions total. The morning was spent at the east pass surfing small hot-dog waves that got progressively bigger throughout the day. Afterwards we entertained dozens of village kids that had paddled their dugouts and rafts up to our stern. I grabbed Elvis's beat up Gibson knockoff and plunked out a few barely remembered Beatles and Bowie tunes. They seemed intrigued, or simply stunned.

Later we took the dinghy into the village for a walkabout. A broad road, covered in ground bleached coral, ran down the middle. Most of the houses were simple cement-block government knockups but a few had been built of driftwood and palm thatch in the traditional Papua fashion. Louis said the original village had been located across the pass but had been wiped out by a tsunami about 30 years ago. Missionaries and the Indonesian government had helped rebuild the village on the other side.

We were shadowed by a large flock of kids who were fascinated by Aamion's towering 6'4" frame and Mark's incredibly pale skin. They seem to be their own tribe, paddling out on their own canoes, foraging their own food from the gardens.

Keith and Aamion sit outside waiting for the biggest set while we ready the boat for departure. This is our last day, and we have 36 hours of intense point-to-point sailing ahead of us in order to catch our flights back to Bali and beyond. Yet there seems to be no urgency to pull up anchor and head back to a dubious civilization. Whatever we were looking for, we found it.

This small atoll turned out to be inhabited by a handful of fishermen who lived in shacks cobbled together from rusting Marsden landing strips abandoned by the Allies. There were bunker emplacements and an old generator marooned in the shallows. The wave, which 45 years ago likely threatened to swamp convoys of Allied landing craft, now became "Celeste's Left," named after Hans' newborn niece.

Just as I could not have imagined the villager's world before this morning, I doubt that they would comprehend mine or the state of numbness required to survive in a civilization locked on fast-forward scan. They deal with sun and reef and stars and babies plopping out slimy as newly caught fish on dirt floors. I grapple with blur in a culture caught in the endgame of consumerism.

But for now, in this cloistered mirrored lagoon, we share the same heartbeat. And from somewhere over the horizon it's beginning to rain.

Postscript: In November 1956, Corporal Kishi and his squad surrendered to the Indonesian police. An adjunct from the Japanese State Department arrived shortly thereafter and formally relieved Kishi of his protracted post. Kishi returned to Tokyo where he married and had a son. One day he visited his grave. Kneeling down he made a small burning pyre of his death certificate and posthumous decorations.

Back in the jungle on Morotai, Private First Class Tereo Nakamura, of the 5th Takasago Volunteers, would hold his vigil for another 18 years.

Surfing and Sex

By Sam George · SURFER Vol. 43 No. 3 · Feb. 2002

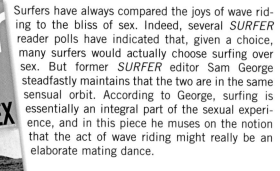

Surfers have always compared the joys of wave riding to the bliss of sex. Indeed, several *SURFER* reader polls have indicated that, given a choice, many surfers would actually choose surfing over sex. But former *SURFER* editor Sam George steadfastly maintains that the two are in the same sensual orbit. According to George, surfing is essentially an integral part of the sexual experience, and in this piece he muses on the notion that the act of wave riding might really be an elaborate mating dance.

It is, by far, the strongest drive in our lives. It pervades our deepest thoughts and dreams with a hot desire that makes it hard, so hard, to concentrate on anything else. The supreme passion, elemental, rampant and, for all our thin veneer of civilized behavior, uncontrollable. For this simple act we will do anything, sacrifice everything in the pursuit of fleeting, potent gratification. Betray lovers, brothers and friends. Cheat, lie, scheme . . . risk. All for that blinding moment of pleasure: hot, wet and naked. Or wrapped in rubber—we don't care, just so long as we can do it and keep doing it, over and over again.

But the pressure, the relentless pressure, in a culture that has taken this most private moment and turned it into a very public obsession, warping values, turning ours into a world where "hard-core" is the new ideal. A false, unrealistic ideal that in its purely graphic depiction has set an almost impossible standard of participation, giving rise to international cult of fantasy. Magazines, videos, the more hard-core the better. Full-color, in-your-face, full front-lit super action; don't we all love to watch? And if we can't watch, we call up and get it over the phone.

And yet it's a beautiful thing, this fluid dance of desire, hardly diminished for how its been chronicled. This is accessible romance, a kinetic romance. Whether done alone (a perfectly natural urge) or shared with close friends, it is still the most sublime of couplings, the timeless pattern of attraction, arousal, penetration and release never more eloquent. This passion—this true essence—has, in turn, been reflected back on our culture, marking it in ways no X rating ever could. Romance that has colored our most creative expressions: music, poetry, art and fashion. It has changed the way we look at ourselves, how others look at us, how we regard others. Quite literally, it makes us.

We're talking, of course, about sex. What? You thought we were talking about surfing? Couldn't blame you if you did, surfing having been, and still the most erotic of all sports. Always has been, historically, philosophically, emotionally and physically wrapped up tight with that *other* basic human drive, twin serpents on a cultural caduceus which, upon examination, are virtually impossible to separate.

We're not going to even try. Because even the most proprietary look at the sport reveals that surfing isn't just like sex.

Surfing *is* sex.

Is That an *Olo* in Your Pocket or Are You Just Happy to See Me? 400 A.D.–1920

It's been said that passion comes in waves, and for that we have to thank the ancient Hawaiians—those lusty, liberated, sexually uninhibited Hawaiians. This remarkable culture, having after their long trans-Pacific voyagings found themselves in such fertile climes, took leisure-time activities and turned them into an art form. The most extraordinary thing, however, is that unlike virtually every other culture of the 5th century A.D., Hawaiian men and women played together, and not just in the bed chamber.

"The thatch houses of a whole village stood empty," wrote 19th century missionary William Ellis, who in his 1831 account *Polynesian Researches* described the arrival of a new swell. "Daily tasks such as farming, fishing and tapa-making were left undone while an entire community—men, women and children—enjoyed themselves in the rising surf and rushing whitewater."

Key phrase: enjoyed themselves. Keep in mind that it was customary to surf naked in those days, and the erotic effect of all that sun-kissed, exercise-toned, glistening skin, heightened by the stimulation and exhilaration of shared strenuous sport, combined with the Polynesian's inherent sensuality and lack of shame, must have been . . . formidable. Writes cultural anthropologist Ben Finney in his seminal 1966 work *Surfing: A History of the Ancient Hawaiian Sport*:

"This equality and sexual freedom added zest to the sport and were important to its widespread popularity. No doubt many a Hawaiian, who on some day didn't feel at all like surfing, found himself paddling for the break line in pursuit of his lady love, knowing full well that if a man and a woman happened to ride the same wave together, custom allowed certain intimacies when they returned to the beach."

"Laying out" on the beach certainly would've had an entire different connotation back then. And had moralities not changed since those amorous times, can you imagine how much more crowded the surf would be today? But changes did occur that rocked the Hawaiian sport of kings to its foundations, the true nature of which has never been seriously examined until now. To do so is to accept a radically new perception of surfing and its erotic essence.

The effect the white man's arrival—most specifically missionaries of various denominations—had on 18th and 19th century Hawaii has been widely discussed, and much lamented. Traditional surfing lore has told us that uptight Calvinists effectively banned the sport along with just about every other frivolity Sandwich Islanders seemed to enjoy. Undoubtedly surfing's permissive atmosphere outraged the pious newcomers. Yet the Puritan devil-dodgers made pains to point out that the white man's God didn't oppose surfing per se.

"The decline and discontinuance of the use of the surfboard, as civilization advances, may be accounted for by the increase in modesty, industry or religion," claimed pioneering Calvinist missionary Hiram Bingham in 1847, "without supposing, as some have affected to believe, that missionaries caused oppressive enactments against it."

So it wasn't surfing this new convention sought to rub out, but something of its essence. In an illuminating passage from his surfing text, Finney theorizes that in fact it was surfing's erotic elements—the nudity, the commingling of sexes and the ensuing sexual freedom—which led to the cultural clampdown and the eventual demise of the sport by the late 19th century.

"With these activities forbidden," he writes, "interest in surfing quickly died. The Hawaiians apparently found little value in the sport when it lacked these attractions. One explanation of the decline admits that 'as the zest of the sport was enhanced by the fact that both sexes engaged in it, when this practice was found to be discountenanced by the new morality, it was felt that the interest in it had largely departed.'"

In short, the sport was love-sexy right from the get-go, and at its hardest of cores meant to be shared and enjoyed without shame between men and women. Only when they separated the surfing from the sex did they f—k everything up. Or at least try to. Because surfing's sexy self would not be denied, and with its rebirth in the early 20th century—and the beginning of its modern history—it wasn't just the big boards that got stiffer.

Why Do You Think They Called Them Woodies? 1920–1950
During surfing's rebirth in the early 20th century, a very strange thing happened: we got back into the water on our boards, but without the women. Who knows why this is so, other than to understand that by the turn of the century women as a gender suffered much greater cultural suppression in Hawaii, with women's rights everywhere at an all-time low. Regardless, as the Modern Era developed on the shores of Waikiki throughout the 1920s and '30s, a new archetype rose up out of the foam and took its place as the sport's most enduring erotic icon: The Beach Boy.

"Without these remarkable people the island would be nothing . . . they are perpetual adolescents of the ocean, the playboys of the Pacific."—James Michener, *Return to Paradise* (1951).

These tumescent playboys of that Pacific got that way simply because when they stopped paddling out with women, they began paddling out for women. This distinction has defined surfing's sexual seascape ever since; only today, with the rise of the Roxy Girl, has the tide begun to turn back to its original high-water mark (but more on that later). Unlike more conventional masculine role models, however, surfers were uniquely endowed to wow the babes. For one, they performed virtually naked, "bronzed Mercurys," rippling muscles toned by the sea and the sun. And straddling their huge, hard, redwood phalluses, how could, say, a baseball player of the same period compare in sex appeal with his droopy-bottom pantaloons and puny bat? Surfing's sensual climate in both Hawaii and California was further reinvigorated by hunks like Tom Blake, once described by a female friend as "outrageously handsome." In the first half of the 20th century the legendary waterman established himself as the modern sport's first serious eroticist. A collection of Blake photos, published in *Tom Blake: 1922–1932* (Adler Books, 1999), reveals a surf scene literally throbbing with sexual tension and imagery. The famous *National Geographic* self-portrait of super-buff TB posed against his redwood quiver, each board growing in ascending proportions as if in various stages of arousal, is perhaps surfing's single most potent image. And believe it, the beach boys knew how to use all that wood.

"The real secret was the water," reported one sandy stud in Grady Timmons's *Waikiki Beachboy* (1989). "Wahines have a thing about it. Get a woman in the water and something happens. Every woman I ever met wanted to make love in the water. A lady once told me, 'When I was 19, you took me tandem. Can you imagine what it was like for me, going to a Catholic school on the Mainland, to have a man take me surfing? To lay on top of me, on the back of my legs . . . skin to skin. In the water.'"

Well, when you put it that way . . . but as in the decades following the beach boy's Golden Era of the 1930s and '40s the sport flourished beyond Waikiki's lusty shores, the overtly masculine stereotype grew. In *Surfing San Onofre to Point Dume: 1936–1942* (Adler, 1986), a collection of photos by the late Dr. Don James, there are plenty of sexy photos: surfer guys posed with their planks a la Blake, surfer guys cuddled up with their girls on the beach, said girls dancing hula for their surfer guys, posed alluringly for their surfer guys—not one photo of a girl surfing. It's clear that in the post-WWII surf scene, and with very few exceptions, a women's place was on the beach, preferably lying on a blanket with her, well, let's say arms opened wide.

This sexual economy was the root, if you'll pardon the expression, of the modern sport's most far-reaching cultural epoch, when in the late 1950s it was made clear that it really was all about getting laid.

Gidget Was a Virgin. 1957–1963

By the mid-1950s, surfing's modern sensuality was simmering just under the surface of its raciest scene: Santa Monica and the surrounding beaches.

Proximity to the Hollywood fantasy-factories, and perhaps more influentially, the Little Bohemia that sprang up where Chautauqua Blvd. meets the Pacific Coast Highway, touched the fledgling lifestyle with a patina of forbidden pleasure. The beach was the thing—many of Tinsel Town's most scandalous trysts climaxed in sultry, salty, seaside Malibu bungalows. But surfers lived on the sand; the bonfire, blanket and bottle of cheap wine were their stock in trade. Small wonder the breathless ingenue who eventually went on to become the 20th century's Ultimate Sex Goddess explored early erotic nuances around the embers of a Santa Monica beach fire, wrapped in a low-neck sweater and the muscular arms of L.A. proto-surfer Tommy Zahn, who knew the future Marilyn Monroe merely as Norma Jean.

To a generation of '50s parents in gray flannel suits (and matching pleated skirts) the beach was a dangerous place where virtue could find no purchase; the free-spirited, free-loving surfers who made it their stage, dangerous people. This pervasive vibe of sexual intrigue was at the heart of perhaps the single most dramatic punctuation in the sport's history: the 1957 publication of *Gidget*.

Do you really think that the hordes of eager teens who flocked to coast in Gidget's wake—and later, following the 1959 feature film of the same name—did so because they couldn't wait to get out there in that chilly Pacific? No, it was the sex, the sex and titillation that provided author Frederick Kohner with the undercurrent necessary to elevate this tale of his young daughter's Malibu adventures above more typical teenage love stories. Consider this heated passage:

"*Malibu Mac, a regular sex-hound, was the next to give voice.*
'Let's drag her down and give her the time . . .'
Well, as I said, I pretended not to listen but lapped up every word of that sexy talk, every single syllable of it . . .
'Why should she mind?' said Hot Shot Harrison. 'She's a good girl.'
'I don't know,' mused Golden Boy Charlie. 'Maybe we're all wet—maybe she's a nice girl.'
They all looked at me expectantly and, like a dope, I fell for it.
'What's the difference?' I asked.
'Let me explain,' said Schweppes. 'A good girl goes on a date, goes home, goes to bed.'
'A nice girl,' his Lordship continued, 'goes on a date, goes to bed, goes home.'
'So, what kind of girl are you, Gidget?' Malibu Mac asked with a leer."

It was obvious that Gidget was in much greater danger of losing her virginity than drowning off her balsa board, and both the book and the movie underscored this clearly. Most significantly, however, was how the plot of the movie departed from the book. *Gidget* the book—probably the best book written about surfing, for what it's worth—ends with our heroine's discovery that while courtly love might be fleeting, love of the sun and the surf is forever. *Gidget* the movie skipped this surfing coda, focusing instead on the more lurid device of Gidge quite innocently playing "Kahoona" [*sic*] off "Moondoggie," with nothing less than her chastity at stake. In the end, Gidget gets "pinned" by her surfer-guy-turned-frat-boy, the childish surfing side of things cast off with her training bra. Small distinction, perhaps, but one that had a huge impact on the sport's sexual sensibilities to come.

Beach Blanket Bonking. 1965–1975

Can you imagine how different surfing culture might have turned out had Annette Funicello been a slut?

Beach Party, Beach Blanket Bingo, Muscle Beach Party, How to Stuff A Wild Bikini; yes, those old American International surf-and-sexploitation movies, when viewed in retrospect, seem so corny and campy that they approximate deliberate farce (how real-life beach-buddies Tommy Zahn and Marilyn Monroe, blond bombshells both, were translated into Frankie Avalon and Annette Funicello, two dark hair–and–nosebrowed Italian-Americans from New York City is beyond all but a studio head's comprehension). Yet in the early 1960s, with the hard-core surfing world still reeling from the popularizing effects of the *Gidget* boom, these wildly popular films did more than focus even more of the world's attention on our previously exclusive club. On the heels of Sandra Dee's Gidget and James Darren's Moondoggie (what's with all these Italian surfstars?), frisky Frankie and virginal Annette inadvertently established sexual stereotypes that lasted well into the next decade. Can anybody out there even remember the plot of 1963's *Beach Party*?

In that seminal "beach movie" an anthropologist played by comedian Bob Cummings, set on studying the "mating habits" of modern teenagers, naturally chooses the Malibu set on which to conduct his research. And why not? While the rest of America's youth fumbled and groped with Playtex Living Bras in the gloomy back seat of dad's Delta 88, surfers—who didn't just yearn for but existed in Bikini World—were making love on the beach, leaving turtle tracks in the sand without shame. What could be more natural? As *Beach Party*'s poster art proclaimed, "It's What Happens When 10,000 Kids Meet On 5,000 Beach Blankets!"

Despite the erroneous depiction by Frankie and Annette, real surfers established themselves at the cultural vanguard of the "free love" era, the pervasive aura of sexual permissiveness that more than any peace movement or environmental awakening defined the era we know as "The '60s." Surfers, uninhibited and already partially naked, were baring their white butts to the stars (or the sun, in some cases) long before any Woodstock hippies jumped on the bandwagon. But in one crucial area surfers lagged behind the civilian world, and that came with the development of "the chick."

In the context of the sexual revolution, lucky Hippie Chicks were able, for the most part, to adopt as role models a whole generation of assertive female rock and roll stars. Sure, there was plenty of inequality to go around in the music industry, but the message was by and large empowering. Surf Chicks, on the other hand, inexplicably took their cue from Annette Funicello's "Dee Dee" character (one of *Gidget*'s "good girls" if there ever was one), content to wait chastely on the sand while their love interests did battle against the mighty sea and even mightier "nice" girls who waited like sirens in the shadows to drag faithless boyfriends to their doom. Here, in what could've been a very liberating period, was born a new archetype, the B.G.S.O.: Beach Girl as Sexual Object. So far removed from their original role as surfing and sexual equals, girls now simply filled out their bikinis—and the collective fantasies of at least two generations of surfers who spent as much time in the bathroom with early-'70s Eeni Meeni Bikini ads as with today's Reef Brazil girls. This stereotype, which lasted well into the 1970s and '80s, still exists in many ways. But in the mid-1970s a new wave of sexuality swelled up that actually eclipsed *Beach Party*'s surf chick.

Suddenly, we all went pro.

Not That There's Anything Wrong with It . . . 1976–1996

If we have professional surfing to thank for anything, it's for lifting us out of the only truly unsexy period in surfing history: the early 1970s. Oh, sure, crocheted bikinis were hot, and there was that topless O'Neill wetsuit ad, circa 1970. Another high point was the development of tuberiding, a Freudian slip if there ever was one. "Sometimes a cigar is just a cigar," quoth Sigmund, the father of both modern psychoanalysis and the theory of sexual sublimation. But if he considered trains roaring through tunnels potent symbols of turgidity, Lord only knows what he would've made of tuberiding—spit and all.

For the most part, however, the soul surfing era was pretty limp, libido-wise. All that philosophizing and intellectualizing, as if we had more important things to think about than the trusty beach blanket. And the travel—driving a Volkswagen Bug south of the border to Puerto Escondido was hardly an erotic pursuit, especially seeing as how Tijuana's infamous donkey bars had long since closed down.

Luckily surfing's next sexual halcyon was just around the corner. The advent of modern professional surfing and the subsequent surf-wear explosion jacked up the sport's sexuality quotient in several important ways—none of which could have been predicted. It would be too easy to point to the growth of the international pro tour and its early playboy pioneers, traipsing around the pre-AIDS beach-scapes, ravenous groupies trailing like wolves following the buffalo herd (the name

Margaret DePraved still sends a shiver up the urethras of plenty of the over-40 vets who may have visited her tent at Burleigh's '77 Stubbies Pro). The Action Sports Retailer convention (our industry's bi-annual Sodom and Gomorrah but with a spring juniors line) could, since its inception in 1981, provide enough tales of depravity to fill a surfing version of "Who's Done Who." And let's not even factor in the development of the European tour in the mid-1980s, when visiting pros descended upon Hossegor's topless maidens like a horde of invading Visigoths (although if the truth be known, the rapine was often reversed, with many a young pro dragged down to the beach bunkers by predatory mademoiselles with bad teeth and armpit hair). Yet in actuality, these eras of excess affected relatively few surfers, and even those primarily with an exotic array of STDs. What the subsequent growth of pro surfing did spread to the mainstream was a new economy, built almost entirely on erotic imagery that changed the way we looked at the sport and ourselves. And in ways you might not have imagined.

First and foremost, the 1980s and early '90s ushered in the era of the male pin-up, the burgeoning surf-wear manufacturers choosing, strangely, a strategy of homoerotica to sell their trunks. In 1980, Gotcha, for example, featured in their first few major ads a series of vamps, posed submissively in front of a strapping, young Cheyne Horan like horny love slaves. But in the months to come, Cheyne, Martin Potter and the rest of the company's all-male harem were eventually shown playing with themselves.

The Video Epoch reinforced this ethic. Groups of guys gathered around VCRs, poring over titles that, virtually without exception, feature nothing but boys, boys and more boys: surfing together, traveling together, partying together . . . toweling off together. Scoff if you will, but then watch this year's acclaimed film *Shelter* and ask yourself if Gidget would've had anything to worry about in that merry farmhouse. Better yet, rent Zalman King's *In God's Hands*, in which Mickey obviously loves Shane. Granted, we're a male-dominated sport, but if the advertising and video imagery of the past 20 years has accurately captured the romance of surfing, it's of the sort that dares not speak its name.

On the other hand, the growth of the surf-wear industry also brought us the Reef Brazil Girl, that lone bastion of female sexuality, however objectified, in a surf world gone curiously conservative. Irate mothers and librarians are still writing us to complain about those tawny cheeks. Considering the explicit sexual overtones that pervade practically every other medium—from VH1 and "Lady Marmalade" to the latest cover of *Hot VW* magazine—it could be said that surfing, once the sexiest sport in America (as described by this author on the front page of the *Wall Street Journal* in 1989—you can look it up) had gone a little soft.

Kelly and Lisa, Sittin' in a Tree . . . 1996–2002

Demographically, by the mid-1990s surfing was setting itself up for another very unsexy period. Blame it on longboarding if you want. Not longboarding itself, which is the sexiest of all surfing disciplines (riding upright, arching, leading with your hips, the obsession with anything 69 and lower), but the more widespread cultural implications of the subculture—family surfing. With more and more older surfers either staying active beyond traditional age limits, getting back into the sport or learning for the first time, the whole mating ritual thing got thrown out of whack. Today, on a good day at Rincon, the average surfer would be as old as Cummings the anthropologist in *Beach Party*, not sexually charged-up Frankie and Dee Dee. And while the endorphin high from a good session still might occasionally translate to a "naughty night" with the spouse back home, for many of the aging surf demographic the waves became a place to alleviate sexual tension, rather than heighten it. Couple this new mood with the mid-'90s grom explosion—kids of former hard-core kids now reaching surfing age—and it's easy to see how the legacy of saltwater sensuality was in danger of premature completion.

Enter two Floridian surfers, Kelly Slater and Lisa Andersen, who together brought sex back to the forefront where it belonged.

During his rise throughout the '90s, Kelly Slater fostered a sensual persona the likes of which hadn't been seen since Blake's "standing erectile" poses. Forget the series of sexy Quiksilver ads: Kelly, eyes seductively downcast, skin warm and wet, trunks perched precariously on narrow hips, Channel Islands thruster upright and rampant. It's not about his splashy stint on *Baywatch*. Disregard, even, when Slater was featured, in 1991, as one of *People* magazine's 50 Most Beautiful celebrities. No, Kelly's contribution to our Sexy Millennium can be summed up in two words. One, actually: Pamela.

This has nothing to do with the fellow *Baywatch* bimbette's perceived sexuality, nor her overexposed, overaugmented characteristics. (Ever wonder why, when discussing Anderson's notorious home porn movie, all anybody talked about was the size of hubby Tommy Lee's schlong? We know the real thing when we see it.) Like Marilyn Monroe before her, Pamela Anderson's sex appeal was mass manufactured. Kelly, on the other hand, was already proving himself as the greatest surfer in the world—the ultimate Real Thing. By dating an uber-sex symbol, Slater was making a much bigger statement about his sexual self than that of his famous consort. Surfers were once again sexy; Kelly even made bald sexy, bare testimony to the breadth of his influence in a notoriously blond world. In that sense Kelly Slater has brought us back to the beach blanket where we belong. Lisa Andersen, however, helped reshape history.

The shape in question was of her hips. In 1989 Lisa, young, spritely and tired of having to surf awkwardly in women's bathing suits, put on a pair of men's trunks and found that they hugged her hips quite nicely, thank you. And boom—the Roxy Girl Revolution was born.

Keep in mind that up to this point in surfing history, women were being judged by how much they surfed like men. It was to be expected that eventually many began to take on masculine characteristics to facilitate this. So far as role models were concerned, by the 1980s female surfing sexuality (heterosexuality, at least) had almost disappeared from the sport; the B.G.S.O. again reigned supreme. At the Op Pro, for example, the bikini contest drew more entrants than the professional women's event.

The Surfer Girl Movement inspired primarily by Lisa Andersen changed all that. It was great that she surfed great—but a lot of female champions have been hot. The difference with Lisa was in how she was perceived by male surfers. It could've been the trunks, but for some reason Lisa always seemed like she belonged out there with the men. She was comfortable in the water. Her confidence was palpable, and there's nothing sexier than confidence. Paradoxically, Andersen liberated a new generation of women surfers with her sexiness.

The girls who have come into the sport during the past five or so years have brought with them that same confidence, and in doing so, inaugurated an entirely new era of Sexy Surfing. Then again, we've felt this vibe before. Six hundred years ago men and women rode the waves together, the shared experience of surfing a rich and sensual component in the timeless ritual of attraction and mating. Somewhere along its timeline the sport lost its mojo and surfers, both male and female, were categorized, objectified and ultimately segregated. But we're back in the water together these days and it feels so good. To paraphrase that randy old beach boy:

"Every surfer I ever met wants to make love in the water."

So get it on. 🔲

Everybody Surfs: Episode V:
To Boldly Tow

By Dave Parmenter · SURFER Vol. 46 No. 12 · Dec. 2005

It is in the gray zones between truth and fiction that good writers find fodder for satire and farce. As surfing slowly inched its way into mainstream acceptance, the gray areas exploded, and no writer mined these areas better than Dave Parmenter. Parmenter's "Everybody Surfs" serial, launched in 2005, is a surfing version of P.G. Wodehouse's and S.J. Perelman's classic satires—a hilarious send-up of modern surf culture that proved to be the perfect outlet for Parmenter's misanthropic wit. Here, he tackles the explosion of wanna-be tow-in surfers.

"What I can't abide," exclaimed a Retro Fish and NorCal Beanie, "are those goshdarned Toaats."

He and the Old Legend, Hoppy McBride, sat basking in the afternoon sun on the little wooden deck in front of Surfdoggie's Surf Shop, the Old Legend absently flipping through a back issue of *Golf Digest* while the Retro Fish and NorCal Beanie seethed over a new issue of *GlobalSurf*.

The Old Legend's weathered map registered confusion.

"No doubt you refer to some recalcitrant tribe of South Sea islanders," he replied, "throwing their weight around in the copra market."

The Retro Fish and NorCal Beanie shook his head.

"No, no, it's *tow-ats*—you know, like 'tow-in.' Except now, these miscreants are using Jet Skis to fling themselves into ordinary waves on regular surfboards."

He shoved the magazine in front of the Old Legend and stabbed a finger at the center-spread, explaining that more and more surf photos were staged by the unseen hand of a Yamaha.

"I mean, look at that spray! Are we to believe that this surfer, built on the lines of Ichabod Crane on a juice fast, is responsible for a roostertail like the middle flume of the Hoover Dam? Must we now appraise every surf photo with the skepticism normally reserved for the Piltdown Man or tortilla stigmata?"

The Old Legend nodded in understanding and pointed to an advertisement in his golf magazine for a sure-fire titanium carbon-fiber driver.

"It's the American Way," he sighed, "to seek shortcuts in mastering a lifelong pursuit."

A perfect case in point (went on the Old Legend) is the account of one of my nephews, Hughie Catsbreath. Like so many of the quasi-professional surfers residing behind the Orange Curtain, young Catsbreath kept body and soul together with the help of fat photo-incentive checks bestowed by one of the enormous surfwear corporations that sprawl everywhere in the Southland by the city block.

It was a golden life. All he had to do was stay frontlit at f/5.8 and never go left, and the checks would materialize in his postbox.

Then one summer, Fate gave Hughie Catsbreath the sleeve across the windpipe. A pall of wet gray June Gloom settled over the coast, creating what would come to be known as the Summer of Ektachrome. For four dreary months not a single frame of Kodakchrome 64 was exposed. By the end of summer my nephew had slid from number 12 to number 116 in the *SurfBiz Monthly* "Exposure Meter."

And so on the first of the month young Catsbreath opened the mailbox to find that his monthly envelope was stuffed not with the anticipated stipend, but rather a pink slip, a Whirley Gear sticker and a coupon for 10 percent off the purchase of a pair of cargo pocket walk-shorts.

Hughie Catsbreath was devastated. All professional surfers are unwitting Marxists, believing "to each according to his needs, from each according to his abilities." The money spigot had abruptly gone *phut*, and when that happens in Orange County the vultures begin circling overhead. That night he tossed in a fitful doze, and try as his febrile brain might to squirm from the inevitable, he knew just one course of action remained.

If he were ever again to nuzzle up to the swollen teats of the billion-dollar surf industry, he would have to become a commercial big-wave rider.

Back in the Early Years, when a young man found himself cast out and destitute, he stowed away on a tramp steamer and went off and joined the Foreign Legion. Today, he just moves to Maui and buys a Jet Ski.

In the morning he crawled from bed, resolute; he took the phone off the hook, brewed a pot of strong black coffee, wrapped a cold washcloth 'round his neck, opened his savings passbook and, licking a pencil, began scribbling furious figures onto a notepad. Recently, Burleydong Boardshorts had offered a $1,000-per-foot bounty on big waves: their annual "Big X" prize would be awarded to the surfer who, during the stated period, was photographed occupying space on the tallest wave. A 50-foot wave, calculated Hughie Catsbreath, if it won for him the coconut and cigar, would see him through at least two years of Big Gulps and Blink-182 CDs.

Owing to having spent his entire life along the shores of Orange County, my nephew had never ridden a wave larger than 8 feet. But, he reasoned, everyone was a tow-in surfer now—surely it was easier than it looked. And the new method of measuring wave size emboldened him: applying this modified tape measure his 8-foot personal best became a respectable 17.3 feet.

So Hughie Catsbreath booked passage to Kahului, Maui, and alighting there one sticky October afternoon he immediately headed off, like a prospector fresh off the boat in the Yukon, to the local outfitters to acquire the equipment vital to his new trade.

Back in my day, when a man left hearth-fire and home-acre to go with the old gray Widow-maker, he needed only a heart of oak, a board of balsa, and a pair of M. Nii trunks. From a list of essentials two pages long, Young Catsbreath purchased a new Yamaha WaveRunner and a quiver of tow boards graduated in two-inch increments; he bought six kinds of foot straps, an assortment of leashes, a rescue sled, and a dozen towropes in neon yellow and international orange. Having little sales resistance, he also procured life vests with matching helmets, oxygen bottles, a case of air horns, a waterproof two-way radio, a first-aid kit, bathymetric charts of Jaws, and an EPIRB.

It only remained for my nephew to find a suitable tow partner. He scoured the local supermarket bulletin boards and newspapers. There, in the latter, he found sandwiched in the personal ads between "Men Seeking Women" and "Women Seeking Women" a column with the heading, "Men Seeking Tow Partners." After half a dozen interviews, young Catsbreath found his man, a Brazilian surfer also recently arrived on Maui. Ronaldo Saladbarre spoke little English, but claimed to have repeatedly viewed all the Hollywood big-wave motion pictures.

"I see *In God's Face* seexty-seven times," he said.

"Hands," corrected Catsbreath.

"What?"

"It's 'Hands.'"

"What is 'hands'?"

"What God holds you in when the waves are really big."

"No, I think you make wrong. Hands for measure horses."

"Nevertheless," Catsbreath assured him with polite firmness, "the film in question is called *In God's Hands*."

Ronaldo Saladbarre shrugged.

"Eh, eet's all good."

Having thus found a partner and completed his outfitting, Hughie Catsbreath sat back and waited for Jaws to rear up on its hindquarters and start spewing money into his empty purse.

It was then that a tremendous mass of high pressure broke out of its Arctic prison and smothered in its crib the first nascent low-pressure trough of the season. Then the anticyclone settled over the storm track and the entire North Pacific Ocean yawned and went to sleep for a year and a quarter.

Time, said the sage, is the reef upon which all our frail mystic ships are wrecked. His meager savings depleted, young Catsbreath was forced to seek temporary employment if he was to survive the wave drought. He soon found a position on the southwestern shore of the island giving surf lessons at one of the posh tourist resorts.

There is something about the tropical air that lulls the un-inoculated *malihini* into a drowsy complacency. Young Catsbreath waded into the pleasant and faintly dull routine marked chiefly by rustling palms, copious sunshine, discounted cocktails at the beachside bar, and pushing his Pillsbury clientele into the gentle rollers off the hotel. Soon the tropics had slipped the chloroformed rag over his face, and he thought less and less about the Big X Bounty. By the following autumn, he was out of shape, 20 pounds overweight, and no longer wished to be dragged into a wave big enough to knock Godzilla on his bottom.

Finally, the balloon went up one day the following December, when the phone rang and a frantic voice gibbered on the line.

"What if I told you," recited a breathless Ronaldo Saladbarre, "there was a wave so beeg . . . "

Buoy One, he went on, was sending out readings like a seismograph hauled by a dump truck over potholes, sending half of the inhabitants of Maui pulling trailers piled with Jet Skis to Jaws—and the other half of the population following to watch.

When they crept idling into the channel a few hours later, Jaws resembled a major sea battle crossed with the grand opening of a McDonald's in the Sunni Triangle. Seventy-five Jet Skis, 42 powerboats, three helicopters and a zeppelin streaked, hovered, and jockeyed for position amid the towering swells marching in aflame with streamers of spray. Things, it could be said, were hopping.

His blood frozen in fright, Hughie Catsbreath watched horrified as a tow-surfer skittered down the face of a 35-foot mountain, only to have the lip swat him as if he'd been a biplane strafing a particularly ill-tempered King Kong. At the center of it all was international tow star Lars Hammertan and his Band of Merry Men; they dodged cross traffic and effortlessly snatched the biggest and best waves. It was like watching the Harlem Globetrotters filch the basketball from a group of elderly bird-watchers.

It was Ronaldo Saladbarre that finally broke the spell. Where young Catsbreath was petrified by the monstrous surf, the Brazilian, full of the zest and brio so common in his native land, felt it was the stuff to give the troops. He liked what he saw. He jumped from the seat and began capering on the rescue sled.

"I go first! I go first!" he exclaimed as he unspooled the towrope and wedged his feet into the foot straps of his tow board.

Hughie Catsbreath nodded weakly. Fear had chilled him to the marrow. Shivering, he reached into a compartment and grabbed his wetsuit. Leaving the machine in idle, he swung sidesaddle on the seat and began stuffing his feet into the rubber legs.

I don't know if you have ever tried to put on one of these newfangled zipperless wetsuits when you are cold and wet. It's like trying to cram into tight clothes made of flypaper. And the fact that Hughie Catsbreath was presently an XL trying to squeeze into an ML did not make it any easier. As he struggled, the machine putted along in a lazy circle, occasionally steered by a knee or elbow to avoid traffic. He stuck his arms down the sleeves and with a colossal effort tried to pull the neck hole up and over his shoulders. He got it as far as his upper chest and then, redfaced with the strain, the rubber slipped from his grasp and he lost his balance. He lurched forward, arms pinned helplessly to his side and feet still snagged in the legs of the suit. For a second he tried to arrest his fall, but it was no good. My nephew tells me it resembled one of those old film noir scenes where Richard Widmark jerks a crook's coat down over his arms and gives him a trimmin'. The upshot was that he fell heavily upon the handlebars—right onto the throttle lever, to be exact.

The machine reacted to this sudden spurring of its flanks by coughing a ball of spray and exhaust, rearing up on its haunches, and then streaking like a scalded cat straight into the lineup. It seemed to Hughie Catsbreath, struggling to untangle his sleeve from the throttle, as if all of nature was roaring its disapproval. Ronaldo Saladbarre, who had been yanked out of his foot straps at 35 miles-per-hour and was well on his way to becoming the first tow-in bodysurfer at Jaws, was yelling at him. The occupants of the 75 Jet Skis, 42 powerboats, three helicopters and the zeppelin were yelling at him. The Merry Men were yelling at him. The only person not yelling at him, it seemed, was Lars Hammertan.

He was presently outside about to scoot into the biggest wave of the day.

The Jet Ski, with Hughie Catsbreath draped over the handlebars and his partner screaming Portuguese curses at the end of the towrope, plowed directly toward the trough of the approaching monster just as Hammertan let go of his towrope. Hammertan, as he swung into a series of S-turns preliminary to getting down to brass tacks, was shocked to see heading for him what appeared to be a rodeo clown wrestling with the horns of a berserk bull dragging a shrieking bronco-buster by the stirrups. Seeing little future in continuing his present course, he veered sharply left and hightailed it east-nor' east along a massive left wall.

Meanwhile Hughie Catsbreath, the Yamaha, and Ronaldo Saladbarre sailed over the cresting wave like it was a motocross ramp, each flying into various trajectories according to Newtonian law. When each came to rest three things had come to an end: a new Yamaha WaveRunner, Hughie Catsbreath's aquiline nose, and his welcome on Maui.

While young Catsbreath wasn't actually frog-marched away, I am told the procession leading him to the airport was at least equal to the statehood parade of 1959. And while Lars Hammertan was at the head of this incipient lynch mob, he soon found reason enough to keep Hughie Catsbreath on his Christmas card list. Later, it turned out that when he was forced left on that wave he chanced upon a section that flared up into the tallest wave of the winter. The check, when he received it at the Burleydong Boardshorts Big X Bounty award presentation, was made out for $61,000.

As for Hughie Catsbreath, his career as a commercial big-wave rider was over. He returned with hat in hand to Orange County and Whirley Gear. Inc., where he was recently promoted to Vice-Assistant Sticker-Giver-Outer. It just goes to show you that a man, as "Dirty Harry" Callahan once said, has got to know his limitations. 🔳

Sidekicked

By Chris Mauro · SURFER Vol. 47 No. 2 · Feb. 2006

In the cascade of endless decisions we face in our daily bustle, hindsight often obscures the seemingly insignificant but pivotal choices we have made that set the course for the rest of our lives. What the future held for Chris Mauro when he was 12 years old, he couldn't exactly say; he only knew for certain that surfing would be part of it. Twenty-five years later Mauro found himself answering an intern's query as to how he ended up as the editor of *SURFER*. In this essay he traces the answer back to July 5th, 1979.

No self-respecting surfer will ever consider the tiny bay I grew up in a destination location, yet its thumping little closeouts netted more of my attention than they deserved when I was young. By 10 years of age I was attempting to be the first one on the beach each morning, but there was one person who consistently beat me to it. He was the trash man, the same lucky bastard who got to drive the coolest dune buggy I'd ever seen up and down the little quarter-mile string of sand I called home. In fact, I swore his vocation was my calling as I watched him jump berms, spray water and cut deep scars into the sand at top speeds. Hauling trash, collecting the rotting kelp and sweeping the bathrooms and stairways was hard work for sure, but, I reckoned, a tiny price to pay to get behind *that* wheel.

Never short on nerve, I'd ask the trash man if I could take the buggy for a spin on my way home. He'd laugh, then temper the rejection by congratulating me on my better rides. That was the gist of our relationship for a good year or so. But everything changed one 5th of July. That's the busiest day of the year in the beach cleanup trade, a day when great pyramids of rubbish swallow trashcans whole, smoldering fire pits threaten wayward toddlers and burnt wires from skyrockets and sparklers lurk as dangerous booby traps in the sand. My friend was understandably perturbed. The excess bagging, the sifting of sand and the hauling of hundreds of pounds of trash up the long, steep, switchback stairs would take him all day without some kind of help.

We quickly struck an accord, and having agreed to labor at his side the rest of the morning I finally felt the thrill of wind and sand whipping through my hair that day. The dune buggy had no passenger seat. I sat in the big wooden bin where trash was hauled, but not minding in the least the wretched stench or the gruesome sludge. A few weeks later I flew solo, and I was totally convinced all my dreams were coming true. My 12th birthday was still a week away and yet I was already a trash man's apprentice.

While I was never paid in cash, there were rewards, none bigger than my ticket out of the bay. Funny thing is the only guy who loved surfing more than I did was the trash man—who, it turns out, was really only 16 years old. The old guys in their 20s called him "Nip," short for "Nipper," which was shorter still for "Little Nipper," which he allegedly was at one time. "Nip" had all the surf magazines, and knew all the names of places in them. He also had his driver's license and the keys to a Baja Bug, albeit with holes in the floor and a slippery gear stick, but it could safely cover long distances. For the next five or six years, I accompanied him on his numerous explorations of the vast coastline beyond, effectively becoming his sidekick.

I can't ever recall a more exciting time than being a young innocent abroad, absorbing the coast, its characters and its moods. That's when every bend in the road beckoned, each day was a new adventure, and all my meals were scraped together. As a sidekick, I was subject to terrible abuses. Our trouble usually began early and spread far, yet it didn't matter that I had to freeze outside his house at 4 a.m. midwinter, waiting for the light to go on because I wasn't allowed to knock on the door, or that I had to sit in the car, starving, with no money while he downed a dozen donuts, or that I was forced to paddle out in enormous-size surf before dawn broke and I could lodge a fully enlightened protest. "Look, you have one job," he'd say. "Tie the rubber band there around the stick when we hit fourth gear and just hang on for the ride."

For the next few years I did.

Sadly, our summer job came to an abrupt halt during the legendary El Niño storms of 1983. From the cliffs above our bay, we watched in horror as an angry ocean plucked our dune buggy right off the beach (along with the entire shed, the lifeguard tower and countless trashcans). She was afloat for a while, hanging upside down by her big tires while getting sucked out to sea. Sadly, she was never replaced, and the job quickly lost its luster.

Looking back on it all now though I realize the rides she offered are still going. My early escape from the bay paved the way for further adventures all around the world, and being stuck behind this desk, and "Nip" would go on to find terrific success as a competitive surfer. Today, however, most of you know him as "Snips," a.k.a. Mike Parsons, the guy who charges big Todos Santos and Cortes Bank. We're still good friends, the trash man and I. But years ago I cut way back on my 4 a.m. sessions, so we don't ride together nearly as often. Still, every now and then he sucks me into one of his crazy big-wave sessions and my old sidekick role haunts me. Especially when the horizon turns black and I hear his familiar screams ordering me into position: "Deeper! Deeper, you pussy!" Suddenly, the memories of past abuses come flooding back to me . . . but I savor every one of them.

Acknowledgments

Exploring *SURFER*'s very colorful past in great detail is a thoroughly enjoyable process. It's literally like catching up with old friends. We'd like to thank all the *SURFER* magazine writers, editors, and photographers, former or present, who contributed their valuable feedback and insight to this collection. Without them, this undertaking would not have been nearly as fun.